Insights From Music Therapy Practice and Research

Jessica Atkinson

# Insights From Music Therapy Practice and Research

## Other Knowing

palgrave
macmillan

Jessica Atkinson
High Wycombe, Buckinghamshire, UK

ISBN 978-3-031-86219-9    ISBN 978-3-031-86220-5 (eBook)
https://doi.org/10.1007/978-3-031-86220-5



This Palgrave Macmillan imprint is published by the registered company Springer Nature Switzerland AG.
The registered company address is: Gewerbestrasse 11, 6330 Cham, Switzerland

*In memory of my mother, Anna.*

# Preface

Some years ago, I set out to explore a topic through research: experience, evidence, and what counts in music therapy. At the end, I discovered that it was not the results that seemed most important, but the journey of exploration. This was because my guides and inspiration were the nonverbal people who I had worked with over twenty-six years as a music therapist, and because the context was the non-verbal medium of music therapy itself.

In order to investigate this topic, I looked for research approaches that could in various ways honour the non-verbal worlds of the many people who had inspired me: I used arts-based methodology, focusing on creative writing, painting, glass fusing, making a mobile and more. In addition, I drew upon other research traditions, including phenomenological enquiry, looking deeply at my own experiences of this arts-based work to learn more about the experiences we offer others in music therapy. A key question was whether these experiences might in themselves be regarded as evidence of therapy. It was this learning about what we offer as music therapists, which came about through my own creative research activities, which seemed to be the substance of my research. It is what I am sharing here.

So, in the following pages, you will find the story of my journey. I did not have a pre-conceived destination, but I was clear about the purpose of my travel. After some time, four Roles appeared: Musician, Music Therapist, Researcher and Carer. They are all me, but they tell the story from different perspectives. I did not invite them, they just arrived and would not go away, and more problematically, they all talked at the same time. As a result you will find that this book contains Dialogues in which they speak, or often argue. In addition, there are Direct Messages: these are sections where the other Roles have granted Researcher permission to discuss certain themes. She does so in the form of a Direct Message to you, the reader, listener, observer.

But this book requests more of you—it invites you to *participate* as a Collaborator. This is because the book is offering you an arts-based journey that reflects the one I took. Its function is not to entertain you. Rather, it hopes to engage you in much of the same experiencing, reflecting and non-verbal, arts-based knowing that I experienced during my research.

It would be reasonable for you to argue that you can't be a Collaborator, because we do not know each other and are not in the same space. By collaborate, I am implying the kind of commitment that we might give when actively listening to a piece of recorded music: without our effort, the creator's purpose and the performer's interpretation will never be fulfilled—we need to share their intention. This is what I am requesting of you. If you prefer the term Explorer to describe your engagement, please use this substitute.

On a practical level, this book did not begin life in chapters, because it is unusual to announce chapters in the middle of a conversation. Instead, Musician had found quotations, all from Shakespeare, that reflected the topic of the following Dialogue—this is part of her dedication to 'artful living'. The Direct Messages had brief subject descriptions so that you, the Collaborator, could know what Researcher was writing about. However, modern publishing requires chapters in order to grant sectional access to online readers. So they now exist, but the quotations and descriptions retain their focal positions and purposes.

In conclusion, I am offering you a book like this because I needed one of this nature when I was practising and researching music therapy, but could not find one. So I have attempted to provide one. If you are an arts therapist, community arts leader or an artist I hope it will offer experiences that both resonate with your work and invite reflection. If you are involved in caring for others, I hope it will affirm the dignity of those you encounter who know, and share their knowing, nonverbally. And I hope it will encourage you to share arts-based experiences with those who receive your care. If you are a policy maker or funder, it is a deep concern of mine that you might feel equipped to advocate for the therapeutic experience of personhood that results from arts-based, non-verbal knowing. This book aims to provide a theoretical framework for why such experience can itself be regarded as evidence of successful therapy. If you are a social scientist, I would be delighted if your engagement with this book encouraged you to believe in the other knowing that can be found in autoethnography and arts-based research. If you are a student in any discipline, I hope what follows will inspire you to explore and reflect.

Before I go, I need to make another request: the Roles sometimes get heated and say things that may appear provocative or unfiltered. This is their prerogative and is what happens in conversation. So, you may read something that grates or feels uncomfortable in the Dialogues. At such times, please be reassured that the conversation is spread out across the whole book: invariably, the Roles return to thorny subjects and Researcher untangles them in the Direct Messages in her more analytical manner. Also, each Role only speaks from her own perspective, offering just one of the four strands of thinking that makes up any of my arguments. I would therefore be grateful for your patience and good will.

Thank you for your interest. Thank you also to the many people who have helped me on this journey, particularly Nick Wilson, Nicky O'Neill, Stuart Wood and Miranda Dodd for your generous interest and support, Laura al Bandar for your insights, Jen, Peter, Anna and Mary for giving me quiet spaces to work in, Helen and John for your inspiration and kindness—though you have gone on ahead and cannot see where I have arrived; and thank you to my family for your patience and care. Above all, I am grateful to the many music therapy participants and their families and carers that I have been privileged to work with over the years.

Jessica Atkinson

… introducing the Roles:

Musician (M)
Researcher (R)
Music Therapist (MT)
Carer (C)

MT: What happened to the introduction?

C: What introduction?

MT: Exactly!

R: There isn't one…

MT: What? Listen, Researcher, after all this effort, don't you think it would be sensible to help people navigate this whole thing. You know, Chap. 1 will be about this, and Chap. 2 about that. It's only fair.

M: (*Showing irritation*) For goodness' sake. Whose side are you on? I've been making the point again, and again for ages now that it's the music that makes a difference to people… and the painting and the stories and the mobile. Getting absorbed in them is what will get the message across, not all the talking. If you spell it all out in the introduction it's like saying: hello everyone, here's a book about discovering what happens when you taste something unexpected – only, just so you know it's going to be cinnamon, then mushrooms, then coffee. I mean, it ruins the whole point!

(*Researcher seems offended.*)

C: Don't worry, Musician. I think Music Therapist was just trying to make things a bit easier for the Collaborators and make them feel welcome. You know, they could have opened another book and then they would never know what matters to you … to us. And you're right, - the things that matter most to you have turned out to be the whole point of this story…

M: I don't know why I got involved in all this. It's not what I've spent hours practising for.

C: But I think you're wrong, Musician. It really *is* what you have given all that time and care and commitment to. You care so much about the people you meet in music therapy that you want to validate their knowing and their artful being. You always talk about it.

MT: So do I!

C: Yes, yes of course, and you Music Therapist. (*Pause*) I think it will be ok. Let's just begin and if things get really muddled, we can put some sort of signposts in, can't we, Researcher?

R: Definitely. For a start, the plan is all there in the Contents page (*Musician sighs*). And yes, we can give a bit of description so that people can navigate. I never said we couldn't do that. And there is an index because I know I've gone to books with a particular focus in mind and wanted to find bits to do with that. … So, (*Cautiously*) are we ready?

High Wycombe, UK Jessica Atkinson

# Competing Interests

The author has no competing interests to declare that are relevant to the content of this manuscript.

# Contents

# About the Author

**Jessica Atkinson** Jessica trained as a classical musician and linguist and was always puzzled by the distance from stage to audience. As a student, she discovered the writings of Nordoff and Robbins, pioneers in music therapy, and longed to think about people and music in the ways they did. This led to music therapy training and over the last twenty-six years she has met and worked with participants who experience learning difficulties, life-limiting illness, emotional difficulties, bereavement, traumatic injury, physical disabilities and more. Jessica began research in order to understand better the nonverbal and arts-based knowing which lies at the heart of music therapy encounters. She completed her PhD at King's College London.

# List of Figures

CHAPTER 1

# Beginning the Journey

## Direct Message 1

### *Background to This Book*

Dear Collaborator,[1]

In the Preface, Musician briefly identified what mattered most to her in the research exploration contained in this book, namely the arts-based engagement which led to the making of pictures, poems, stories, fused glass pendants, a mobile, a video and a sound-track. This engagement also led to a deeper recognition and theorising of the nonverbal and arts-based knowing that is both generated by and validated in music therapy experiences, and which I will suggest could be construed as evidence. As Researcher, I found that these features proved to be both the substance and findings of my investigation, and that Musician's instinct was powerful.

In order to share these experiences of engaging, which matter so much to Musician, I need to explain why I set out on a journey of research in the first place. As you know, I am Researcher and I am addressing you as 'Collaborator' because I am grateful for your involvement and I realise I need your willingness to *experience* this arts-based exploration if the book

[1] As explained in the Preface, this book is offered as an arts-based experience in which you—reader, engager, participator—are invited to be a Collaborator. The author's involvement is presented by four Roles, each representing a part of her experience: Musician, Music Therapist, Carer and Researcher.



J. Atkinson, *Insights From Music Therapy Practice and Research*,
https://doi.org/10.1007/978-3-031-86220-5_1

is going to communicate in the way it needs to, that is if you are to have the opportunity to experience this other knowing and potentially value it. However, I realise that however great my interest is in engaging you as a Collaborator, and whatever curiosity I may have about your experiences, I cannot expect you to share these as there has been no process of informed consent, and your involvement is not that of research participant.

As I am writing to you, and not discussing issues with the other Roles in a conversation, I will use headings and references as I think they may bring some clarity.

*The Focus of Exploration in This Book*

This book came into being because I wanted to understand more about the experiences that occur in music therapy: what is their nature, how are they experienced, what knowing is involved or emerges, why might any of this matter? In particular, I wanted to investigate the notion of evidence, because as a practitioner I intuitively felt there must be a link between a participant's *experience*, and *evidence* of their therapy, yet I found it hard to discern this link within dominant attitudes to evidence.

*The Field of Study*

In this research I take a broad definition of the field of music therapy, in respect of who and what is involved. I conceptualise the field as a collection of people and activities which nurture the musical therapeutic encounter between music therapists and participants, and which encompass all the interactions and happenings that occur in order for those who need music therapy to participate: the other actors involved are as varied as medical, healthcare and allied-healthcare staff, formal and informal carers, fundraisers, care-takers, researchers, service providers, commissioners, third sector partners, transport providers, interested public and more. The happenings and interactions are numerous and diverse, including focused listening, sharing, and communicating in music, supervising, training, informing the public, building provider partnerships, sharing skills with families, researching, presenting at conferences, accounting, budgeting, planning events, cleaning instruments … the list is long. I fully describe the field of music therapy, as I understand it, in Section "Direct Message 2".

*Telling the Story of This Enquiry*

This book is an autoethnography.[2] All research tells a story (Thomas, 2009, p. 2) but autoethnographic stories are a particular type: they seek to use and explore the subjectivity of the researcher in order to represent reality as a collection of contextualised subjective parts, rather than as an objective whole, and thereby 'expand the understanding of social realities' (Chang, 2013, p. 108). The emphasis on the researcher is important. However, this became problematic early on in this project. Being a researcher is a role, like being a shopper, or a friend. Nobody is ever *only* a researcher, at any given time, and as I explain in the Preface, other roles quickly demanded a place in my exploration, without my expecting it. This happened when I found myself writing a conversation between myself as a musician, music therapist, carer and researcher. In this manner, the Roles emerged and each speaks in the first person. It is not fruitful to regard their narratives as separate: they are threads of a whole and belong together.

As I explore in Section "Dialogue 3", I have been a musician since I was five years old, a music therapist for twenty-six years, a carer—though I do not use the term—at different points of my life, and conversation was not harmonious! Strong opinions and attitudes were expressed by different Roles and, over time, I began to use this approach as an integral part of the study, conceiving it as an arts-based approach to research (see Chap. 6). Gradually, the concept of a neutral or overarching narrator seemed to be inappropriate. As you have already discovered, I therefore indicate which Role is speaking to you, Collaborator, or to another Role, at any point.[3]

*How My Investigation Took Shape*

I feel passionately about music therapy. Many aspects of my work and thinking are explored in detail later. However, in order to set my interest in experience and evidence in context, it is necessary to share some details at the outset. It is important to note that I trained and practise music therapy in the UK. Some of what follows in this book is specifically

[2] See Chap. 3.

[3] Towards the end of my journey, I became aware of a master's thesis by an unnamed researcher who dramatised a fiery marriage between 'Music' and 'Therapy', with multiple endings (cited in Forinash, 2016, p. 41). Shortly before submission, I discovered Gilbertson's queering of the music therapist identity, presented as a play between two characters (A and B) and Chorus (2022). I have drawn much encouragement from these precedents.

relevant to this culture. However, I hope that other themes and insights may have more universal relevance with regard to the essence and significance of interpersonal musical and arts-based engagement.

I began exploring the unique way of being with people and music that music therapy offers when I was sixteen and, as mentioned, I have worked in the field for twenty-six years, as a practitioner. For many years, I followed the advice of my training, worked hard and questioned little. When I had practised for around fifteen years, I collaborated with a colleague to provide service to families with autistic children.[4]

Everything that happened in this shared work changed my thinking about music therapy. Although I lacked the following concepts and terminology at the time, I encountered an ethic of care[5] in the family carers, became uncomfortable with the illness ideology[6] that dominates Western healthcare and although our service was fully inclusive, I had a dim consciousness that inclusivity and anti-oppression[7] are not the same, and I wanted to work anti-oppressively. Once I started exploring research, I soon became aware of an overwhelming dominance of verbal accounts in music therapy. Where did that leave the insights of our many nonverbal clients? As I moved further into research, I became concerned that there were colonial foundations to Western research processes and methodologies.[8] In short, I realised I was acquiring '"dangerous knowledge," that is; knowledge that challenges taken-for-granted assumptions in clinical practices' (Stige & Aarø, 2011, p. 27).

In particular, I became exasperated with the music therapy profession. We had had choices when we shaped our interaction with the

[4] See Section "Dialogue 3".

[5] See Section "Direct Message 4".

[6] Rolvsjord (2010) explores this concept within music therapy—see Section "Direct Message 2".

[7] I understand inclusion to mean the removal of barriers to participation. I am drawn to Roni Strier's exploration of anti-oppressive practice in social work as it highlights the same dangers faced by music therapists, namely that the power imbalance inherent in both practice and research 'may replicate the structural conditions that generate oppression' (2007, p. 859).

[8] Numerous scholars identify the domination of colonial settlers over indigenous peoples in various locations, and the consequent imposition of settler ideologies and methodologies (Carlson, 2017; Hart et al., 2017; Chilisa, 2020; Seppälä et al., 2021; Thambinathan & Kinsella, 2021).

neighbouring fields of therapy, medicine, arts in health, community music, and the interwoven field of research. We could have remained loyal to our unique identity, but we chose to align ourselves to the attitudes and practices of psychotherapy and to adopt medical model, linear research designs, and later a fixation with outcomes.

This is a gross oversimplification, and I accept the accusation that I have contributed nothing to the discussion and development of our profession, and in fact have benefitted enormously, on my own account, from the tireless effort of those who pioneered the work and others who have later fought for professional and financial recognition from sundry commissioning organisations, institutions and regulatory bodies.

However, fifteen or so years into my work as a music therapist, this status quo started to become uncomfortable, particularly as it felt so at odds with the types of interactions, relationships and musical encounters we were having in the service for families. After four years, the organisation providing this service abruptly changed its priorities and working practices, and the service was terminated. I was not able to reconcile myself to this occurrence and left the organisation. I felt a sense of shame and compromise that was exceedingly strong: I felt divided and 'dis-integrated', because my beliefs were totally at odds with my required behaviour. I became aware that there had been other events in my working life that had led to this dividedness in myself, and I wanted to explore whether there was anything about me, music, music therapy, or anything else, that linked them and that I could learn from. The concept of 'integrity demand' grew from these questions, and is explored in detail in Section "Direct Message 5". It refers to a need to be, or do, in a certain way in order to retain a sense of personal wholeness.

All through this time, whilst I was continuing to work with people and music, offering therapy sessions to numerous participants, the shift to 'evidence-based practice' was taking hold (Bonde et al., 2002, Chapter 5.4; Vink & Bruinsma, 2003, pp. 15–23; Bunt & Stige, 2014, pp. 201–4; Aigen, 2015, p. 14; Baker, 2015, Chapter 9; Wheeler & Bruscia, 2016, p. 9).[9] This was apparent to different extents in different settings, but I was most starkly conscious of it in a neurological rehabilitation setting.

[9] See Section "Direct Message 2" for a discussion of evidence-based practice in music therapy.

Here, measurement seemed to take priority over relationship in music therapy. Goals were required and constantly updated when desired measurements were achieved. I was confused and still am, by the requirement to pre-determine the outcome of therapy in this way.

The journey from distress and disappointment to this book has been long and full. For many years of research and practice, I have been living with a network of questions around what evidence might be, what knowing may be like, what allows a participant's integrity to remain intact (whether therapist or client or any other stakeholder), what may or may not oppress others or be valued by them, what system of ethics is guiding whom, all in relation to the arts-based medium of music making. I was not conscious of it, but in the years leading up to this investigation and the early years of exploration, I had started to feel a particular urgency around these issues when I thought about participants who are nonverbal, or do not use language.[10] More recently, through examining literature, reflecting on practice and discussing ideas in supervision, I have recognised that the phenomenon that is common to all of these questions is *experience*: my integrity demands are provoked by experiences; I fear the loss of wisdom that could result from neglecting the nonverbal experience of others; an ethic of care, like the wind, can only truly be experienced—description is not enough.

But what of evidence? I am grateful to my friend, the educationalist and scholar Miranda Dodd[11] for first asking the question 'aren't evidence and experience the same thing, in music therapy?'[12] I am fascinated by this proposition. It probes into the musical encounter at the heart of music therapy. But it also probes into the cultures of music therapy as a

[10] Language users have skills to formulate meaning through the use of words and shared structures. They may communicate this verbal meaning through speech, or pictorial systems, or sign, or more personalised solutions. Some fluent users of speech may lack meaningful language skills, because they have lost them through a stroke or accident, or because they were unable to learn them. Some people who are capable of spoken language choose not to speak. In this study, I use the term 'nonverbal' to describe people who have no, or very limited, language skills as well as no recognisable speech.

[11] Dodd's doctoral thesis uses dialogue between Researcher and Practitioner in Chaps. 2, 6, 8, 10 and 11 (2014). She credits as her inspiration the dialogue format of ancient Greek philosopher Plato's writings, for example *The Republic* (2007). Dodd, in turn, greatly influenced my decision to allow the Roles their voices.

[12] This question arose in a discussion on a Northumberland beach at Easter, 2022.

whole—what assumptions and value judgements dominate, why do they arise, are these assumptions and judgements tacit or openly acknowledged, who benefits from them, who does not? On an ontological level, the proposition additionally asks what sort of things *are* experience and evidence.

The issue of evidence matters, because I perceive a self-perpetuating cycle: evidence-based practice lends itself to evidence-based research. Funding follows evidence-based research. Funding enables therapists to continue pursuing evidence-based practice, and so on. The notion of experiential, emergent therapeutic change, which I was trained as a music therapist to facilitate, is increasingly hard to justify as the purpose of therapy: the unique experience of relational music making becomes a *context* for measurement rather than a *source* of knowing and healing. This upsets me.

It is clear that Gary Ansdell and Mercedes Pavlicevic share my concern (Ansdell & Pavlicevic, 2010; Ansdell, 2017). These authors highlight the exact problem that music therapists often 'replac[e] the phenomenon [of music therapy] with abstractions (be they words or numbers)' when undertaking research to 'evidence of the efficacy of music therapy' (2010, p. 131). They provide a strong 'rebuttal' to this trend by exploring the '"gentle empiricism"' developed by Goethe, embraced by Steiner, and carried into Nordoff Robbins music therapy practice and research by Paul Nordoff and Clive Robbins themselves. This approach emphasises deep attention to a phenomenon as it emerges, a reverential attitude to this emergence, and an avoidance of preconceived theoretical stances (p. 134). Ansdell further probes at the purpose of evidence by questioning whether it is to 'show or prove?' (2017, p. 126).

However, I am still left with questions. I began by clarifying that I regard the field of music therapy as comprising all the interactions of diverse actors, and all the happenings that occur in varied activities in order that people who need it are able to participate in a musical therapeutic encounter. Perhaps it is stating the obvious to explain that all interaction, occurrences and participation that happen in the socially constructed, socially mediated field of music therapy, necessarily draw upon *and* generate experience. Personally, I do not think it is too obvious to state. However, there is virtually no existing music therapy research which seeks to make this point. Nor have I encountered any literature that explores the relationship between experience and evidence in music therapy. Indeed, although there is much in Ansdell and Pavlicevic's work that speaks to my interests and concerns, I still have questions concerning *what the experience of music therapy is*, at an ontological level. Furthermore, whilst there is some research that investigates culture, I have not found any that focuses on the cultures of the profession. I therefore intend to address these issues in this book.

It is my hope that this will be of interest to music therapists and all the other people who are involved in making music therapy happen, according to my broad definition: this is my primary intended audience. In addition, I hope it might appeal to anyone who is interested in evidence-based care and the experience of personhood, as well as people navigating academia when their research involves art-full, nonverbal communication. Moving beyond my specific field of study and the particular topics involved, I hope this study will encourage all those who are drawn to research to explore different ways of knowing in order to honour the widest possible diversity of wisdom and experience in others.

Thank you again for collaborating,
Best wishes,
Researcher

PS A note on the term 'experience' (Experience as a concept is fully discussed in Chaps. 3, 4, 5 and 6.)

It is difficult to give you my definition of the term 'experience' at this point, because this book is committed to providing an experiential journey through which the notion can be explored, identified and described, within the context of music therapy. So, at this point of departure, I use the term in the vernacular sense of *something I have gone through, or apprehended or that has happened*. I agree with Ansdell (2014, p. 57) who identifies two usages of the term in everyday speech, discussed in Chap. 3:

1. Experience as 'something personal we accumulate (as in, "After thirty years, I'm an experienced pianist")'; Later in Chap. 3 I personally conceptualise this as 'embedded experience' (my term).
2. Experience as 'something more immediate and particular that we undergo in the present, and that leaves a vivid impression (as in, "I had this extraordinary experience this morning!")'. I personally conceptualise this as 'in the moment experience'.

## Dialogue 1

### *Some Tensions Emerge Between the Roles and They Discuss Their Motivations for Contributing to This Book*

Are we all met? Pat, pat.[13]

MT: Hey, what just happened?

*Silence*

MT: I mean, what *was* that?

M: What?

MT: We sort of zoned out. It was … I don't know. … what was it?

*Pause*

R: It might have been me?

MT: How? In what way?

R: Well, I was Direct Messaging the Collaborators.

M: What does *that* mean?!

R: The people engaging with this book…

M: Oh, the audience.

MT: The listeners?

C: I thought they were readers…

MT: Anyway, why? I thought we were all part of everything?

[13] Shakespeare, *A Midsummer Night's Dream,* Act 3 Scene 1 (1986, p. 361).

R: But you know what it's been like. The rest of you get so up-tight when I talk about theory.

MT: That's not really fair…

R: Sorry, not you, Carer…

C: Sorry?

M: So? What's with Direct Messaging?

R: It's just something I thought would be helpful. Then when *we* get together, we can just talk…

M: Instead of sleeping through all those endless ideas?

R: That's what I mean. You hardly relish the experience … I figured it wasn't your favourite part, so I just thought it could help to message the Collaborators with my thinking.

MT: But how will *we* know what you're thinking, then?

R: Music Therapist! What are you on about? We four are together all the time! We debate all this stuff constantly. It's only the Collaborators who are limited to these pages.

MT: Oh … confusing…

R: Not really…

MT: I suppose it's fair enough, then.

R: Believe me, you didn't like it. It's been pretty tough throughout these years, particularly since trying to get this book together.

C: Sorry, Researcher. It shouldn't have been like that.

R: Oh, don't worry … But anyway, that's what it was—a Direct Message—and there will be more.

*Pause*

M: So long as you don't tell them anything that we don't know, or don't say that anything comes from one of us, when it doesn't.

R: Why would I do that?

M: Just checking…

*Pause*

R: It's particularly you, Musician. Do you even remember the number of times you complained that you didn't want to be part of footnotes and the like. Remember? You said you'd only join in this exploration if it would be about music, and that *that's* what you care about?

*Pause*

R: Music Therapist, why are you here, for that matter? Musician's here for it to be about music. What about you?

MT: Well, … I suppose I'm here for the people. I want their voices to be heard. I know them through music, so being here for music goes without saying. But I'm here for them really—I want them to feel valued.

*Pause.*

R: And you, Carer?

*Pause.*

M: Has she gone?

C: No, I'm here.

R: But *why* are you here? I just want to check.

C: Because we need to do this. You know. There are people who need a chance to know themselves in music. It makes a difference. But it is always a fight to get there. So we need to do this together and make the case. That's why, really.

R: Thanks, Carer.

*Pause.*

C: Researcher, why are you here?

R: Me? Well … the thing is … it's because of minding about it. I want people to know I'm not researching because it's quite interesting, or because I want a new job, or because I think I have any particularly special message. I'm doing it because I'm worried what will happen if I *don't* put my tiny drop in the ocean. We may lose something I care about if we don't make a stand.

C: I think it's all about motivation, isn't it?

M: What is?

C: Why we are here, you know. We all have different motivations, and we could each keep track as the writing goes along. Just an idea.

M: OK. It would be better, anyway. It wouldn't be all of us just tagging along after you, then.

R: What! That isn't….

MT: *(Interrupting)* Musician, *please!* We've been through this. No-one's trying to waste your time or pull rank. Why the agro now? Can't we just give Researcher a chance? There's another eighty-odd thousand words to complain in. Please let's just get started for now. For goodness' sake…

M: Maybe, but you….

C: We were talking about our motivations.

R: Yes, I know.

C: I think that if we record our motivations it will help us keep this investigation doing what we want it to do. … actually, what it needs to do.

R: Oh. Interesting. You're probably right. Will you start?

C: OK—you probably know this, but as a Carer, I really can't be doing with the oppression that flows from our ableist, neurotypical social structures and values. I see music therapy as offering something to counter this. We lose this, and we regress.

R: Well, that's your background, what's your motivation—I think we'll need it if we're going to hold each other to account throughout the project!

C: Fair enough. My motivation is this: as a Carer, I'm here to ensure that people living with impairment or disability or difference are heard on their own terms, and to advocate for an approach to music therapy that honours these voices. Is that snappy enough!

MT: It's good, it's clear. Musician, what's your motivation?

M: I believe that the relational encounter that occurs within music making is a human need: it's un-replicable and contributes uniquely to fullness of life; and fullness of life is denied to so many of the people who participate in music therapy.

R: Yes, and that's your belief. What is your motivation?

M: *(Thinking)* My motivation is this: as a Musician I am here to insist that nothing else contributes to fullness of life in the way that music making does.

R: Thanks, Musician. That's good. Do you want to go next, Music Therapist?

MT: Yes. My motivation is this: as a Music Therapist, I am here to find out what the experiences in music therapy actually *are* and what they are evidence *of*.

R: OK, and as a Researcher, I want to explore what it is about the cultures of music therapy that leads to some experiences being accepted as evidence, others not, and whether there is scope for re-thinking this.

M: That works. Are we done?

MT: I'm not sure. Our four motivations cover a lot of the concepts in the introduction, but there is another, mainly to do with *how* we do this research.

M: Oh come on, we're getting these motivations out in the open so we can check up whether we are actually keeping on track. Surely four is enough. We won't manage more, it's getting overloaded.

MT: No, I'm not thinking of motivations. More like a promise. I'm thinking our Promise is that it's a non-negotiable integrity demand, for all of us, that in this research we'll always avoid oppression of others and foster an ethic of care through the music therapy and research practices we use.

R: OK … but it's all getting a bit full and clumsy…

MT: I know, but that's why: it's *because* this project feels big and unwieldy and could easily vanish down rabbit holes. I just want to make sure we do what we say, because otherwise it won't align with our motivations.

C: True.

R: Well, if you think so…

MT: Thanks.

*Pause.*

R: By the way, who found the quotation?

M: I did.

MT: It makes me laugh, that quote ... you remember? A bunch of craftsmen meet to rehearse a play. Think of this as a rehearsal, and for goodness' sake, do start...

R: Me? What's going on?

C: Don't worry. Can you just answer the question?

R: What question?

C: Whether we are all 'met'?

R: Oh, that ... (*Long pause)* I suppose some of us are 'met', but not all of us yet. I wanted to investigate these aspects of music therapy because I have worked as a music therapist for twenty-six years.

MT: Well, I have, in my role, actually.

R: (*Frustrated*) This is what I mean: every time I try and say something, another Role butts in and complains that I'm speaking out of turn. Sorry, not you, Carer. Anyway, I do think it's OK to say that I'm a music therapist, because music therapists do research work as well. In fact, most music therapy research is done by practitioners—I can hardly think of any that isn't.

MT: True, but...

R: Anyway, are we all met? Actually, there are loads more people involved in their own ways in this research: caretakers of spaces, neighbours and others who suggest music therapy to people who need it, therapists, participants of course, carers of every sort—formal, informal, young, older—commissioners, service providers, researchers, supervisors, trainers, multidisciplinary team members, everyone. They join the book in the stories, poems and vignettes, later on. So that's who we all are—the cast list, if you like...oh, and all the people whose books and articles I talk about.

*Silence.*

MT: There's a way to go before that, though.

R: I know, let's move on.

## Direct Message 2

### *Music Therapy: Purpose, Practice and Profession*[14]

Dear Collaborator,

I am sorry you have been drawn into what must seem quite a fractious start to this book. As Researcher, I did not expect it to be like that, but that is how it has turned out anyway. I am quite glad to have the chance to talk to you directly, in fact. It is fairly chaotic trying to explore a topic with three other Roles all wanting to have their say and shape the research.

I know you will be expecting a clear theoretical framework, and there is plenty to share with you. This message will mainly be about music therapy itself. Sorry if it comes a bit late. I realise it is essential for you to understand the field of exploration—it is a fairly unfamiliar field for many, so I will try to explain it as fully as possible.

It is a relief to have the chance to write a little more formally. However, I know I will upset the other Roles if I engage in analysis or broader discussion here, since we have finally agreed that any discussion is going to happen in the Dialogue conversations.

Please do get in touch if there is anything that does not make sense, or anything that you would like to know more about.

*My Background in Music Therapy*

When I was sixteen, I heard of music therapy. I had vaguely known about Nordoff and Robbins because my mother had explored music teaching in special schools as part of her training as a music teacher. A few years later, after taking a degree in German and Italian, I followed suit and trained as

[14] It is important for me to reiterate that this section will inevitably be affected and biased by the fact that I trained and practise in the UK (see also Section "Direct Message 1"). I hope that there are sufficient aspects that resonate with the fields of music therapy in other locations. I know I have read about music therapy elsewhere that shares central features of purpose, practice and profession with those I recognise in the UK.

a teacher of music and drama (secondary). I was inspired by my mother's stories and followed her example, setting up a placement in a couple of special schools.

The problem with this experience was that I did not know what I was doing. I did not have skills to offer meaningful music making to the children with severe physical and learning difficulties that I was meeting. I started reading about music therapy and was profoundly moved by Nordoff and Robins' *Therapy in Music for Handicapped Children* (1973). I wanted to know how to think about both people and music the way they did. Five years later, after teaching in a secondary comprehensive school and a 6–18 special school, whilst also working as a violinist and violin teacher, I was accepted for training as a music therapist at Nordoff Robbins centre in London.

*My Concept of Music Therapy*

As I mentioned in the conversation, I regard the field of music therapy as comprising all the interactions of diverse actors, and all the happenings that occur in varied activities in order that people who need it are able to participate in a musical therapeutic encounter. I have at some point in my working life occupied almost all the roles that I can think of: I have been both therapist and client in music therapy, as well as carer of someone receiving music therapy. I have provided administration support, fundraised and acted as caretaker for a music therapy space. I have been lecturer, student, supervisee, supervisor and trainer. I have worked as part of a multidisciplinary team, been a lone worker, and had both employed and self-employed status. I have been a service provider on location and a peripatetic therapist. I have been an evaluator, writer about music therapy and now researcher. By referring to music therapy, I include the entire field—practice, profession and academia.

*Defining Music Therapy*

For practitioners, this is a rich and ever present problem. Kenneth Bruscia has devoted an entire book, in three editions, to the subject, identifying over one hundred current definitions. He concludes that, at its heart, music therapy involves a therapist and participant(s) in a musical encounter for a beneficial purpose. He offers the following 'working definition' for the profession:

> Music therapy is a reflexive process wherein the therapist helps the client to optimize the client's health, using various facets of music experience and the relationships formed through them as the impetus for change. As defined here, music therapy is the professional practice component of the discipline, which informs and is informed by theory and research. (Bruscia, 2014, p. 36)

*The Purpose of Music Therapy*

Healing is central to the current meaning and purpose of therapy, drawing on the original Greek word *therapeia* (healing). How such healing is achieved in a musical context is much debated (see below—Approaches to Music Therapy).

*Being a Music Therapist: Musical Activities, Formats, Settings, Client Groups and Funding*

In the UK, trainees typically learn improvisation skills to a high level, and there was a very strong emphasis on this in my own training. However, in this country, music therapy involves a wide variety of approaches, including improvising, playing pre-composed music, composing, song-writing, story-telling, listening to music, discussing music, moving/dancing, performing. The format can be individual work, small or large group work, including drop-in or open groups, and family work. The settings range from people's homes, to institutions (hospitals, schools, colleges, prisons), to community settings (charity drop-in mornings, community rehabilitation centres) to supported living (care homes) and even on-line sessions.

Client groups are varied: I have personally worked with adults with learning difficulties, adults in hospice care, people who are bereaved, adolescents with emotional and behavioural difficulties, autistic children, adults in neurological rehabilitation, families with children with additional needs, adults with mental health difficulties, and in clinics which offer music therapy to anyone in need. In these, I have worked with people with issues as diverse as mapping cochlear implants, social isolation, anxiety, physical disability, learning difficulty, autism spectrum disorder. The youngest child I have worked with was six months old, the oldest adult received a telegram from the late Queen for reaching her hundredth birthday whilst I worked in her care home. I have worked alongside numerous different kinds of carers who support others (informal, formal, paid, unpaid, young, older) as well as many different multidisciplinary team professionals, including physiotherapists, speech and language therapists, occupational therapists, psychologists, medics, nurses, healthcare assistants, teaching assistants and more.

Some music therapy is funded by schools and the NHS (in mental healthcare in particular). However, the third sector is a major funder and it is not uncommon for a school or prison, for example, to host a service that is paid for by a third-party charity. This can mean that the working lives of therapists can be insecure. Often, charitably funded music therapy pilot projects are very well received, but no ongoing funding can be found and self-employed therapists, in particular, can experience difficulties in this way.

For the first fifteen years of my work as a practitioner, I set up all the work I did, and had no regular contact with other arts therapists of any kind. I then joined a large music therapy team for four years and later moved to my current employer—a national, not-for-profit music therapy provider. I have been part of this large team for eight years, now.

*Reasons for Participating in Music Therapy: How Can Music Therapy Help?*

Music therapy takes as its starting point the notion that a vast majority of people respond to music (Roth & Wisser, 2004, pp. 52–4; Koelsch, 2014, pp. 170, 178; Egermann et al., 2015, pp. 7–8). With this in mind, music therapists seek to engage the participant in music in any way that is meaningful to them, and which can help address the particular difficulty, vulnerability or need that they are experiencing. Because music is a realm of sensory, creative and aesthetic experience involving people in time, music therapy can address difficulties in many different areas of people's lives: developmental, social, functional, spiritual, emotional, psychological, cultural. For example, the structure provided by an early-years greeting song can help autistic infants to develop the social and functional skills of listening, turn-taking, planning, sequencing and coordination (as they prepare to gap-fill using the drum they are offered when the predictable gap arises). Or, a vocal blues in a neuro-rehab group can help participants extend their pitch range and outbreath (essential for sustaining speech), thereby offering emotional, psychological and physiological support: the participants gain confidence and self-esteem as they enhance their breath control and realise that they are communicating successfully, making sense in music, without needing words. The developmental skills of playfulness, problem solving, memory, self-control, initiating and following can all be experienced and developed by young adults with learning difficulties rehearsing their band for a performance.

Exactly how this 'help' is measured, whether as part of a 'treatment' or research programme, depends on the setting. Changes in all the areas mentioned are observable and, above all, audible, hence the occurrence of music CDs or download links in music therapy books (Nordoff & Robbins, 1977; Ansdell, 1995; Bonde et al., 2002). Self-reporting, by participants experiencing music therapy, is included to some extent in the majority of studies in which participants have this capacity and is used by therapists in their own assessment and evaluation. Studies from medical settings demonstrate that physical and chemical changes in the body and brain can occur during and after music therapy (Aldridge, 2003; Chou et al., 2003; Chang & Chen, 2005; Sendelbach et al., 2006; Chuang et al., 2010; Liu et al., 2010; Loewy et al., 2013; Aigen, 2014b, pp. 17–22). Both the form of the measurement, and its reporting, will be influenced by the intended audience for that information (Wood, 2016, p. 127).

What the role of *music* is in this therapeutic journey of change depends on the therapist's approach to their work.

*Approaches to Music Therapy*

There are a variety of different music therapy approaches. Broadly speaking, many practitioners trained in Nordoff Robbins music therapy often describe their work as 'music centred'. Those whose work draws heavily upon psychotherapeutic theory and concepts tend to refer to their work as 'psychodynamic music therapy' (Aigen, 1999, 2014a, Chapter 3). Other specialist approaches have developed for specific client groups. In reality, many therapists might nowadays have a basic approach, but use insights from other approaches to broaden their work.

## Music Centred Music Therapy

Nordoff and Robbins themselves defined their work as 'creative music therapy', rather than 'music centred'. Their writing (1971, 1973, 1977) reveals their profound anthroposophical belief in the unique value and communicative potential of every person, and this emerges as the guiding principle in the work.[15] The approach that Nordoff and Robbins

[15] Students in the Nordoff Robbins approach still learn the fundamental principle of the 'music child', that is, 'the individualized musicality inborn in each child' (Nordoff & Robbins, 1977, p. 1). Whilst Nordoff and Robbins based this claim on their empirical obser-

pioneered in this early stage forms the foundation of the Nordoff Robbins music therapy that is practised across the world today (Simpson, 2007, Chapters 2, 3, 4).

I will describe this in detail as it is the approach that I take in my work. What it means is that the actual phenomenon of the music that is made between participant(s) and therapist is seen as the locus of therapeutic change (Ansdell, 1995, p. 4; Aigen, 1998, p. 291; Verney & Ansdell, 2010; Ansdell, 2014, pp. 46–7; Bunt & Stige, 2014, pp. 49–51). Aigen refers to this as music *as* therapy (2014a, p. 56 'Interventions through music or as music'). A foundational belief of music centred music therapy is that, whilst we all have musical preferences, a healthy person is able to move flexibly between the different roles (leading, following, initiating, co-creating) and elements (pitch, pulse, metre, rhythm, motif, timbre, mood, style, phrase, cadence, genre and articulation) inherent in music making. Because most of the people who come to music therapy are in fact living with some form of difficulty, and are not enjoying full health, well-being, or potential, the music centred music therapist can assess the participant's musical profile, noticing which areas are avoided, difficult or blocked, and work for flexibility in these areas. So, for example, an adult with mental health difficulties might beat percussion loudly, apparently avoiding a therapist's attempt to draw them into shared musical phrase or cadence. The music therapist may well engage the participant with talking on a common sense and social level, but would not seek to work towards flexibility primarily through speech. Rather, the therapist would devise as many opportunities as possible for the participant to become aware of their own part in the music, their inflexibility, and the scope of music for offering a different, phrased, nuanced and fluid world of experience. In this way, the therapist can work to give the participant a new, more flexible experience of self, within music.

### Psychodynamic Music Therapy

'Psychodynamic', or 'psychodynamically informed' music therapy (Sobey & Woodcock, 1999; Aigen, 2014b, Chapter 3; Kim, 2016; Metzner,

vation of the many children they worked with, it is significant that since then, prominent researchers in the fields of psychiatry, psychoanalytic theory (Stern, 1977, 1985), psychology, psychobiology and music psychology (Malloch & Trevarthen, 2009) have corroborated the claim with numerous forms of evidence. For an overview of contributors to this field, see Aigen's *The study of Music Therapy* Chapters 13–15 (2014b).

2016) refers to music therapy that allows for the locus of therapy to lie within aspects of the therapy other than the music making itself: a typical focus for this work could be interpersonal dynamics, as experienced both within and outside of the music making between therapist and participant(s). These dynamics are explored for personal growth and change, and as such, the approach would constitute an 'intervention *through* music' (Aigen, 2014b, p. 56).

The origins of this approach are both ideological and historical. Early pioneers in UK music therapy were drawn to psychotherapeutic and analytic concepts, notably Juliette Alvin (1965 Chapter 3), Mary Priestly (1994), Marjorie Wardell and Peter Wright (cited in Hadley, 2003, p. 2). However, in addition, it has long been recognised within the profession that early practitioners sought validation for their work by adopting theories and practices from the pre-existing and widely accepted field of psychotherapy (Aigen, 2014b, pp. 218–19; Bunt & Stige, 2014, p. 15). In particular, the notion of the therapeutic frame (Gray, 2013, pp. 5–7), the concepts of transference, counter transference and projective identification in interpersonal dynamics (Yalom, 1995), and the professional expert persona of the therapist, all became central to UK music therapy in the early decades (1960s–1990s) and were influenced by psychotherapeutic and medical approaches. Indeed, until the late 1990s, when Pavlicevic, Ansdell, Stige, Wood and others involved in the development of Community Music Therapy (see below) began to offer new literature that challenged both the notion of expert therapist, as well as an interpretation of the therapeutic frame which assumed that therapy happened behind closed doors, and notions of 'clinical' versus 'other' music, many music therapists would probably have regarded the psychotherapeutic model of music therapy, named the 'consensus model' by Ansdell and Pavlicevic (Ansdell, 2002; Pavlicevic & Ansdell, 2004, pp. 21–23), as the only *real* music therapy—other approaches were somehow outside accepted practice.

Theory building in early psychodynamic music therapy also turned to the neighbouring profession of psychology for explanation and inspiration. In particular, Winnicott's concepts of 'the facilitating environment' and of play (1991, 2018), Bowlby's theory of attachment (1982), and Stern's investigations into early infant interaction (1977) formed key conceptual foundations which are still relevant, and taught, today. In summary, from the earliest days of music therapy, widely differing ideas of 'what counts' have been expounded and developed.

**Specific Approaches**

In America, where music therapy grew out of rehabilitation services for ex-service men and women in postwar hospitals, a behaviourist approach has developed (Hanser, 2015) and receptive music therapy is utilised, i.e. the use of listening to music for clinical purposes. Guided Imagery and Music (GIM), an approach founded by Helen Bonny, combines Jungian and transpersonal theory with active listening to music and visualisation (Ventre & McKinney, 2015).

More recently, some specific approaches to music therapy have developed for particular contexts. Thaut (2010), for example, has pioneered 'neurologic music therapy' programmes in which music is used in systematic activities to enhance cognitive and physical rehabilitation. Additional training is required for this work. Rolvsjord has championed 'resource-oriented' music therapy in mental health settings (2010): building on 'wellness ideology' of health promotion (Chap. 2), as opposed to the 'illness ideology' prevalent in contemporary Western healthcare (Chap. 1), she advocates music therapy which celebrates strengths and empowerment in the participant and seeks equality between participant and therapist as music makers (pp. 42–44). Rolvsjord is a further strong influence in my work.

**Community Music Therapy**

A growing branch of music therapy is known as Community Music Therapy (Ansdell, 2002; Pavlicevic & Ansdell, 2004; Stige & Aarø, 2011; Ansdell, 2014; Wood, 2016). In her introduction to Part III of *Music Therapy Handbook*, Barbara Wheeler (2015) summarises the scope and ideology of Community Music Therapy:

> Community Music Therapy (CoMT) is distinguished from traditional music therapy by its participatory, ecological and sometimes also activist orientation. The focus on how music therapy can function outside of normal boundaries, often in non-traditional ways in the community, implies that social change, not only individual change, is part of the agenda. The author [Brynjulf Stige] says that CoMT "encourages musical participation and social inclusion, equitable access to resources, and collaborative efforts for health and wellbeing in contemporary societies". Because sensitivity to context is highly valued in CoMT, it is practised in diverse ways around the world. (Stige, 2015, Chapter 19 cited in Wheeler, 2015, p. 131)

The Community Music Therapy approach strongly informs my own work and much of my working life has been committed to offering this musical meeting-place to participants[16].

*Evidence-Based Practice in Music Therapy*

My own awareness of evidence-based practice (EBP) in music therapy has been gradual. During my training, I cannot remember any discussion of the concept and its practical ramifications. This is perhaps not surprising, given that I gained my qualifying diploma in 1998 and my Masters in 1999. For it is relevant to understand the phenomenon in the context of developments in policy, research and social life in general.

Bochel and Bochel (2017) comment,

> The idea of evidence-based policy was strongly promoted by the Labour governments from 1997, in particular following the publication of the White Paper *Modernising Government* (Cabinet Office, 1999), with their 'what matters is what works' mantra (Davies et al., 2000), seeking to highlight a shift away from what was portrayed as the dominance of ideology during the Thatcher years … The move also reflected an increase in the number of groups and organisations, such as pressure groups and professional organisations, trying to exert influence on government policy, and using evidence as a way to do this, and a growing distrust among the public towards professionals, responsible for service delivery, who had hitherto largely been seen as experts. It could also be seen as linked with the increased use of audit and inspection in public services (for example, Dorey, 2014). (p. 112)

[16] Community Music Therapy is inspired, in part, by the concept of 'music(k)ing' (Elliott, 1995; Small, 1998). These authors argued strongly, and influentially, for a re-imagining of music. They asserted that UK music education pre-1990s was overly focused on music as 'art object', with a historical 'canon' to be found in the classical Western tradition alone. They argued that this established an elite who had access to this tradition, but who were nonetheless 'outsiders', learning about composers of elevated talent and expression, unlike themselves. In contrast, they suggested that art, dance and theatre were more inclusive—notice the verbs 'dancing' and 'sculpting', for example, which avoid the reification of the object and emphasise the process, hence their almost simultaneous coining of the term 'musicking' (Small) and 'musicing' (Elliot). These ideas were starting to find currency when I trained as a teacher in 1992—the first year of the National Curriculum in England, which promoted a shift from music education as music 'appreciation', towards music learning as 'doing', through composing, performing, listening and appraising.

These observations seem of considerable importance to me—when I trained, music therapists were indeed seen as 'experts'. Yet in the same period, as a profession, we were eager for statutory recognition and registration and the opportunities this would afford for 'exert[ing] influence on government policy'. In reality, I perceive that this eagerness has played out with music therapists expending more effort on trying to influence other secondary bodies who influence government, such as the medical and education professions, than on directly influencing government itself. As the authors indicate, we have done this by 'using evidence' from our work, with the result that evidence-based practice has indeed developed, whether or not this has been in response to relatively distant policy. My own experience might suggest that evidence-based practice has often been driven by the pragmatic need to secure contracts. *Presenting the Evidence* (Pavlicevic et al., 2009), corroborates my perception, as it intends to be 'The up to date guide for music therapists responding to demands for clinical effectiveness and evidence-based practice' and provides guidance, theoretical frameworks and examples.

Whatever the causes of the growth of evidence-based practice, this situation is challenging for me, as I explore throughout this study. Various music therapists consider this phenomenon in the literature. Procter describes the tensions involved in the editorial to *The British Journal of Music Therapy* 'evidence' edition (2006, pp. 74–5). Also in the early days of this approach, Vink and Bruinsma explain evidence-based practice and its reliance upon randomised control trials (RCTs) (2003, pp. 15–23). Bunt and Stige confirm my observation that evidence-based practice has been adopted by music therapists to provide 'external validation … greater professional credibility and … greater academic recognition' (2014, p. 202). They also start to question whether the methodologies used in RCTs 'limit the nature of evidence', and ask 'are there other kinds of acceptable evidence for music therapy?' (p. 203). Wheeler and Bruscia echo these thoughts and relate them directly to a music therapist's practice, noting that for 'some music therapists … the types of evidence that are generally acceptable in EBP do not reflect the goals that they have in therapy and thus their work with clients' (2016, p. 9). Baker (2015, Chapter 9) and Bonde et al. (2002, pp. 257–265) describe the process of EBP and the types of evidence which inform the approach. Interestingly, Baker notes that across healthcare, 'EBP introduced a paradigm shift … that downgrades intuition and unsystematic clinical experience, suggesting they are inadequate for clinical decision making' (p. 103).

The strongest ideological critique of the turn to evidence-based practice in music therapy comes from Aigen (2015). Drawing on his early scholarship in philosophy of science and psychology, he highlights the inherent researcher bias in the construction of RCTs and participant bias in engaging with them. He fundamentally questions the hierarchy of evidence explicit evidence-based practice: of the seven levels in the model he cites (Melnyk & Fineout-Overholt, 2005, p. 10 cited in Aigen, 2015 p. 17), the top four constitute quantitative data, with only the bottom three focusing on qualitative. This situation effectively relegates and invalidates the voice of the very people it is seeking to empower—the clients—so he regards it as unethical. Added to this, Aigen questions the notion that RCTs are a 'gold standard', and critiques the concept of a gold standard, per se, since it refers to a failed and abandoned economic policy, whereby national wealth used to be pinned to the value of gold reserves. But above all, he challenges the attempt to extrapolate evidence for music therapy through RCTs, whose dominant quantitative ideologies deny the unique, qualitative properties of musical engagement, itself (pp. 3–10). De Nora and Ansdell pursue a similar argument in their article 'What can't music do?' (2014) through their exploration of how musical engagement affords flourishing.

It is important to share what is meant by evidence-based practice in music therapy, as well as what grounds have been offered for critiquing the theoretical and practical foundations of this approach, because this book is exploring what counts as evidence in music therapy. However, my investigation is as much concerned with what counts as experience—and asks in particular whether any forms of experience could count as evidence. To this end, Abrams' article 'Evidence-based music therapy practice: an integral understanding' is particularly helpful. Abrams explores Wilber's 'epistemological domains of evidence' (Wilber, 2001 cited in Abrams, 2010, p. 353) highlighting the need for music therapists to become conscious of our own epistemological positions, i.e. our beliefs about what can be known and how. For, Wilber illuminates some distinctly differing epistemological frameworks, or conditions, that emerge when we assert what does or does not constitute evidence in a given situation. He divides these conditions or frameworks into four domains—subjective and intersubjective, which involve individual and collective 'interior' experience of evidence, and objective and inter-objective, which encompass individual and collective 'exterior' manifestations of evidence (p. 354).

I find it exciting that Abrams emphasises how definitions of evidence depend entirely upon (1) our position in relation to the events and experiences from which we are seeking this evidence, and (2) our beliefs about what can be known and how. I am also encouraged that Abrams explicitly and precisely identifies 'experience' as a dominant feature of subjective and inter-subjective domains of evidence. It is curious to me that I have found little follow-up to these ideas since Abrams addressed them in 2010. I hope this book will play a small part in this. Perhaps the clearest articulation of this gap comes from Baker (2015):

> Still missing from our evidence base are systematic reviews of qualitative studies. ... of what our clients experience and value from their participation in music therapy. (p. 113)[17]

*Tensions Encountered by Music Therapists*

Being a music therapist is a difficult professional role to hold. Musicians that we meet can become upset, imagining that their music is thought to be un-therapeutic. Education staff can question what is seen as a soft timetable—probably no more than six one-to-one sessions in a day. Medical staff can become frustrated that music therapy is unmeasurable. Volunteers in various settings can be non-plussed that this therapy can be fun, and see it as competition for other activities. And it is not uncommon for anyone encountering music therapy to be surprised that it is paid, because surely we know that music is a blessing and a joy and we are lucky if we can do it and have had the chance. I have come to expect regular moments of discomfort relating to all these attitudes, wherever I am working and in whatever role.

So, this is a broad background to the field of study. As I said before, I feel entitled to write about the practice of music therapy even though I am also a researcher, because my Researcher role has grown out of practical experience. I apologise if this overview is bland or dry. I find it fascinating! It is such a small profession, but there are numerous approaches and theories and people feel strongly about them. I know that Music Therapist feels very closely aligned to music centred work.

[17] Interestingly, in the field of nursing, David Evans argued as early as 2003 for researchers who are creating 'gold standard' systematic reviews to draw on studies offering a much wider combination of methodologies, including qualitative and descriptive (Evans, 2003, pp. 79–83).

With regard to our status as a profession, we are registered as 'healthcare professionals' under the Health and Care Professions Council and have various legal obligations, including a duty of care to our participants, adherence to safeguarding regulations, and a commitment to music therapy supervision from an appropriate professional, though interestingly this need not be a music therapist. 'Music Therapist' is a protected title and can therefore only be used by people with recognised training and registration.

It seems only fair to say that I acknowledge that this is my personal take on the music therapy field: I write as a researcher engaged in autoethnography and cannot disentangle myself from my impressions and insights—nor do I wish to. But other commentators may paint a different picture.

Thank you again for agreeing to be part of this. I will write again when the conversation turns to care ethics.

With best wishes,
Researcher

## DIALOGUE 2

### *The Audience for the Book is Considered and the Focus is Discussed*

Where should this music be? I'th'air, or th'earth?[18]

*Researcher is absent.*

C: Is it as dull as Musician thinks?

MT: What? Music therapy theory?

C: Yes.

MT: Dull! (*Laughs*) *No*, actually. Well, *I* don't think so. It's about music therapy. In fact, I think about it every day that I work, and talk about it with supervisees and with my supervisor all the time.

C: Honestly?

MT: Yes. It's what we do. It's important.

[18] Shakespeare, *The Tempest,* Act 1 Scene 2 (1986, p. 1322).

*Pause.*

C: I love that quote. It's when Ferdinand comes round after the tempest, isn't it? And music fills his ears and calms and restores him. It creates a sort of beautiful, magic realm after his ordeal. It reminds me of music therapy, really.

*They all smile.*

C: Before we go on…

MT: Yes…?

C: Would it make any difference how you worked … I mean … you say you were trained in music centred music therapy and do a lot of Community Music Therapy. But would it make any difference to us being here if you worked a different way—what was it … psychodynamic…?

M: Obviously!

C: What?

MT: No, it's OK Carer. I agree with Musician, it would make a difference, quite a big difference.

C: Why?

MT: *(Thinking)* It's because … the thing is … I've told you about music *in* therapy, or music *as* therapy. I use psychodynamic thinking in my work all the time. But my deepest belief, in terms of therapy, is that it's to do with the shared music making. It's something that's so hard to describe because it's not about words. But it's the connectedness that happens in music making: for me, that's where the therapy happens.

C: So would that connectedness not happen in other ways of doing therapy?

MT: Oh, I'd never say that. No, definitely it would happen. It is more to do with how you think about it, how you frame it as therapeutic. It would be better to ask someone who thinks of themselves as basically a psychodynamic music therapist, or from another approach. It's interesting—there's so much to learn…

C: But you still think of yourself as, what was it, … 'music centred'?

MT: I do, it really matters to me.

C: Is that why you and Researcher got into that argument about whether to put 'music centred' into the title?

MT: Yes, that was tricky!

C: Why?

MT: I think it was to do with who would read this. I know what she means. If I look for an article or something, I scan down the database and if something has a client group or therapy approach that isn't the one I'm looking for, I move onto the next. So I think Researcher thought people would just scroll over this research if we put 'music centred' in the title.

C: Yes, but isn't that missing the point. I mean, if this is about music centred work, then we should say so, and that way the people who need it will stand more of a chance…

MT: Well, actually it wasn't only about excluding readers, it was because she knows that lots of therapists have musical encounters that they are trying to theorise and explore, not just music centred therapists. It is *music* therapy, after all. And she felt that people who aren't trained in music centred work might feel their practice doesn't count and that the ideas in this book aren't for them, … you know, if we put 'music centred' in the title.

C: I'm sorry you didn't get the words you wanted.

MT: No, it's fine, really. I think it's better this way. I was more worried about using 'nonverbal' in the title and limiting it to being about nonverbal participants. I never intended that when we started.

C: What did you intend?

MT: ...honestly?...I think this way of thinking works for *any* participant. I worked for nine years in a hospice. Those participants could talk. But the relatedness in the music making, – that was what counted, ... I know it. They used to tell me, in fact! So, I had imagined that this investigation would be about all participants...

C: ...So why did you pretty much only write poems and stories about nonverbal ones? And right from the start you and me were in there, arguing for nonverbal people to be understood on their own terms. It's what *I* care about, anyway. I mean, I care about everyone, but that really matters to me...

MT: I don't know why I wrote those stories and why all the participants were nonverbal. I didn't think about it. ... at all ... I just wrote. They were the characters that came to mind ... just sort of arrived and I needed to tell their stories. It wasn't until six years in, and Researcher was chewing over what the title should be, that I realised.

C: Really? I noticed it straight away. It was plain as anything. But I think you shouldn't worry about it. It's all about valuing people and meeting needs, isn't it? Someone might read this and find out there's a focus on nonverbal people, but they might think 'you know, I could use these ideas with this or that other client group'. In fact, that's exactly what you have done with those ideas about personhood—they all came from dementia care, wasn't it? But they have helped us think together along the way. Really helped.

MT: Yeah, – thanks, Carer.

C: Anyway, I don't want to hold things up … I just wanted to ask … I'm interested…

MT: Thanks…

C: Just one more thought…

MT: Yes?

C: I think those people would have come to you as characters because you really, really mind. People who use language, they can actually say what they want, at the end of the day. But nonverbal people really can't. I wonder if you wrote about those people because they are most at risk of not being heard—it's like, if you can make the case for them, with all the prejudice and discrimination and lack of interest and understanding that surrounds them—then the rest should fall into place.

MT: That's a kind way of thinking about it. You might be right. I just don't know: like I said, it just happened.

C: No worries. I think Researcher is waiting…

*Pause.*

M: Huh!

MT: What?

M: I've got one!

MT: One what?

M: A quote … the next one … you did want me to find more quotes to guide us, didn't you?

MT: I guess so. I don't know. You keep asking me things. It's stressful. I wish Researcher would come back. And … sorry, but … why Shakespeare? It's a bit pretentious, isn't it?

M: (*Irately*) I actually cannot *believe* you just said that. You!!! *Music* therapist who wants everyone to experience music making … What's wrong with Shakespeare? He was a jobbing playwright, paying his way like anyone else. I'm going to ignore that remark.

## Direct Message 3

### *Critical Realism and How Retroductive Argument Brought Structure to This Enquiry*

Dear Collaborator,

I hope that the field of music therapy, and the participation of the Roles in this study, are now more familiar to you. In this message, I would like to revisit the aim of this book and share the conceptual frameworks that I have used to establish some boundaries, such that the aim is addressed.

*Tensions in This Investigation*

As you will be aware, there are many tensions in this investigation, between evidence and experience, between arts-based knowing and academic, verbal knowing, between the different Roles that are involved and the roles we all occupy in different situations. In addition, there is the tension between the status quo of the prevailing cultures of music therapy, and the imagined potential for these cultures to change, which seems to matter in different ways to all the Roles. Throughout this, there is a tension in the relationship between an ethic of care and personal integrity demands—but I will address these in due course.

I have found the act of preparing this book to be exceptionally complicated. I am frustrated that language is linear and that it is both impractical and socially unacceptable for multiple speakers to talk at the same time. The reason for my frustration is that I am trying to describe something—experience—for which there is no one explanation and no single narrative. In order to do justice to the different kinds of experience that happen and the different ways of understanding them, I would need to write my exploration in the format of a Western classical music score, in which multiple parts are written, one beneath the other down the page, so that all their musical lines sound simultaneously in performance. As a tool for sharing ideas and exploration, this would clearly not work. I have therefore needed to separate things which do not occur in isolation, and create something homophonic from something which is inherently polyphonic.[19]

One of the things I have found to be helpful in dealing with this frustration, has been the philosophy of critical realism. I was introduced to the philosophy by my supervisor[20] when I first explored my interest in doctoral study. I did not settle on the topic of experience for a long time afterwards. However, from the start, I responded to the critical realist celebration of complexity and its embracing of multi-layered thinking. I had a gut feeling that my research would need this and in my reading, I was drawn to the focus on ontology, or the underlying nature of things, which the philosophy offers.

Critical realism has influenced every aspect of this book's content and presentation. There are few examples of critical realism as a philosophical approach to music therapy research (Porter et al., 2017; Potvin et al., 2018; Ghetti et al., 2021; Atkinson, 2022; Epstein et al., 2022), so in part I hope to contribute to the awareness of critical realism in this field and contribute new knowledge. First, though, I will explain my understanding of the philosophy and why I feel it is appropriate.

*Exploring Reality Through a Critical Realist Lens*

Critical realism provides a comprehensive philosophy of what is, and of our knowledge of what is. Its founder, Roy Bhaskar, strongly critiqued prevailing attitudes that confused reality itself with human *accounts* of reality. He named this the 'epistemic fallacy' (2016, p. 23). Instead, he clearly defined the realms of the real (everything that is), the actual (everything that happens) and the empirical (our knowledge of reality and of what happens).

Bhaskar's purpose was pragmatic and emancipatory: he described critical realism as an 'underlabouring' philosophy that 'aspires to clear the ground a little, removing, in the first place, the philosophical rubbish that

[19] In music, homophony denotes a single part or voice whereas polyphony denotes multiple interwoven parts.

[20] All music therapists are obliged by law to have regular supervision. Therefore for a music therapist, 'supervisor' usually implies a clinical supervisor. However, in this book, I do not make reference to my clinical supervisor. A story will follow involving a fictionalised clinical supervisor. Apart from this, all other references to 'supervisor' denote my academic supervisor.

lies in the way of scientific knowledge, especially but not only the social sciences' (p. 2). This is a 'serious' endeavour that aims to identify this 'rubbish' by challenging other approaches on their own terms and demonstrating their flaws through a process Bhaskar calls 'immanent critique' (pp. 2–3). Bhaskar writes,

> It is the characteristic task of critical realist philosophy to explicate ... higher-order or abstract features which are for the most part taken for granted in, or unreflectively but tacitly presupposed by our practices. (2016, p. 3)

*Looking for Generative Mechanisms*

The feature of this philosophy which I am particularly drawn to is the emphasis on the transcendental, or the questions 'why' or 'under what conditions...' do certain things occur. Bhaskar describes a 'transcendental argument' as one that asks 'what must be the case for some feature of our experience to be possible, or more generally what must the world be like for some social practice (as conceptualised in our experience) to be possible' (original brackets)? To address these questions, critical realist researchers look for 'generative mechanisms' in the *real* domain that explain why things happen in the *actual* domain and are perceived in the *empirical* domain (p. 3).

I am exploring experience and evidence in music therapy. Thinking about these phenomena from a critical realist perspective enables me to look beyond *what* different stakeholders are experiencing, and to ask the question *why* stakeholders are having these experiences and not other ones, under what circumstances other ones might arise, and why other phenomena may or may not be recognised as an experience or evidence, depending on *what* values people hold and *why* they hold these values. It gives the researcher tools to propose likely generative mechanisms through the process of 'retroductive argument' and to learn more about the three coexisting domains: the nature of underlying reality, the things that happen and our understanding of these.

*Retroductive Argument*

Retroduction—this activity of uncovering the underlying generative mechanisms which explain events and occurrences and our experiences of them—is defined by Bhaskar in the following manner:

> A retroductive argument asks what would, if it were real, bring about, produce, cause or explain a phenomenon; and retroduction is the imaginative activity in science by which the scientist thinks up causes or, as we shall say, generative mechanisms which, if they were real, would explain the phenomenon in question. (2016, p. 3)

Bhaskar insisted that critical realism was first and foremost a philosophy, and not a methodology (p. 87). However, in promoting retroductive argument, the philosophy also points towards its own methodological approach—one in which the researcher theorises or 'thinks up' explanations for things.

*How I Use Retroductive Argument to Structure My Exploration*

The journey from my interest in critical realism to gaining some insight into the topic of experience and evidence has been surprising. In different phases of my investigative journey, I have focussed in turn on carers, ethic of care, integrity, academia, and turned to *experience* as something of a last resort, for it was the one thing that united them all. However, along the way, I had embraced arts-based methodology, fallen into autoethnography, committed myself to engaging with phenomenology, and grappled with Aesthetic Critical Realism. I did this in obedience to the retroductive requirement to 'think up causes'. I kept thinking up! In fact, this whole project is an imaginative activity.

When the point came to create the story of my exploration, I became overwhelmingly stuck. As indicated, everything seemed to be interwoven and simultaneous and I could not find a single narrative that I could tell in linear fashion. Out of necessity, I decided to present four sections of analysis (Chaps. 3, 4, 5 and 6), each focusing on one of the methodological approaches listed, and what it revealed about experience, evidence and what counts in music therapy. I was reluctant to bring about this simplification of a complex issue, but realised that autoethnography is useful for sharing the *story* of a happening and how such stories weave together; phenomenology is a useful concept for understanding the *experience* of phenomena that happen; Aesthetic Critical Realism is useful for understanding our *awareness* of what happened and *why* some occurrences are valued and others not; arts-based research helps in understanding the *knowing* that comes from an arts-based happening.

When I was feeling particularly dispirited, I suddenly gained some clarity: the critical realist approach of retroductive argument had not, in fact, *accidentally* led to the dismantling of my ideas. Instead, it had deliberately and helpfully led to the defining of different aspects of experience: I thought I was separating sections of analysis according to methodology. In fact, I was separating them according to type of experience, and had reached this point directly as a result of critical realist retroductive argument.

*Further Thoughts About Data and Analysis in This Book*

Because of the nature of experience—the fact that it *is* the substance of our lives—everything that has happened in the course of my enquiry has unavoidably become data. With regard to analysis, I am attempting to be obedient to the root meaning of the Greek word 'analysis', in which 'ana' signifies 'throughout' and 'lysis' signifies 'loosening'. I perceive my work as gently loosening the fibres of a complex topic so as to feel their nature and see their connections. Importantly, this is not the same as untangling, which would be to simplify the topic: I am keen to preserve what tangle there is, because that tangle is part of reality. However, by imagining the generative mechanisms of these tangles, that is, what might have given rise to them, I hope to understand them better, and perceive how they have contributed to what counts in music therapy.

*A Note on Critical Realism and the Concept of Experience*

Critical realism is concerned with understanding the whole of reality, where reality includes everything material, conceptual, known, unknown and possible, even if absent. Experience is obviously a part of this whole, and a vital part because it is so intimately connected to our knowledge of reality. However, as Nick Wilson observes, critical realism itself has lacked a robust theory of experience, stemming from Bhaskar's writing of '*A Realist Theory of Science* [1975] … as a response to what he saw as philosophy's (and more especially, positivism's) overreliance on experience' (Wilson, 2020, p. 15 original brackets). To address this shortcoming, Wilson thoroughly explores the concept of experience from a critical realist perspective, additionally linking it to a critical realist examination and definition of the concept of art. The result—Wilson's theory of Aesthetic Critical Realism—has been a significant influence on my investigation and will be discussed later in Chap. 5.

I hope this background is helpful to you in your role as Collaborator. One of my greatest concerns is that I might inadvertently upset you by responding to pressure from the Roles and 'performing' the noisy muddle which has been this project. That is why I am glad for these spaces to share ideas in a more formal way. I personally would find great reassurance in something more linear and sequential. However, I am persuaded by the other Roles that our topic has a different nature and that these somewhat spiral visitings and revisitings of different features of the study are in fact inseparable from the topic of experience. I hope that critical realism might to some extent provide a thinking framework for some of your responses, as well.

With many thanks, again—
Researcher

## Dialogue 3

### *The Risks of Autoethnography are Debated and Different Roles' Experiences of Care and Caring are Shared*

All the world's a stage.[21]

*Researcher is still absent.*

MT: I don't get it.

M: No? … As You Like It?

MT: No. We do music, not drama.

M: Oh! (*Looking genuinely surprised*). Music Therapist … take a break.

MT: And who is going to keep this book going? I've no idea where Carer is.

M: I will.

MT: Really?

M: I just said so. I've prepared a monologue!

[21] Shakespeare, *As You Like It,* Act 2 Scene 7 (1986, p. 717).

MT: What! How will that help? Can we focus on the topic?

M: You're talking like a music therapist. Where's the musician in you? Come *on*! We are just starting to make headway with Researcher. We don't have to be straitjacketed, at last. Get creative!

MT: I'm going to wake Researcher up…

M: Oh calm down. She's not asleep, she's just writing her Direct Messages. Anyway, it's only a short explanation of my background as a musician. I'm surprised at you. Relax!

MT: But we know your background.

M: But the Collaborator doesn't. Come on! … Look, I'm going to say it anyway. (*…During which Music Therapist leaves*). You can go if you like … (*Addressing the Collaborator*) I have been a musician all my life. I started music lessons when I was five, on the violin and six, on the piano. I hated the violin. Fortunately, an early scientific experiment—seeing what would happen if I cycled over a brick—landed me with a broken collar bone and I couldn't play for some months. Once I returned to the violin, I loved it and have loved it ever since. But I didn't want to play the violin, really. I was desperate to play the clarinet, which I heard on the radio, again when I was six. To this day, I think it is the most beautiful sound there is. More than that, though, when I heard the clarinet, I somehow sensed the world getting bigger—as if there were more possibilities than I could imagine. It was very powerful, and I can trace my interest in music therapy right back to that moment.

I jumped through the various hoops that are placed in front of people who show promise at Western classical music—exams, leading orchestras etc.—but I always knew that I was not primarily interested in playing concerts of other people's music. It is not that I don't value these amazing experiences, because I do, and I fully recognise the enormous privilege of my musical education and opportunities. It's more that there's something about being with others who never thought that participating in music could offer them anything, and seeing and hearing them come alive in shared music making, that's one of the most exciting things I know.

Music Therapist? Can you add about how our interest in music therapy arose?

*Silence.*

M: Is anyone there?

*Silence.*

M: Oh great, … I didn't mean 'leave me to it'. For goodness' sake … this isn't going to work if I'm on my own. It stops being a conversation. Why? … (*Thinking*) … It'll have to be me and you, Collaborator, who are engaging with this for now, then. I guess that's a conversation of sorts. Sorry about that. I'll just have to tell you stuff, till they come back.

C: I'm here.

M: Carer? You kept that quiet.

C: Well, I wasn't, but now I am. Where have we got to?

M: It was going to be how our interest in music therapy came about. But Music Therapist isn't here, nor is Researcher, so if this is ever going to get off the ground, I suppose we ought to tackle autoethnography.

C: Meaning…?

M: Why we are all in this and how to do it safely and reliably.

C: Oh.

M: There are ways to make this autobiography, and ways to make it autoethnography. Researcher told me.

C: And we're going for autobiography?

M: No, autoethnography.

C: OK, I don't mind.

M: It's not about minding, it's about whether it is research.

C: And Researcher read about it and has written about it?

M: Yes.

C: Then that sounds helpful. Can't we use it?

M: Yes, of course we can. But…

C: Where is Music Therapist, anyway?

M: Taking a break.

C: Oh, is she OK?

M: Fine, but I think she didn't like my quote this time.

C: All the world's a stage. Shame. I like it.

M: Good. Why?

C: Well it's honest, isn't it? I mean we are always in one role or another. Friend, worker, sister.

M: Helper, resident, passenger,

C: Care-giver, care-receiver.

M: Do you feel that's a role?

C: Of course.

M: How?

C: In so many ways. But, basically, there's so much more to a person than what they're doing at a given time, or having done to them.

It closes down so much of what matters when you see leaflets about 'carers' or 'care-receivers'. But I know it's meant well.

M: I didn't realise. Sorry. Are you happy with the name of your Role?

C: Well. I'd prefer 'human being', but that won't help what we're trying to do.

M: Sorry, I didn't realise.

C: It's OK. I never use the word: I don't think of things as 'caring'. I've had a role at different stages of my life that others might use the word 'carer' for. Twice it was quite a short time. But once it was a lot longer. But it's just loving people, really. Trying to. It's hard in the middle of the night! ... Actually, that's not true. It's not hard loving people, ever. But it is hard when the world expects you to bounce into cheery extrovert mode straight after. But you have to do that, or people keep away and that's worse ... I think that's why Music Therapist asked me to join in with this. I wasn't going to because I'm more of a practical person. But I guess it's important to think about what's behind the scenes.

*Pause.*

M: Shall I keep going?

*Pause.*

M: Carer, I'm getting confused.

C: I'm sorry. Why?

M: It's since we've started doing this whole investigation as a conversation.

C: What's the problem?

M: Well, it can become ... I'm not sure how to describe it ... there's a fine line.

C: Between what and what?

M: Between being ourselves, – roles that Jessica has and has brought to the work—…and just making it up.

C: But we're not making it up. I'm not, at least.

M: No, I know. But it is starting to feel as though it might be easy to do so. It was happening when I was getting up tight about musical experience, and Music Therapist was being all "I mind *so* much about this" and you were, … well, … I'm not sure where you were … but I found myself thinking: what's the difference? What's the difference between just making up four roles who might have an interest in music therapy, and actually representing Jessica and how she experiences different roles? The people engaging with this wouldn't know the difference. They wouldn't know that not all music therapists get stressed about musical experience and not all musicians get irritated by research. And it would be so easy to just run with this grumpy musician character, for example, but it wouldn't be my Role any more. And that scared me, because it would mean that in arts-based research you can basically invent stuff and, if you like, claim that it's real, and no one would know.

C: (*Thinking*) I think they would know.

M: How?

C: You just mentioned it. Didn't Researcher talk about being reliable? Reliable and valid, or something. I remember a phrase of that sort. I think people will be able to tell whether we're representing Jessica, or just some fictional person, by whether it sounds and feels likely and true.

M: Yes, but think about it … how many novels have you read, or how many films or plays have you seen, where the characters are completely and totally believable.

C: But that doesn't matter, because we *know* that they're not real.

M: And that's my point. In autoethnography, there's a danger we might *say* something is real and true, but actually it isn't.

C: I hear you. But I don't think we can get round that. It seems like just something the readers will have to take on trust. We just say: "these roles are all drawn from Jessica's own experience" and that's all we can do, really.

M: OK. Well, it's out there now.

C: Let's keep going. It'd be nice to show the others that we've covered some ground. And maybe bring in the bits about reliable and valid. It will be there, somewhere, in Researcher's writing.

M: Thanks, Carer. It helps me, talking to you. What is it … why … how do you stay calm and make people feel better?

C: Do I? … I guess I stopped worrying a long time ago whether I was going to get much of my own stuff done. And I like people. Researcher started telling me about a theory of care. Something … ethic of care … I think. She was quite into it, but I don't really think that way. I don't mind if she does, though, she seems to like theories.

M: Ethic of care … yes, she went on more than a bit about that. Anyway, where have we got to … was it: (1) autoethnography theory; (2) our story; (3) valid and reliable stuff; (4) ethic of care. Researcher will eat her hat when she knows I'm helping with this…

*Carer looks intently at Musician.*

C: Actually, Musician, you don't need to.

M: …need to what?

C: Go into all of this. Researcher's writing her messages. It's what we need: then we don't have to pretend to do her bit. And then our conversation won't keep stalling.

M: (*Looking irritated*) Well, I was only trying to help…

*Music Therapist returns, seeming reflective.*

MT: Thanks for the break, (*Pause*) ... You know, I've been thinking: if all the world is a stage, then I think it was probably me who started this play.

M: Could be. How d'you mean?

MT: D'you remember ... I had been a music therapist for a very long time—fifteen years—when I joined the team in that regional music therapy centre which individuals, families and other professionals could make referrals to. For the first time, I had music therapy colleagues in my place of work.

C: Yes, I remember you telling us about that.

MT: I began to meet a lot of informal carers,—you know, parents, grandparents, siblings, neighbours, friends. Music therapy is fairly well known in the field of autism support[22] and loads of families had referred their young autistic children for assessment. As a rule, the service I had joined tended to offer an individual assessment session, followed by a course of individual therapy. If the family chose, the therapy could then continue in a group, where appropriate. The trouble is, that this pattern is time consuming and when I was working there, it meant that families lower down the list were waiting for over a year for assessment. We felt this wasn't acceptable and so that's why a colleague and I piloted a different approach: we explained that it was untried and we would need the patience, help and understanding of the parents or carers. We then grouped the children as best we could and asked the parents and carers for their hopes and dreams for their children. We started with eight families and ended with forty. It was the most challenging, stimulating, exciting and moving work I've ever done.

M: You've always lit up when you talk about it. What was so special?

[22] A Cochrane review has suggested some benefit to this client group (Gold et al., 2006).

MT: What stands out is the collaboration with the parents and carers, as well as the learning from them. My colleague and I were honest about everything—what musical resources we could and couldn't offer, what we were trying to do in the music making, when we felt there were significant steps towards the hopes and dreams, what we noticed in the children and families' responses: it soon became a whole family affair and we often had large groups of several families with mixed neurodiverse and neurotypical children and a variety of supporting adults. But just as important, maybe more so, we continually listened to the carers' feedback, what they noticed, what was significant to them and what they valued about the whole experience.

We worked with these families for over four years, and during this time my colleague and I realised that something different was going on in the interactions between us as therapists and the adult carers. A sort of different quality to the relationships. When we reflected on it, we realised that we felt more vulnerable, because we were always actively and deliberately trying not to come across as the expert professional; but at the same time we felt more connected and even held. It was strange, because it's traditionally the therapist's role to hold the space and the participants within it.

C: Yes, it would be.

MT: We thought carefully about whether it was appropriate: were we actually condoning, or even creating, a burden of responsibility for the carers to carry? But, we came to think the opposite. It's quite easy for therapy to fall into a pattern where the 'strong' therapist works to heal the 'weak' client. This can work, and even be important, sometimes. But it can be unhelpful, too, and therapy can be other things as well, to do with empowerment, agency, co-creation and ownership. We wanted to be transparent and honest, so we discussed all this with the adult carers and they reported that they didn't feel burdened. In fact, they felt relieved to have an hour in the week when they felt normal and didn't have to apologise for their children's behaviour.

M: It's sad to hear that. I mean, it's good they felt supported.

MT: Yes, true. And it meant we started to think more deeply about why the adult carers felt normal in this approach to music therapy. We were really aware that a lot of the typical tensions in the therapist-carer relationship were missing: there's often stress at the time of discharge and pressure around providing reports, but this didn't occur and we wondered whether it had something to do with deliberately trying to collaborate in this way. So, for example, we just told the families when the waiting list was building up and *they* volunteered to opt out for a while so that new families could join. It was a completely different way round.

We didn't have a thinking framework for our experiences at the time, but looking back, it's clear that as therapists, we were learning from the families that for them, daily life was all about caring but not expecting anything in return. It felt so radical and liberating that even before we understood the ethics of all this, I was drawn to researching the experience.

C: Then you *are* the reason we are all here. We seem to keep forgetting that.

MT: Don't worry. But really this project isn't mainly for me. It's because of the people I have worked with—all the people in that service, and all the many, many others over the years. And particularly the ones who don't use language.

C: Oh yes, of course. We haven't even spoken about them for a while.

MT: Well, it's been a bit noisy around here!

M: Sorry, Music Therapist. But we're on the same page, right? We need to be noisy about keeping the music as the thing that matters…?

MT: Yes, that too.

*They all reflect a while.*

C: Shall we take a break?

MT: That'd be good.

C: Thanks for sharing, Music Therapist…

*Pause. Music Therapist looks at Musician, enquiringly…*

M: It's OK, don't ask: I'll find another quote. I've got it already, in fact … it's a bit obvious, maybe…

## Direct Message 4

### *An Ethic of Care as Theory and Experience*

Dear Collaborator,

I need to explain what an ethic of care means to me. It could not be more important to this book. The reason is this: music therapists are allied healthcare professionals—care is embedded in our title. I am completely certain that every music therapist is committed to providing this care. But can we be certain that all our practices and attitudes reflect those of the informal carers I had worked with (see Section "Dialogue 3"), who cared without expecting anything in return? If the answer is no, how many of us are longing for this? And where a music therapy participant is nonverbal, what ethical framework are we using if we are not honouring the nonverbal knowing and wisdom that they possess? Wouldn't an ethic of care demand that we do, even if it affected what we expect to 'take' from our work?

As I described in my last message, I had been experiencing this ethic in the attitudes and interactions of the informal carers and their care-receivers and it had profoundly influenced the way I was practising as well as my relationships to participants and the other therapists I worked in sessions with.[23] I had not heard of the theory of care ethics when I began thinking about informal carers in music therapy as a research topic. Yet I strongly wanted to understand and share what felt to me like an almost revolution-

[23] I was trained at a time when 'co-therapy' was common among Nordoff Robbins music therapists. It involves two therapists working with participant(s) in the session, one leading the music, the other facilitating the participant's involvement and arose from the collaborative activities of Paul Nordoff and Clive Robbins who adopted this approach in their pioneering sessions.

ary possibility for developing music therapy practice. It was on my doctoral programme that I encountered the theoretical foundations of care ethics and began to define the ways in which this thinking was becoming non-negotiable in my research attitude and undertakings.

I now wish to explain my understanding of care ethics, because it is so central to this book, but I want you to know that I am drawn to an ethic of care in an instinctual and personal way. My insights have developed entirely from my being exposed to this ethic, and thereby having the chance to *experience* it deeply, as a quality of relationship. In turn, this experience has significantly shaped the questions that guide this investigation: they focus on the kinds of experience that occur in music therapy, why some do and others don't count as evidence, and what this can tell us about the cultures of music therapy.

*Ethics of Care*

I read Carol Gilligan's book *In a Different Voice* (1982). As an ethicist and psychologist she proposes a new morality, based on a feminist analysis of the differences in ethical development observable in girls and boys. She argues that Freud, Piaget, Erikson and Kohlberg, amongst others, have defined and established a dominant concept of moral development that is based entirely upon observations of boys and male adolescents (Chaps. 1, 2 and 6). This ethical framework stems from a fundamental separateness that these theorists believe boys experience in infancy, early years and puberty, when they recognise and assert their difference to their care-giving mothers. The resulting individuation leads to an ethic in which autonomy is prized and one's rights are protected by rules of justice (p. 21). The ethical framework which results can be regarded as transactional. I reflected on this, and started to observe all kinds of interactions in work, at home, in many situations, where a more or less transactional approach seems to be almost unconsciously at play.

In contrast to this, Gilligan traces the ethical development of girls in the work of scholars including Nancy Chodorow, Janet Lever, Matina Horner and Georgia Sassen (Chaps. 1 and 2). Whereas Freud and Piaget regard girls as morally underdeveloped or deviant because their development does not correspond to that of boys, these theorists perceive a different explanation and suggest that girls do not seek separation from their mothers, instead developing a continued relationship which forms the foundation of their morality. Instead of seeking rules to protect their autonomy from interference by others, girls seek to maintain relationship with others, favouring what Gilligan describes as an ethic of care (Chap. 1), based on a sense of responsibility.

This early exposition of care ethics, regarded as 'first generation' exploration by Olena Hankivsky (2014, p. 253), has been widely developed over the past thirty years. Joan Tronto (1993) expanded the ideas into a 'second generation' conceptualisation, asserting the political ramifications of care ethics: a feminist alternative to perceived male-shaped and -dominated political systems is proposed, based upon human connectedness and relationships, and supported by responsibilities of care, rather than rights to justice.[24]

Up to this point, I had not observed the Western life we lead through a feminist, political lens. I am aware that mine is a late start and a very incomplete understanding, but I find it hard to ignore the ideas and thinking framework it presents. I am wary, too, of falling into an 'ethic of care, good; transactional ethic, bad' binary, because I probably lack understanding of transactional interactions. But I have worked in an allied healthcare profession for twenty-six years, and have definitely experienced the tension between these two approaches.

*Further Development of, and Challenges to, Care Ethics*

What emerges from care ethics is a turn from notions of care as the right of a separate and individual care-receiver, supplied at a cost by care-givers until such time as this burden can be relinquished, to a system of care as ongoing relationship, in which universal human vulnerability is acknowledged. One dictionary definition identifies care as—'a cause of… a disquieted state of mixed uncertainty, apprehension and responsibility' (Merriam-Webster Online Dictionary). To the twenty-first-century Western citizen, the immediate cause of the 'disquiet' could be regarded

[24] Tronto develops this concept further, throughout her writing, applying the principles of connectedness, mutual vulnerability and responsibility to the whole social sphere in *Caring Democracy: Markets, Equality and Justice* (2013). She summarises her arguments in her article 'Democratic caring and global care responsibilities' (2015), where she decries neoliberal economics, which confound our ethical thinking, for we relinquish all notion of 'common good' in order to cherry pick only those care solutions which do not damage us as individuals. Furthermore, the integrity of the state as a fair provider of care is also compromised as we condone 'porous' boundaries which allow migrant carers to enter, whilst simultaneously demanding 'impenetrable' ones to keep other migrants out. In this way, we pass the care deficit 'down the line', allowing poor countries to shoulder the 'burden of care' in richer ones, despite the fact that many of the poor ones face their own care crises.

as the burden of providing care for another within a care crisis. However, seen from the perspective of care ethics, the 'disquiet' could equally be a suppressed recognition of our shared vulnerability in a system in which shared responsibility is still absent.

Care ethics have not been without critique. Whilst care (Phillips, 2007; Bunting, 2020; Chatzidakis et al., 2020) and care ethics continue to be explored (Feder Kittay & Feder Kittay, 2003; Hamington, 2004; Held, 2006; Slote, 2007; Boris & Salazar Parreñas, 2010; Barnes, 2012) and the contribution of care ethics to contemporary thinking about care and society is widely acknowledged (Hankivsky, 2014, p. 253), Marian Barnes questions the appropriateness of the mother-infant dyad as the primary model of care because it perpetuates inequality between participants in the care experience: the strong adult and the weak infant (2015, p. 32). Instead she offers concepts of 'networked care' (original speech marks), which involves all those connected to an individual, and 'collective care' which involves groups with similar care needs caring for each other—e.g. a mental health group (p. 35). This inversion of weak care-receiver and strong care-giver challenges preconceptions and assumptions about people, and indeed describes the experiences that my colleague and I had in our work with the families. Barnes emphasises the need to 'value the spaces' where this sort of collective caring can happen.

In addition, care ethics has faced critique from intersectionality theorists. Here, the fundamental feminist tradition of basing care ethics on gender models is called into question. In her article 'Rethinking care ethics: on the promise and potential of an intersectional analysis', Hankivsky (2014) concludes that it is irrational to prioritise gender over any other form of difference or oppression when seeking to explain human experience, whether of care or anything else:

> Few care scholars explore the extent to which systems of oppression interact and mutually reinforce each other, that is, the extent to which they are indivisible as would be consistent with an intersectionality perspective. (p. 259)

What Hankivsky favours is an approach to care ethics in which all 'interlocking' experiences of difference and oppression are recognised as constituting hidden or manifest experiences of power systems, and therefore need exposing and addressing through an ethic of care (p. 260).

*The Relevance of Care Ethics to the Exploration in This Book*

In spite of these objections, adopting an ethic of care has become, and remains, important to me. It is not an optional theoretical concept, but represents everything that I try to bring to my work with participants, who I have long since avoided referring to as 'clients' because of the inbuilt financial transaction implicit in this word. As I alluded to at the start of this message, I have begun to question numerous habits and assumptions in the practice of music therapy. Everything, from insuring ourselves against potential client litigation, to using diagnostic labels in reporting, has started to feel uncomfortable. The role of neoliberal economics in dictating the provision of treatments and therapies on the basis of cost-benefit has become challenging. This questioning has extended to my involvement in music therapy research, as well. Whilst studying on a doctoral programme, I started to feel uneasy about processes within academia—is a PhD course more interested in new insights, or in upholding approved research structures? Is its ethical framework transactional or caring?

I began to reflect on my experiences in music therapy and started to see a pattern in which, from time to time, something distinctly uncomfortable would happen. These were always specific events and cannot be attributed to any particular work setting, type of relationship (i.e. participant-therapist, or multidisciplinary team-therapist) or way of working. Instead, they were episodes in which I felt somehow challenged, as a therapist and as a person. This is not particularly unusual: therapists need to work alongside others and there are bound to be tensions. However, there was something about the nature of these tensions that caused me to think more deeply. Many of these types of tension are fictionalised and included in the poems that I present as arts-based data and in the short story, *Chloe's Story* that explores a fictional episode from the viewpoint of nine different characters (see Chap. 2, Section "Poems, Stories and Vignettes"). My hope is that these works speak for themselves and, for this reason, I will not elaborate on them here.

What became apparent, through careful reflection with my supervisor, was that the episodes that stood out in my memory were all times in which my attempts to engage with others through an ethic of care were compromised.[25] These experiences all took place before I had encountered the

[25] During these discussions, it was of utmost importance to maintain the confidentiality of the music therapy participants I had worked with, as required by my training and state regis-

concept of care ethics, and for that reason were perhaps even more uncomfortable than they would be now that I have this thinking framework.

Perhaps it would help to clarify exactly what an ethic of care means to me, in practical terms, when I interact with others as a practitioner, researcher or in any other type of music therapy role:

- I attempt to listen attentively to participants and their carers, as well as to colleagues and all music therapy stakeholders.
- I attempt to engage from a position of humility, rather than expertise, always honouring the expertise of participants and carers who live daily realities of care-giving and care-receiving.
- I attempt always to be mindful of the power I exercise as a person of privilege in numerous ways, particularly regarding musical experience and opportunity, socioeconomic and educational opportunity, and professional status. I try to challenge systems and structures where I believe that they are oppressive, and where I have opportunity to do so.
- I attempt to not expect things to go 'my way' in return for trying to offer this kind of care.

The truth is, I nevertheless continually fail in these attempts. Music therapists are trained to follow the lead of the participant, so within music therapy sessions I have some confidence that I am at least trying to limit what I expect in return for my music therapy interactions. It would be naïve to claim that I expect nothing in return, for these issues are subtle, and I am aware that I have sundry predispositions—for example, towards structured phrases and cadences, away from cymbals and electronic sounds—which I both consciously and unconsciously satisfy in music therapy music making. Furthermore, I will explore later (in Chap. 5), how there is a danger that therapists can so absorb a tacit culture of music therapy that we do in fact determine and prejudice the therapy in some ways—by pursuing goals, or grouping peers together at the expense of mixed age groups, or adhering to the 'norm' in whatever way.

I know I have at times inclined towards a lack of listening to research stakeholders because of my preoccupation with my own agenda, and have experienced supervision as a care-full and caring space to explore this

tration. I therefore changed all identifying details relating to people and settings. My supervisor maintained a confidential supervision space.

tendency. But the relationships within which I find it most difficult to maintain my ethic of care are those with other professionals involved in music therapy—commissioners, fundraisers and multidisciplinary team members. Conflicts of purpose, outlook and measurements of success can be stark. When I experience an impulse to proceed with music therapy in a way that is contradicted or blocked by other professionals, I can listen, notice power systems, challenge them with respect, but I admit that I can find offering an unconditional caring response difficult at these times, although I hope I try.

I also very much hope that you might have experienced some attempt at care in my invitation for you to engage with this study, Collaborator. Please believe that I truly appreciate your time and effort.

With best wishes and thanks,
Researcher

## Direct Message 5

### *Integrity Demands and Acknowledging the Normative Dimension of This Enquiry*

Dear Collaborator,

I hope you have had a pleasant weekend?

I have been quite encouraged by the quietness of the Roles since they asked me to write to you. I perhaps should have explained in the first Direct Message that I expect I will need to write several times in order to 'convey the information'—I believe that was the task I was given.

*Reflections on the Role of Theory in This Study*

I am conscious of my constant reference to, and exploration of, different theories in this study. I do not include these theories as external props to support my own story: rather, discovering these theories, getting to know them, mulling them over, trying to use them as a lens for my looking, or as a home for my ideas, are all activities that *make up* my story. In a way, my research journey has been an ongoing and circular experience of feeling the absence of theoretical foundations, searching for explanatory or inspirational theories, finding potentially helpful ones, trying them out in the context of my study—i.e., proposing retroductive arguments—questioning some more and looking again. I do not believe that theory must be exposed for an idea to be useful, any more than the structural mechanics of a building must be exposed for the space to be occupied. However, the Pompidou Centre in Paris, or the Lloyd's Building in London do, in fact, deliberately reveal their structural workings, thereby challenging the people that use them to re-think their assumptions about the built environment and architectural form. In the same way, I have found that exposing the theoretical framework of my study is what I want to do, because I am inviting readers to challenge their theoretical assumptions about music therapy and its purpose and value.

*Integrity*

You know by now, that the research which I share in this book came about as a PhD project. This message will share a little about another important theoretical focus—the concept and experience of integrity. I have thought deeply about the jarring experiences I have had over the years as a music therapist: you will see later in the poems, stories and vignettes (Chap 2, Section "Poems, Stories and Vignettes") that many of these focus on situations in which I strongly wished to offer care to a participant in my music therapy work in a certain way, but this care was not facilitated by the system, environment or institution in which I found myself. In some instances it was a simple case of my wanting to celebrate the communicative creativity of an individual in a setting in which a deficit model of pathologies and labels was dominant; in other instances there were more complex situations of professional territories and misunderstandings that made my caring efforts seem naïve or inappropriate.

After a while I began to concentrate on the notion of integrity, by which I mean wholeness or undividedness, and I started to formulate the concept of integrity demands. This is my own term for a type of experience which I will explain more fully below, but which occurs when some element(s) of a situation which would be non-negotiable if I were to experience wholeness, or undividedness, are missing. The term 'integrity demand' has probably already come up in the Dialogues without explanation or context, which I realise is unhelpful: part of the trouble I experience with this book is that the Roles continually talk as if we are all many years into this journey, but I am acutely aware that you are probably only an hour or two into it, and somehow I have to provide some sort of 'back story' for their arguments.

The part that the idea of integrity has played in this enquiry is a complex one: I have discovered that integrity, or undividedness, is vital to my own wellbeing, but it also provokes a tension when combined with an ethic of care (Section "Direct Message 4"). This is because the *demands* for integrity that I experience—for example the need to respect a participant in a particular way, or to honour their experience in a particular way—can clearly be at odds with the needs of another person involved, who might value different things. How, then, can I maintain an ethic of care towards all involved, by making space for their integrity demands, when this would cause me to become divided myself?

After years of this exploration, I am convinced that there are no easy answers to this conundrum. Instead, I believe that awareness of and attention to the integrity demands of self and others is essential. In addition, a deeper understanding of the cultures of music therapy and their foundations would greatly help as they could explain our systems of value recognition, i.e. 'what counts', and how these systems contribute to our personal integrity being satisfied, or coming under pressure.

I have thought a great deal about how other people experience their own integrity demands. It seems likely that we all think our own demands are normal, yet we do not speak about them. In fact, we do not speak about feeling whole, or divided, or compromised very much at all, whether as therapists, neighbours, friends, researchers. I have started to imagine a giant balloon of status quo which we more or less unthinkingly inhabit, or tolerate much of the time. I use the image of a balloon, because the status quo has started to feel quite fragile to me, at least in my own music therapy practice.

However, this will be addressed later, in discussions of the cultures of music therapy (Chap. 5). At this point, it is necessary for me to briefly share my understanding of integrity and what I mean by integrity demands. I believe there is considerable scope for misunderstanding this phenomenon, and whilst integrity is no longer a central topic of my investigation, it has become an important concept and *experience* in my research. In critical realist terms, it is 'underlabouring' for the project as a whole.

*Some Theories of Integrity*

An initial search of the concept of integrity yields literature in two broad areas: philosophy and research ethics. This study is not exploring the latter, for research ethics is a separate field which I believe could be regarded as applied integrity. Nevertheless, I hope that I will achieve integrity in my own research, in the applied sense, as well as in the sense that I am aiming to approach the whole study in a way that is consistent with my integrity demands.

The essay on integrity in *The Stanford Encyclopedia of Philosophy* begins 'integrity is one of the most important and oft-cited of virtue terms. It is also perhaps the most puzzling' (Cox et al., 2001). The authors proceed to identify the three main ways in which the term is used: (1) to describe a 'quality of a person's character' ('virtue term'), although the authors acknowledge that immoral acts can sometimes be done by people whose characters have the quality of integrity; (2) to imply the 'wholeness, intactness or purity of a thing' (when describing objects, but they concede that this can also be applied to people); (3) to refer to 'various parts or aspects of a person's life' (e.g. professional integrity). The authors explain,

> ...ordinary discourse about integrity involves two fundamental intuitions: first, that integrity is primarily a formal relation one has to oneself, or between parts or aspects of one's self; and second, that integrity is connected in an important way to acting morally, in other words, there are some substantive or normative constraints on what it is to act with integrity. How these two intuitions can be incorporated into a consistent theory of integrity is not obvious, and most accounts of integrity tend to focus on one of these intuitions to the detriment of the other. A number of accounts have been advanced, the most important of them being: (i) integrity as the integration of self; (ii) integrity as maintenance of identity; (iii) integrity as standing for something; (iv) integrity as moral purpose; and (v) integrity as a virtue.[26]

[26] Cox et al. examine 'Integrity as the integration of self' through the work of Frankfurt (1998, cited in Cox et al., 2001, Section 1) who proposes that in order to achieve integrity, a human being must choose between different orders of 'desires' and 'volitions': it is necessary to commit to the highest order desires and volitions with self-knowledge, and through this commitment, the human being starts to become one with them. But there are no limits to what the content of these desires and volitions might be. Thus, it is theoretically possible that someone may experience a fully integrated self, whilst in pursuit of a desire that is utterly harmful to self or others. This problem persists in the third theory of integrity above—(3) Integrity as standing for something. Within this view, it is possible for a fanatic to have 'integrity', whilst contemplating or enacting substantial harm. Theory (2)—'integrity as maintenance of identity', similarly considers the relationship between the human being and their 'commitments'. The authors explore philosopher Bernard Williams' notion that some of our commitments (our 'identity-conferring commitments') are more important to us than others, and that integrity lies in staying true to these, that 'to act with [Williams' view of] integrity is just to act in a way that accurately reflects your sense of who you are; to act from motives, interests and commitments that are most deeply your own' (Williams, 1973, cited in Cox et al., 2001 Section 2). Importantly, Williams does not bring a moral dimension into his explanation. It is significant that Williams makes this connection between 'who you are' and 'acting': although there is more emphasis on integrity as a state of being, there is still the expectation that having integrity requires ***doing***.

Cox et al. identify a problem: these theoretical 'accounts' reveal the implication that integrity is something that is recognised by others and attributed *by others* to an individual. If these 'others' perceive that the beliefs which underlie the individual's commitments are spurious, then they will not attribute the individual with integrity, no matter how steadfastly they hold to their commitments.

*My View of Integrity*

Much of my exploration of integrity so far has been devoted to trying to find a theoretical foundation that is not overwhelmed with the concepts of good, bad and evil which dominate virtue ethics and many theories of motivation. The reason for this is twofold: firstly, my personal experience of undividedness or integrity, is not one of aspiring to goodness, but of *being whole*. Similarly, my experience of lacking integrity, or of being divided, is one of *being fragmented*. Secondly, this book involves concepts of integrity demands in music therapy. Participants in music therapy frequently do not communicate with speech and language in a mainstream way, or at all. The theories of virtue ethics and moral theories of integrity which I have encountered have been highly conceptual: making sense of them has required the use of language, and there is also the implication that in order to act in keeping with these concepts of integrity it would be necessary to organise one's thought in a language-based and cognitive way. As discussed above, I am undertaking this investigation from an ethic of care and wish to remain consistent in every aspect of the enquiry. It is therefore unacceptable to me to subscribe to a concept of integrity which is based on language, for in effect this would exclude many of the participants I work with and deny them their integrity at the outset of the project.

With this in mind, it is important to consider where the locus of integrity lies. If it is not in a language-based thought process, then where? In my experience, undividedness is the locus of integrity: consequently integrity is the undividedness we recognise—they are the same thing. Many theories seem to imply that integrity is somehow the product of reconciling inner conflicts, or staying true to what you believe. But my starting point is different, and I prefer a notion of integrity which is something like 'self', 'identity' or 'personhood': I propose that it is a state of being, not doing, enabled, fostered and allowed by certain situations and circumstances, but challenged by others such that it can be lost.

*Some Theories of Integrity Which Can Help This Study*

Schwartz's (2016) theory of compromise integrity is helpful. He is concerned that human beings often encounter complex situations in which it is not clear what principle or rules should be followed. For example, 'when does courage cross into foolhardiness? When does caution cross into cowardice?' (p. 4). Schwartz wishes to include the notion that 'etymologically, "integrity" means wholeness' (p. 3), but sees the very real likelihood that we will experience dividedness in these complex situations if we adhere to the principle-led-virtue-understanding of integrity. To overcome this difficulty, he proposes the alternative virtue of 'compromise integrity', which 'adjudicates between self-interest and virtue' so that we 'can avoid a psychic split ... Compromise integrity just adds that sometimes even professed principles must be abandoned and that a virtue is required to decide when these rare exceptions are warranted' (p. 4). But this integrity is still verbally mediated—through 'professed principles'.

The most useful theory I have found is Pianalto's concept of 'practical integrity' (2012). He critiques notions of 'psychological integrity' which regard integrity as the tranquillity that comes from the resolving of inner conflicts and competing desires or values. The reason for this is that people may reasonably live with deep conflicts in life, such as belonging to two very different cultures, or having overcome addiction but still recognising the urge to abuse a substance. Following the logic of psychological integrity, it would not be possible for these people to have integrity. Pianalto rejects this notion as inappropriate. But more than this, he proposes a different understanding of integrity 'as a kind of practical wholeness or harmony evinced by the way in which one confronts the various conflicts and tensions that arise' (p. 4). He continues, 'the difference can be expressed thus: psychological integrity emphasizes the elimination of conflict and inner struggle; whereas, practical integrity emphasizes what it means to struggle *well*' (p. 5 original italics). Pianalto concludes:

> ...importantly, then, the person of (practical) integrity may not know where she is going, or where she will end up, but she does know that there are ways of getting wherever she might go that are not, for her, an option. In that respect, such a person will have a sense of who she is and what she stands for, even as who she will become and what shape her life will take remains in many ways a mystery which only the living of it can reveal. (p. 28)

This description of someone who has practical integrity is deeply relevant to this study. Some of the people I have worked with in music therapy have ways of being in the world that I find particularly hard to imagine in that they do not seem to relate to the language-focused environments that tend to surround them. For example, I have worked with autistic people throughout my working life. One young boy was wary of the sessions which he shared with a small group of other autistic children and their carers. He would often circle the room for the full forty-five minutes, ostensibly avoiding the musical interaction, and using coping strategies that made an interactive relationship with others difficult. For the whole group, the principal aim of the work was to enable us to gather in a small circle before the session ended. On one memorable day, the boy in question circled the edges of the room with his parent, as usual. But shortly before the end, he came forward to where a girl of his age was sitting in the 'gathering' space. He knelt down and put his arms round her in a brief hug. This startlingly powerful gesture of connection brought both his mother and me to tears. My understanding is that he had an impulse to experience wholeness through human connection that was so strong that he was willing and able to overcome his distancing-coping-strategies in order to fulfil it. It often seemed he was struggling in music therapy, but on that day he was able to share his practical integrity, his 'struggling-well' with 'conflicting' instincts which were not 'known' in language terms, but which stemmed from a 'sense' of who he was and what he 'stood for'. Furthermore, he knew which ways of getting to such integrity were 'not an option' and he lived bravely in the 'mystery' of the present moment.

I believe his integrity was not the *product* of struggling well—he was not lacking integrity until the point that he performed the 'mainstream' act of connecting with a peer. Rather, his intact, inner integrity was made up of an ongoing state of needing to avoid interaction often, but embrace it sometimes. On this day, it demanded that he be and behave the way he usually did, as well as reaching out and connecting with his peer, which so clearly seemed to be a necessary part of his wholeness that day. I include this example, because it illustrates Pianalto's proposition that integrity doesn't *involve* struggle on the path to attainment, but actually *is* a struggling-well. With this illustration in mind, I therefore suggest that integrity is not merely a value or state of being, but is a fundamental human *need*—one that demands to be enabled and allowed.

*Note to Collaborator*

Collaborator, I would understand if you were growing a little weary of all these theoretical reflections. The thing is, this book is about music therapy, nonverbal and arts-based knowing, relationship. They are themes that belong in the world of sensory perception, intuition, experience. In order to gain any insights into them, I have found it necessary to attend closely to my own nonverbal, sensory, intuitive, experiential being. In many ways, wrapping concepts in language does them a disservice and complicates this investigation. But I cannot fill a book with unwritten intuition—I do not think it would be published. So I am trying to find the least inaccurate verbal descriptions and definitions of experiences I have had, not because I regard myself as the main focus of the book, but because I believe these essentially nonverbal experiences must be acknowledged and taken seriously when we are looking for evidence of therapy in nonverbal participants, or any participants for that matter. My point is that these experiences are not in fact specific to nonverbal people, but are universal, although the verbal world tends to overlook and undervalue them.

*From Needs to Integrity Demands*

I am not exploring integrity because I think that for me and others it is an interesting point of reflection. I am exploring it because I believe it is a human need,[27]—indeed I have experienced it as such. I suggest there are two needs that arise in connection with integrity. Bradshaw, in 'A taxonomy of social needs' (1972, pp. 72–4), identifies that needs may be 'felt' or 'expressed' and I propose that the first need is to feel integrity. Secondly, if we know or apprehend in some way what being undivided or having integrity is like, then tension arises when we perceive it to be missing. For example, we may feel at ease, undivided and whole deep down, but at the same time external circumstances conspire to confound us, throwing

[27] The concept of 'need' in social science has been heavily influenced by the 'hierarchy', proposed by Maslow (1943). He outlines human needs, beginning with physiological needs, and moving as if up a ladder, to safety needs, belongingness and love needs, esteem needs and self-actualisation needs. He suggests that 'man is a perpetually wanting animal' and that 'the average member of our society is most often partially satisfied and partially unsatisfied in all of his wants' (p. 395). This theory has been revisited by numerous scientists of different disciplines, resulting in a concept of needs that are biologically rooted, often unconscious (Kenrick et al., 2010), socially embedded and inclusive of a transcendent or spiritual dimension (Koltko-Rivera, 2006) and 'necessary' for 'survival or wellbeing', whereas a want is a desire that 'may be inimical to flourishing' (Bhaskar, cited in Hartwig, 2015, p. 324).

obstacles in the way of our inner integrity. At this point the integrity which we know, but which is challenged, can prompt us to clamour for the conditions which will allow it to thrive. Perhaps the margin between the ***need*** for integrity, and the ***demand*** for integrity-enabling conditions, is slim. However, in my own life I experience a point at which the discomfort of integrity-threatening circumstances turns into a clamour for enabling ones, and at this point the clamour is non-negotiable and not open to compromise. This is what I call an 'integrity demand'.

*Summary Reflections*

I do not know whether other people experience any, many, weak or acute integrity demands. I know that I do, and that this causes practical difficulties in situations as they arise, as well as ideological difficulties in times of reflection. There is nothing whatever that validates my own integrity demands, other than my own experience. The same is true for everyone else. When one of my integrity demands is the deep impulse to try to interact with others (as well as with myself and the environment) from an ethic of care which gives without expecting return, life becomes a continual puzzle of questions and possible pitfalls. Virtue ethics are irrelevant. Conflict and compromise abound, particularly as I expect that all the Roles would identify, and prioritise, different integrity demands at different times: Music Therapist may want to empower music therapy participants, but does she have the right to assert her need to abandon written consent forms which she perceives as perpetuating a power imbalance, if this will undermine and provoke anxiety in her colleagues? If she honours her colleagues' needs, what does she do with her frustration and loss of self-respect, not to mention shame on behalf of participants?

This dilemma has dominated my enquiry. At one stage, my integrity demands were such that my research supervisor's resounding and repeating comment on my writing was 'avoid binaries': I had pursued my own integrity demand agenda to such an extent that everything that did not afford my integrity became part of the problem. It was a learning phase that I hope I have moved beyond. What it has shown me, however, is that there are issues of competing and conflicting integrity demands wherever there are relationships in the field of music therapy: between officers of the professional bodies and therapists; between carers and fundraisers; between researchers and officials of academic institutions; between supervisors and participants and so on. Some stakeholders have greater responsibility, others greater power, others more time to reflect. Ultimately, each person constructs their sense of dividedness, or wholeness, from their experience. More than ever, therefore, it seems essential to explore and understand experience in music therapy.

*The Normative Dimension of This Research*

I cannot side-step the fact that for me, this book seeks to address a 'normative need' (Bradshaw, 1972): I am not simply interested in what people experience in music therapy and how decisions are made about what counts. I *mind* about this and strongly advocate that all of us involved in the field, but particularly those who are paid to be involved, commit to scrutiny of ourselves and our practice, be it financial operations, providing therapy, delivering communications or other activities. In this way, I hope that we could all become aware of how our integrity demands are playing out, whether they contribute to an ethic of care, whether an ethic of care is even being aimed for, how these personal considerations are influencing what is valued and validated in the field as a whole, and how these occurrences in fact constitute the cultures of the field itself.

I am sorry for the length of this section. I believe it is important but understand that it may be trying to read it all.

With best wishes,
Researcher

## Dialogue 4

### *The Roles Argue About Living Artfully and Researcher Identifies What she Hopes to Achieve Through this Book*

The play's the thing wherein I'll catch the conscience of the King.[28]

MT: Musician, why are you so cross?

M: I'm not!

MT: I thought you and Researcher were getting on better these days.

[28] Shakespeare, *Hamlet*, Act 2 Scene 2 (1986, p. 752).

M: We're not!

MT: Can you speak, rather than dragging a thunder cloud around with you?

M: Are you trying to make me feel better?

MT: Please. This is hard work.

M: Ok, you want to know? We decided. It was a deliberate decision. We weren't going to do an 'artefact' plus commentary for this book, because WE BELIEVE that ART is PART OF LIFE. You portion it out and put it in a frame and write a commentary – and what are you doing? Othering it. Making it different, fringe, fluffy. It's exactly what I said I wouldn't be part of.

MT: But Musician … what's the problem. We're not doing that. We're all here, all the way through … what we talk about *is* the art-making. We're not being narrated by some sort of hybrid and there's not a separate commentary.

M: No? Where have you been? Researcher is sidling off, writing to the Collaborator whenever she feels like it. Are *we* invited? Is *your* voice included?

MT: Oh. *That's* the problem. But it's not like that. We asked her to! All her theories were like huge road blocks in the conversation. We've been through this. We asked her to message the listeners, who most likely are interested, and that way we can get on with the discussion of what really matters.

M: And you don't think she's discussing things and deciding what really matters…?

MT: (*Turning to Researcher*) Are you, Researcher?

R: No. I'm not meaning to if I do, at any rate. I don't debate things in the messages. How can I? There's no one there. I need you three to do that. It's not what you dread. And there's absolutely nothing I put in the messages that I haven't shared with you all before, at some point.

*Pause.*

MT: Does that reassure you, Musician?

M: Do I have a choice?

MT: Please, please. What else do you want?

M: I just want it to be real and not lip service. I want us to all sing from the same hymn sheet and be definite that music therapy is about an opportunity for living artfully[29] for people who don't get the chance. And that artful living matters and that music can connect us in a way that nothing else can.

R: I totally agree with that…

M: And I don't want to become the token 'arty one' who is sent off to find quotations from her poetry books because that will keep her quiet whilst the rest of us get on with grown-up stuff.

C: Nobody thinks that, Musician. At least, I don't.

MT and R: (*At the same time*) Nor me … I don't…

MT: Wasn't it you who wanted to do the quotations? I'm sure it was you who came up with the idea?

[29] Musician has taken a particular interest in Wilson's concept of living artfully (2020, Chapter 10; Wilson et al., 2020, pp. 47, 100–1). For Wilson, 'art' is not seen 'as high culture', nor is it confined to artefacts. Instead, art is the 'shareable form' we give to our experiences of 'being in relation to the world': whoever we are, we have the potential for living artfully. This concept resonates strongly with Musician's gut instincts, and is discussed in detail in the chapter exploring Aesthetic Critical Realism (Chap. 5).

*Pause.*

R: So what's with the quotation this time? It's Hamlet, isn't it? Which of us is the villain who poisons his brother? It's a bit pointed, isn't it?

C: No! It's what you're saying, isn't it, Musician. It's about artful living hitting home in the context of daily life. Hamlet gets some actors to enact how his uncle poisoned his father, doesn't he? And his uncle can't cope with being exposed through the theatre. Maybe if he'd been in a courtroom he could have used lawyers to argue away at the surface of things. But he's in the castle, watching a play, and theatre drags your emotion into it,—so his conscience has no way of hiding. It's everything you care about isn't it, Musician?

M: Pretty much.

R: Yes, I understand. I wish you'd used a less violent example.

M: I was in a hurry, ok. You didn't give me long to find the quotes.

MT: No, true. It makes the point, anyway.

*Pause.*

C: It's OK to care so much, Musician.

MT: It's not just about the *presence* of artful experience in life, though, is it Musician? It's not just living artfully that matters. It's about *trusting* the knowing that it involves and that it leads to, isn't it? You know, regarding it as a valid way of knowing.[30]

M: Yes.

[30] In support of Musician's belief, Wood argues that, when viewed as a 'knowledge practice' (Karlgren et al., 2020) and considered in the 'wider context of art history', the music making in music therapy can be regarded as 'found performance': this 're-framing' in turn affords new knowing in healthcare (Wood, 2017, pp. 1–8).

MT: You've mentioned it a lot, all along, when you ask why we're dressing up all the Dialogues, stories, pictures, mobile, as research. But that's your point … well, *our* point,...isn't it?...that the arts-based stuff is not *dressing up* as knowing and researching, it *is* knowing and researching, whether or not people are used to it. We've talked so much about it.

*They think.*

R: You're right, it's the whole point.

M: It's where *I'm* coming from, at any rate.

R: On one level, I think it's probably likely to be a finding.

MT: A finding? How can you discover something you knew when we started?

R: Did we, though?

*Pause.*

MT: Researcher…

R: Yes…

MT: What do you actually want to find out in all this?

R: (*Smiles*) If you asked me what I want to have happened by the time we all end the journey together, or how we would know that the journey had been worthwhile, I would say this: I really want to feel I have untangled the experiences in the whole field of music therapy, but particularly the ones we have when we're in the musical therapeutic encounter. I'm not talking about 'peak experiences'—other people have explored them, and they are important. But for me it's the ongoing, sustained experience of sharing and shaping the music, in a relationship, that matters so much. And I want the Collaborators who are engaging with this work, to feel they have 'tasted' some of this experience, too, otherwise I don't think it will make sense.

M: Ok, I can get behind that.

R: As well as this I want to do *everything* I can to find a way of theorising this experience, so that others don't just assume it's something fluffy ... and so that we can go to people who commission music therapy with confidence and say, 'Listen—this happens and it touches us because this and that is going on at a foundation level, and that's why it's SO important and why it's *therapeutic* experience'.

C: I really do think that will help people access music therapy.

R: Thanks ... And I guess I hope that by the end, everyone including me will understand more about how cultures grow, and how and why music therapy cultures have grown the way they have. Because if we know this, then hopefully we can re-start the conversation about musical experience, and revisit the whole debate about what counts as evidence, and start the process of recognising experience as valuable, even as evidence. And ultimately change the cultures of music therapy.

But apart from all that, I *have* to do this: there are so many people out there whose lives could be enhanced by music therapy, but who either *do* have therapy, but it only focuses on goals and not on experience, or who don't even get therapy because commissioners won't pay for 'just' therapeutic experience, because we've stopped talking about it. And that makes me miserable, quite honestly. So there is advocacy for those people in here, as well.

MT: So we're acting a play to get people's consciences...?

R: (*Laughing*) I suppose that's one way of looking at it!

MT: ...and to bring about culture change?

R: I think it would help...

## Direct Message 6

### *Issues of Methodology, Method, Epistemology and Ontology in an Improvisatory Research Journey*

Dear Collaborator,

When I started out on my journey of research, the part I found most baffling was methodology. It was a term that I encountered in articles, how-to-research books and seminars. I could tell it would provide a bridge from my interests and motivations, to a distant land called Thesis. But I struggled to see the bridge in the work of other researchers, to construct a bridge from the guide books' advice, or to design one of my own from scratch.

Looking back, I believe I did not realise there was another option: the bridge metaphor implies that the journey has been carefully planned. This must be so if the bridge is to reach land on the other side. But there are other kinds of journeys on which you set out not with a route, but with a longing to explore. Instead of building a bridge, you equip yourself with resources and provisions, telescopes and magnifying glasses, food and blankets, phrase books and the odd address in case you travel to the region of a distant relative. The whole point of these journeys is experience: the experiences that inspire you to set out, the experiences that you have along the way, and the experiences you bring home and share.

This is the sort of journey that I am taking in this book. My attempts to find a suitable methodology have been at times confusing, inspiring, exasperating and perplexing. It has been tempting to claim that the entire project is an autoethnography, which is indeed true. However, this valuable methodology does not address certain aspects of the phenomena of experience and culture in the way that I wish to. I have therefore needed to 'equip' myself with several methodological approaches, as already mentioned. More importantly, perhaps, I have needed to commit to total transparency regarding what methodology or method I am using, for what purpose, at which point. Without this, there is a danger that my research could lack focus and be seen to resort to different methodological approaches 'for good measure', rather than because the enquiry needs it.

I will share my thoughts about methodological clarity below.

*The Skittle Effect*

Given the improvisatory nature of this exploration, it is maybe no surprise that I have found my attempts to present ideas in a straightforward manner have invariably failed. I try to name a concept, and find that it is like a skittle—it stands among a group of other skittles and if I target it with an explanation, the 'ball' of my effort continually knocks over all the other skittles, as well as the one I was aiming for. The skittles each seem discrete and individual, but treating them as such can knock them all off balance.

What this means in practice, is that the innocuous sentence—'this investigation looks at experience and evidence in music therapy'—is fraught with problems. Associated concepts demand their place in the line-up: what can be known about experience or evidence? What is such knowledge—is it truth, reality, something else? Is empirical knowledge of experience and epistemological knowledge about experience the same thing? Is either/both independent of me, or do I shape them? How can I find out? What methodologies and methods are appropriate for exploring these things? What am I—mind, body, combination? How do I, you, we communicate all these thoughts? What can be known about anything and how does this epistemological knowledge relate to things that exist and are not known, or that don't exist but are imagined? What is value and how does experience become reconceived as evidence? The questions are many and continually cross refer.

Before proceeding with descriptions of the approaches that I use to examine experience, I will therefore first examine the *concepts* of epistemology, methodology and method and why these concepts are such important resources for my journey. I will then discuss certain methods that are central to my enquiry. I will not focus on methodologies at this point, though—those reflections will occur in Chaps. 3, 4, 5 and 6, as preambles to discussions of the analysis they afford.

*Methodology and Methods*

I like Carter and Little's article 'Justifying knowledge, justifying methods, taking Action: epistemologies, methodologies and methods in qualitative research' (2007), because they provide useful definitions that reflect much of the abstract questioning and concrete seeking that I have undertaken in my project. They refer to research methods as 'research in action', and in particular they quote Schwandt's notion that methods are 'procedures, tools and techniques' (Schwandt, 2001, p. 158 cited in Carter & Little, 2007, p. 1317).

Methods are not random, nor do they constitute methodology: instead, Carter and Little describe how methods are the product of the ongoing, interweaving process within research that 'shapes and is shaped by research questions, objectives, and study design .... and that resonate[s] with particular academic disciplines and encourage[s] or discourage[s] the use and/or development of theory' (p. 1316). This latter, metatheoretical endeavour they define as methodology, and it is concerned with the *justification* of chosen methods in the pursuit of these broader concerns (p. 1318).

*Reconstructed Logic*

Particularly relevant to the exploration in this book, is Kaplan's notion of 'logic-in-use' (1964 cited in Carter & Little, 2007, p. 1317). Kaplan uses 'logic-in-use' to describe any fruitful combination of epistemology, methodology and method that a researcher is employing when things are going well and the research has internal consistency, leading to the production of knowledge. When a researcher attempts to describe and account for this fruitful combination, Kaplan calls this 'reconstructed logic', and cautions that the doing of research and the reflecting on it are not the same thing: instead, reconstructed logic 'is *based* on logic-in-use, can *influence* logic-in-use, and also *idealizes* logic-in-use' (Carter & Little, 2007, p. 1318 my italics).

Reconstructed logic is a fundamentally helpful notion for me as Researcher. It refers to a process of (1) making initial decisions about what to research and how to do the research (2) questioning every assumption, as the researcher, about what can reasonably be known with regard to the research (3) articulating this process. I have felt relieved by the suggestion that this process not only influences the doing (or, logic-in-use) but actually idealises that doing, because this ongoing influencing and retrospective idealisation has been a recurring experience for me. I cannot claim that epistemological belief A has led to methodology choice B and method decisions C. Rather, some bits of the doing have grumbled along, other bits have crashed, some bits have flown; throughout, I have chewed over the ideas and theories that supported my chosen methodological approaches and ensuing methods and this has led to post-hoc 'idealised' revelations as to why some research activities failed, whilst others have issued exciting results. But in all honesty, I was not aware of these destinies at the time. Indeed, giving this feature of my exploration the name 'reconstructed logic' at this late stage, many years into the journey, is itself an act of reconstructed logic. But it is a liberating act and concept, and one that I will return to throughout the specific product of reconstructed logic which is this entire book.

*Tacit Epistemologies and Methodologies*
Carter and Little are explicit about their agenda: they advocate transparency and clarity regarding methods, methodology and epistemology, so that researchers and users of research can 'justify...methods and findings to [them]selves and others ... evaluate one another's contributions, and ... enjoy greater insight'. In other words, they wish to enhance validity and rigour in research. Regarding epistemology, methodology and methods, this agenda arises from their concern that

> reporting is frequently insufficient in all three areas ... [which] suggests a lack of engagement with these important concepts. Methods are generally the best reported. Articles are often silent, and worse, sometimes internally inconsistent with regard to epistemology. Several methodological problems can be observed ... methodological fundamentalism ... post hoc application of a methodological label ... a sense ... that research that is guided by a methodology is more esoteric, less "practical", and therefore less fundable. (p. 1319)

*Epistemology and Ontology*
Carter and Little provide clear illustrations of how epistemology—our belief as to what can be known—fundamentally influences choices of methodology and, consequently, methods. If you believe that it is possible to gain a reasonably accurate understanding of some aspect of the life of another human being by observing it, this will affect every choice you make in the doing of that research, from the ways in which you do or do not collaborate with research participants, to the claims you make for the validity of findings (pp. 1319–23).

However, these authors do not engage with the concept of ontology—ideas about the nature of reality—because they argue that to do so would 'require specialist philosophical treatment beyond the scope of this article' (p. 1327).

But I am particularly drawn to understanding my topic at an ontological level. Chap. 5 is devoted to Aesthetic Critical Realism, which seeks explanations for happenings and occurrences, at the ontological level. In fact, I struggle to see how a study of experience could have any transferable significance if it is only presented as the epistemological observation of the researcher, without any attempt to uncover generative mechanisms of the kinds of experience under investigation. Phenomenology affords ontological lines of enquiry, albeit to address the question 'what is the experience of *x* or *y* phenomenon?' To use Bhaskar's phrase, it is a type of 'epistemic fallacy' (2016, p. 6) to assume that experience has no ontological foundation, simply because we generally associate experiencing with our knowledge of things—that is, at the epistemological level.

*The Dangers of Tacit Epistemologies and Methodologies in Music Therapy Research*

Jane Edwards is a prominent music therapy researcher, whose writing has encouraged me in my search for clarity (2012). She remarks that music therapy researchers often leave out explanation and discussion of their epistemological positions and methodological choices, focusing instead on descriptions of methods:

> in spite of evidence from the music therapy literature that epistemological clarity is understood to be a requirement when reporting studies using social science research methods, an analysis of 92 music therapy research articles and book chapters published from 1987 until 2006 revealed that only 23 of the studies included reference to the researcher' epistemology (Aigen, 2008). Forty five of the reports did not mention any specific research method from the wide range available. Aigen (2008) proposed that the lack of epistemological and methodological clarity revealed in his review is a serious concern for music therapy research, requiring urgent attention. He located responsibility for change in the actions of individual researchers when choosing methods, doctoral supervisory panels, and the editors and reviewers of journals. (p. 386)

In Edward's opinion, this is not just a procedural omission, it actually undermines the validity of the research, because

> Presenting epistemology clearly. … allows critical review and thoughtful understanding of each other's research presentations since the criteria for quality will be differently applied across and between various epistemological approaches. (p. 382)

Furthermore,

> If the researcher's engagement with the fundamentals of the research orientation is omitted then future students cannot learn the capabilities to undertake this research and current researchers might wonder why there is so little regard for their work from peers unfamiliar with these methods. (p. 387)

In other words, perhaps the lack of clarity within music therapy research, regarding epistemology, methodology and methods, has led to the lack of trust from other disciplines. I have myself encountered some mistrust on my own journey. Perhaps achieving clarity in this area would provide our best chance for developing understanding with academic peers from other disciplines?

If for no other reason, it seems of paramount importance to explain my concepts of epistemology, methodology and methods. As discussed, this is continued throughout Chaps. 3 to 6.

I am relieved that it is almost time to share with you many more examples of music therapy work, through poems, stories and vignettes. I hope these will reveal and share the topic of this book: experience in music therapy and its relationship to evidence, with a particular focus on the nonverbal and arts-based knowing that lies at the heart of the music therapy encounter.

I look forward to messaging again in due course.

With thanks and best wishes,
Researcher

## References


Abrams, B. (2010). Evidence-based music therapy practice: An integral understanding. *Journal of Music Therapy, 47*(4), 351–379.

Aigen, K. (1998). *Paths of development in Nordoff-Robbins music therapy*. Barcelona Publishers.

Aigen, K. (1999). The true nature of music-centred music therapy theory: A response to Elaine Streeter's 'Finding a balance between psychological thinking and musical awareness in music therapy theory—A psychoanalytic perspective'. *British Journal of Music Therapy, 13*(2), 77–82.

Aigen, K. (2008). An analysis of qualitative music therapy research reports 1987–2006: Articles and book chapters. *The Arts in Psychotherapy, 35*(4), 251–261.

Aigen, K. (2014a). Music-centered dimensions of Nordoff-Robbins music therapy. *Music Therapy Perspectives, 32*(1), 18–29.

Aigen, K. (2014b). *The study of music therapy: Current issues and concepts.* Routledge.

Aigen, K. (2015). A critique of evidence-based practice in music therapy. *Music Therapy Perspectives, 33*(1), 12–24.

Aldridge, D. (2003). Music therapy references relating to cancer and palliative care. *British Journal of Music Therapy, 17*(1), 17–25.

Alvin, J. (1965). *Music for the handicapped child* (2nd ed.). Oxford University Press.

Ansdell, G. (1995). *Music for life: Aspects of creative music therapy with adult clients.* Jessica Kingsley Publishers.

Ansdell, G. (2002). Community music therapy & the winds of change. *Voices: A World Forum for Music Therapy, 2*(2) https://voices.no/index.php/voices/article/view/1590/1349

Ansdell, G. (2014). *How music helps in music therapy and everyday life.* Ashgate Publishing, Ltd.

Ansdell, G. (2017). Practising Goethe's 'delicate empiricism' in music therapy research: Finding value and saving the phenomenon. In T. Stickley & S. Clift (Eds.), *Arts, health and wellbeing: A theoretical inquiry for practice.* Cambridge Scholars Publishing.

Ansdell, G., & Pavlicevic, M. (2010). Practicing "gentle empiricism"—The Nordoff Robbins research heritage. *Music Therapy Perspectives, 28*(2), 131–139.

Atkinson, R. (2022). *Exploring the role of music therapy in the lives of children with neuronal ceroid lipofuscinosis (Batten Disease).* (PhD), University of Brighton.

Baker, F. (2015). Evidence-based practice in music therapy. In B. L. Wheeler (Ed.), *Music therapy handbook.* The Guildford Press.

Barnes, M. (2012). *Care in everyday life: An ethic of care in practice.* Policy Press.

Barnes, M. (2015). Beyond the dyad: Exploring the multi-dimensionality of care. In M. Barnes, T. Brannelly, L. Ward, & N. Ward (Eds.), *Ethics of care* (pp. 31–43). Policy Press.

Bhaskar, R. (2016). *Enlightened common sense: The philosophy of critical realism.* Routledge.

Bochel, C., & Bochel, H. (2017). *Making and implementing public policy: Key concepts and issues.* Bloomsbury Publishing.

Bonde, L. O., Pedersen, I. N., & Wigram, T. (2002). *A comprehensive guide to music therapy: Theory, clinical practice, research and training.* Jessica Kingsley Publishers.

Boris, E., & Salazar Parreñas, R. (Eds.). (2010). *Intimate labors: Cultures, technologies, and the politics of care.* Stanford University Press.

Bowlby, J. (1982). Attachment and loss: Retrospect and prospect. *American Journal of Orthopsychiatry, 52*(4), 664.

Bradshaw, J. (1972). Taxonomy of social need. In G. McLachlan (Ed.), *Problems and progress in medical care: Essays on current research* (pp. 71–82). Oxford University Press.

Bruscia, K. E. (2014). *Defining music therapy* (3rd ed.). Barcelona Publishers.

Bunt, L., & Stige, B. (2014). *Music therapy: An art beyond words* (2nd ed.). Routledge.

Bunting, M. (2020). *Labours of love: The crisis of care*. Granta Books.

Carlson, E. (2017). Anti-colonial methodologies and practices for settler colonial studies. *Settler Colonial Studies, 7*(4), 496–517.

Carter, S. M., & Little, M. (2007). Justifying knowledge, justifying method, taking action: Epistemologies, methodologies, and methods in qualitative research. *Qualitative Health Research, 17*(10), 1316–1328.

Chang, H. (2013). Individual and collaborative autoethnography as method. In S. Holman Jones, T. E. Adams, & C. Ellis (Eds.), *Handbook of autoethnography* (pp. 107–122). Routledge.

Chang, S. C., & Chen, C. H. (2005). Effects of music therapy on women's physiologic measures, anxiety, and satisfaction during cesarean delivery. *Research in Nursing & Health, 28*(6), 453–461.

Chatzidakis, A., Hakim, J., Litter, J., & Rottenberg, C. (2020). *The care manifesto: The politics of interdependence*. Verso Books.

Chilisa, B. (2020). *Indigenous research methodologies* (2nd ed.). SAGE Publications, Inc.

Chou, L.-L., Wang, R.-H., Chen, S.-J., & Pai, L. (2003). Effects of music therapy on oxygen saturation in premature infants receiving endotracheal suctioning. *The Journal of Nursing Research: JNR, 11*(3), 209–216.

Chuang, C.-Y., Han, W.-R., Li, P.-C., & Young, S.-T. (2010). Effects of music therapy on subjective sensations and heart rate variability in treated cancer survivors: A pilot study. *Complementary Therapies in Medicine, 18*(5), 224–226.

Cox, D., La Caze, M., & Levine, M. (2001). Integrity. In E. N. Zalta (Ed.), *The Stanford encyclopedia of philosophy* (Winter 2016 ed.). Retrieved December 12, 2019, from https://plato.stanford.edu/archives/win2016/entries/integrity/

DeNora, T., & Ansdell, G. (2014). What can't music do? *Psychology of Well-being: Theory, Research and Practice, 4*(23), 1–10.

Dodd, M. (2014). *Making connections: Problems, progress and priorities—A practitioner's viewpoint* (PhD), University of Southampton.

Edwards, J. (2012). We need to talk about epistemology: Orientations, meaning, and interpretation within music therapy research. *Journal of Music Therapy, 49*(4), 372–394.

Egermann, H., Fernando, N., Chuen, L., & McAdams, S. (2015). Music induces universal emotion-related psychophysiological responses: Comparing Canadian listeners to Congolese Pygmies. *Frontiers in Psychology, 5*, 1341.

Elliott, D. (1995). *Music matters*. Oxford University Press.

Epstein, S., Elefant, C., & Ghetti, C. (2022). Israeli parents' lived experiences of music therapy with their preterm infants post-hospitalization. *Journal of Music Therapy, 59*(3), 239–268.

Evans, D. (2003). Hierarchy of evidence: A framework for ranking evidence evaluating healthcare interventions. *Journal of Clinical Nursing, 12*(1), 77–84.

Feder Kittay, E., & Feder Kittay, E. (2003). *The subject of care: Feminist perspectives on dependency*. Rowman & Littlefield Publishers.

Forinash, M. (2016). On supervising arts-based research. *Music Therapy Perspectives, 34*(1), 41–45.

Frankfurt, H. G. (1971). Freedom of the will and the concept of a person. *The Journal of Philosophy, 68*(1), 5–20.

Ghetti, C. M., Vederhus, B. J., Gaden, T. S., Brenner, A. K., Bieleninik, Ł., Kvestad, I., et al. (2021). Longitudinal study of music therapy's effectiveness for premature infants and their caregivers (LongSTEP): Feasibility study with a Norwegian cohort. *Journal of Music Therapy, 58*(2), 201–240.

Gilbertson, S. (2022). Undefining music therapist. In C. Lee (Ed.), *The Oxford handbook of queer and trans music therapy*. Oxford University Press.

Gilligan, C. (1982). *In a different voice*. Harvard University Press.

Gold, C., Wigram, T., & Elefant, C. (2006). Music therapy for autistic spectrum disorder. *Cochrane Database of Systematic Reviews, 2*, 1–21.

Gray, A. (2013). *An introduction to the therapeutic frame*. Routledge.

Hadley, S. (Ed.). (2003). *Psychodynamic music therapy: Case studies*. Barcelona Publishers.

Hamington, M. (2004). *Embodied care: Jane Addams, Maurice Merleau-Ponty, and feminist ethics*. University of Illinois Press.

Hankivsky, O. (2014). Rethinking care ethics: On the promise and potential of an intersectional analysis. *American Political Science Review, 108*(2), 252–264.

Hanser, S. (2015). Cognitive-behavioral approaches. In B. L. Wheeler (Ed.), *Music therapy handbook* (pp. 161–171). Guilford Press.

Hart, M. A., Straka, S., & Rowe, G. (2017). Working across contexts: Practical considerations of doing Indigenist/anti-colonial research. *Qualitative Inquiry, 23*(5), 332–342.

Hartwig, M. (2015). *Dictionary of critical realism*. Routledge.

Held, V. (2006). *The ethics of care: Personal, political, and global*. Oxford University Press.

Karlgren, K., Paavola, S., & Ligorio, M. B. (2020). Introduction: What are knowledge work practices in education? How can we study and promote them? *Research Papers in Education, 35*(1), 1–7. https://doi.org/10.1080/02671522.2019.1677761

Kenrick, D. T., Griskevicius, V., Neuberg, S. L., & Schaller, M. (2010). Renovating the pyramid of needs: Contemporary extensions built upon ancient foundations. *Perspectives on Psychological Science, 5*(3), 292–314.

Kim, J. (2016). Psychodynamic music therapy. *Voices: A World Forum for Music Therapy, 16*(2) https://voices.no//index.php/voices/article/view/2312/2067
Koelsch, S. (2014). Brain correlates of music-evoked emotions. *Nature Reviews Neuroscience, 15*(3), 170–180.
Koltko-Rivera, M. E. (2006). Rediscovering the later version of Maslow's hierarchy of needs: Self-transcendence and opportunities for theory, research, and unification. *Review of General Psychology, 10*(4), 302.
Liu, Y. H., Chang, M. Y., & Chen, C. H. (2010). Effects of music therapy on labour pain and anxiety in Taiwanese first-time mothers. *Journal of Clinical Nursing, 19*(7–8), 1065–1072.
Loewy, J., Stewart, K., Dassler, A.-M., Telsey, A., & Homel, P. (2013). The effects of music therapy on vital signs, feeding, and sleep in premature infants. *Pediatrics, 131*(5), 902–918.
Malloch, S., & Trevarthen, C. (2009). *Communicative musicality: Exploring the basis of human companionship*. Oxford University Press.
Maslow, A. H. (1943). A theory of human motivation. *Psychological Review, 50*, pp. 370.
Merriam-Webster.com. (2023). *Merriam-Webster online dictionary*. Retrieved September 20, 2021, from https://www.merriam-webster.com/dictionary
Metzner, S. (2016). Psychodynamic music therapy. In J. Edwards (Ed.), *The Oxford handbook of music therapy* (pp. 448–471). Oxford University Press.
Nordoff, P., & Robbins, C. (1971). *Music therapy in special education*. John Day Company.
Nordoff, P., & Robbins, C. (1973). *Therapy in music for handicapped children*. Victor Gollancz.
Nordoff, P., & Robbins, C. (1977). *Creative music therapy: Individualized treatment for the handicapped child*. John Day Company.
Pavlicevic, M., & Ansdell, G. (Eds.). (2004). *Community music therapy*. Jessica Kingsley Publishers.
Pavlicevic, M., Ansdell, G., Procter, S., & Hickey, S. (2009). *Presenting the evidence* (2nd ed.). Nordoff Robbins.
Phillips, J. (2007). *Care*. Polity Press.
Pianalto, M. (2012). Integrity and struggle. *Philosophia, 40*(2), 319–336.
Plato. (2007). *The republic*. Penguin.
Porter, S., McConnell, T., Clarke, M., Kirkwood, J., Hughes, N., Graham-Wisener, L., et al. (2017). A critical realist evaluation of a music therapy intervention in palliative care. *BMC Palliative Care, 16*(1), 1–12.
Potvin, N., Bradt, J., & Ghetti, C. (2018). A theoretical model of resource-oriented music therapy with informal hospice caregivers during pre-bereavement. *Journal of Music Therapy, 55*(1), 27–61.
Priestley, M. (1994). *Essays on analytical music therapy*. Barcelona Publishers.

Procter, S. (2006). Whose evidence? *British Journal of Music Therapy, 20*(2), 74–75.
Rolvsjord, R. (2010). *Resource-oriented music therapy in mental health care.* Barcelona Publishers.
Roth, E. A., & Wisser, S. (2004). Music therapy: The rhythm of recovery. *The Case Manager, 15*(3), 52–56.
Schwandt, T. A. (2001). *Dictionary of qualitative inquiry* (2nd ed.). SAGE Publications, Inc.
Schwartz, J. (2016). Integrity: The virtue of compromise. *Palgrave Communications, 2*(1), 1–7.
Sendelbach, S. E., Halm, M. A., Doran, K. A., Miller, E. H., & Gaillard, P. (2006). Effects of music therapy on physiological and psychological outcomes for patients undergoing cardiac surgery. *Journal of Cardiovascular Nursing, 21*(3), 194–200.
Seppälä, T., Sarantou, M., & Miettinen, S. (Eds.). (2021). *Arts-based methods for decolonising participatory research.* Routledge.
Shakespeare, W. (1986). *The complete works.* Oxford University Press.
Simpson, F. (2007). *Every note counts: Thes story of Nordoff-Robbins music therapy.* James and James (Publishers) Ltd.
Slote, M. (2007). *The ethics of care and empathy.* Routledge.
Small, C. (1998). *Musicking: The meanings of performing and listening.* Wesleyan University Press.
Sobey, K., & Woodcock, J. (1999). Psychodynamic music therapy. In A. Cattanach (Ed.), *Process in the arts therapies* (pp. 132–154). Jessica Kingsley Publishers.
Stern, D. N. (1977). *The first relationship: Infant and mother.* Harvard University Press.
Stern, D. N. (1985). *The interpersonal world of the infant: A view from psychoanalysis and developmental psychology.* Basic Books.
Stige, B., & Aarø, L. E. (2011). *Invitation to community music therapy.* Routledge.
Strier, R. (2007). Anti-oppressive research in social work: A preliminary definition. *British Journal of Social Work, 37*(5), 857–871.
Thambinathan, V., & Kinsella, E. A. (2021). Decolonizing methodologies in qualitative research: Creating spaces for transformative praxis. *International Journal of Qualitative Methods, 20.* https://doi.org/10.1177/16094069211014766
Thaut, M. H. (2010). Neurologic music therapy in cognitive rehabilitation. *Music Perception: An Interdisciplinary Journal, 27*(4), 281–285. https://doi.org/10.1525/mp.2010.27.4.281
Thomas, G. (2009). *How to do your research project: A guide for students in education and applied social sciences.* SAGE Publications, Inc.
Tronto, J. C. (1993). *Moral boundaries: A political argument for an ethic of care.* Routledge.
Tronto, J. C. (2013). *Caring democracy: Markets, equality, and justice.* NYU Press.

Tronto, J. (2015). Democratic caring and global care responsibilities. In M. Barnes, T. Brannelly, L. Ward, & N. Ward (Eds.), *Ethics of care: Critical advances in international perspective* (pp. 21–30). Policy Press.

Ventre, M., & McKinney, C. H. (2015). The Bonny method of guided imagery and music. In B. L. Wheeler (Ed.), *Music therapy handbook* (pp. 96–105). Guilford Press.

Verney, R., & Ansdell, G. (2010). *Conversations on Nordoff-Robbins music therapy* (Vol. 5). Barcelona Publishers.

Vink, A., & Bruinsma, M. (2003). Evidence based music therapy. *Music Therapy Today, 4*(5), 1–26.

Wheeler, B. L. (Ed.). (2015). *Music therapy handbook*. Guilford Press.

Wheeler, B. L., & Bruscia, K. (2016). Overview of music therapy research. In B. L. Wheeler & K. M. Murphy (Eds.), *Introduction to music therapy research* (3rd ed., pp. 1–9). Barcelona Publishers.

Wilson, N. (2020). *The space that separates: A realist theory of art*. Routledge.

Wilson, N., Gross, J., Dent, T., Conor, B., & Comunian, R. (2020). *Re-thinking inclusive and sustainable growth for the creative economy: A literature review*. https://disce.eu/wp-content/uploads/2020/01/DISCE-Report-D5.2.pdf

Winnicott, D. W. (1991). *Playing and reality*. Routledge.

Winnicott, D. W. (2018). *The maturational processes and the facilitating environment: Studies in the theory of emotional development*. Routledge.

Wood, S. (2016). *A matrix for community music therapy practice*. Barcelona Publishers.

Wood, S. (2017). "Found performance": Towards a musical methodology for exploring the aesthetics of care. *Healthcare, 5*(3), 59.

Yalom, I. D. (1995). *The theory and practice of group psychotherapy* (4th ed.). Basic Books.

CHAPTER 2

# Meeting Other Travellers

## Dialogue 1

### *The Roles Unite to Provide a Personal Statement in Preparation for the Poems, Stories and Vignettes*

And all the men and women merely players.[1]

R: How are we going to do this personal statement?

MT: Not sure…

C: Are we all going to be 'I'?

MT: Will that work?

M: It's going to have to. It's not like one of us doesn't agree with this, or wants to say something different. It's about the one thing we are all united on!

R: Ok, so, 'I' means all of us.

[1] Shakespeare, *As You Like It*, Act 2 Scene 7 (1986, p. 717).



J. Atkinson, *Insights From Music Therapy Practice and Research*, https://doi.org/10.1007/978-3-031-86220-5_2

M: Sure.

R: And Jessica?

M: Are you joking!! This stuff is going to your head. This isn't all some kind of make-believe. That really would be weird. We are all just being Jessica in different ways, with different priorities. Because that's what life is like.

R: Sorry, just checking. It can be unnerving combining arts-based work and 'straight' research, fact and fiction. It can be confusing.

M: Well, take it from me,—I am Jessica, and so are you, and so are the others. There's nothing fantastical about it: we just couldn't agree which way of thinking and being and doing and prioritising was going to be in charge in this research. So we're all here to do our bit.

R: *(Looking nervous)* Ok…

MT: Honestly, Researcher, it's fine. You're overthinking things. I guess it has to do with integrity—wholeness—and dis-integration—dividedness. We're just naming what goes on when things compete for importance and attention in someone's thinking. Maybe we'll join up by the end. Who knows … no, unlikely … life's not like that…

R: Ok, then … Collaborator,—just to clarify … 'I' is all of us.

*Pause.*

MT: Musician, can we just mention the quotation?

M: Go ahead.

MT: This isn't some sort of gender statement, is it … about there being only two genders?

M: No, of course not. Absolutely not.

MT: It's about the way we humans perform our lives?

M: Yes.

MT: It's important ... to be sure what you mean.

M: I know. Very. It opens the debate around what value there is in artful work from another era or culture or viewpoint. About whether it's OK to use a Shakespeare quote which glosses over non-binary and other identities.

MT: True. Shall we leave that for another time? I think this book is full, as it is...

M: Yes. But thanks for raising it ... I guess I was getting a bit carried away with unfolding the whole soliloquy from *As You Like It*...

MT: Not forgetting the guest appearance from Hamlet...

M: Oh well!

### *Personal Statement By All the Roles, Addressed to the Collaborator*

*My Own Bias*

I acknowledge that I am a cisgender white female of privileged background, in terms of education and opportunity. I do not identify as having a disability and I do identify as a person of faith.

I recognise that it is potentially problematic for someone of my background to represent people, through research, who may feel marginalised in diverse ways as a result of their gender, race, creed, sexual orientation, age, social status, or who experience impairment, disability, illness or disadvantage. Furthermore, it is perhaps questionable whether anyone who uses language can adequately convey what it is like to not use language. The same is true for people for whom a dominating musical tradition is their 'native' tradition: can I understand what music means for people who, unlike me, did not grow up with Western music?

These are important questions and, once again, are concerned with experience. However, I am not seeking to examine the experience of bias and privilege in this book, although I am acutely aware of these issues. Instead, I offer the following stories, and the people who inhabit them, as fiction: in the scenarios I have drawn elements from different situations I have lived through, and I have created every composite character from a minimum of four real people who I have encountered in my work as a music therapist, and added features as well. At the end of the day, I have made up the stories and the characters are fictionalised.

*Author and Character in Fiction and Research*

The criteria for undertaking and writing fiction are different to those for undertaking and writing research. Research writing is cautious as to its ability and claim to represent others, whereas fiction writing is based upon this intention. It is beyond the scope of this study to explore the approach to representing others in both disciplines. However, my own reflections lead me to suggest that the focus in non-fiction research writing is to achieve validity and reliability in research findings through the sharing of others' real voices. By contrast, the focus in fiction writing, is to use characters in stories as both initiators and agents of plot and dramatic effect. Christopher Vogler, emphasises the importance of awareness of the archetype 'masks' that a character is wearing at any given time in a story:

> The concept of archetypes is an indispensable tool for understanding the purpose or **function** of characters in a story. If you grasp the function of the archetype which a particular character is expressing, it can help you determine if the character is pulling her full weight in the story. The archetypes are part of the universal language of storytelling, and a command of their energy is as essential to the writer as breathing. (1999, p. 29 original bold font)

The characters I present in the following pages of arts-based writing are a hybrid of these two approaches. They are fictionalised, but I am anxious that they are not perceived as specially crafted for dramatic effect. Nothing was further from my mind when I started to write in 2020. I cannot deny that this whole book has a 'plot' or storyline of my own making, but I hope this has grown out of my listening to these characters as they emerged. The type of arts-based research writing which I have undertaken therefore lies in a grey area between fiction and non-fiction, autobiography and autoethnography. However, I am clear that what you are reading is an authoethnographic journey, though one which involves many different types of writing.

Many of the poems, vignettes and stories use the first person 'I'. There is always an explanation of who the 'I' in the writing is. On several occasions, the 'I' is the music therapist. In these cases, the music therapist is myself: I write from my own experience and present my own views and responses to the fictionalised characters and settings. It is not the case that I invent people, places and events and insert a fictional music therapist to see how they would respond, perhaps in ways that might differ greatly from my own responses. On the contrary, the music therapist in the writing is as close to me (MT) as I can portray.

*Specific Ethical Issues Regarding Composite Character Creation and Fictionalisation*

I am deeply conscious of the ethical considerations of this undertaking: who is entitled to draw upon the experiences of others? Might anyone feel that they recognise themselves in spite of the fictionalisation? Am I entitled to represent myself as an author of fiction? These questions worry me.

Also, I realise there are particular ethical concerns regarding writing about others in autoethnographic research because an autoethnographer's personal narrative will almost inevitably include the stories of others, but they may not have consented to becoming a part of the research. I encountered two different approaches to maintaining ethical care regarding others in autoethnography. Firstly, a key safeguard against misrepresenting others, or violating their confidentiality or privacy, is an ongoing, open process of relational consent. This was obviously not an option for my project as I decided not to work with real participants. However, I cannot escape the fact that my work and my research are inseparable from the genuine relationships and experiences that have made up my life as a music therapist. Secondly, it can be effective and relatively safe to use 'literary means, such as employing composite characters and fictionalising your narrative' (Hernandez & Ngunjiri, 2016, p. 278). This is distinct from presenting entirely imaginary characters or cases, which can be helpful in situations where a hypothetical case could throw into perspective the case which is the main focus of a study (Becker, 2014, Chapter 6). As already discussed, I therefore made a methodological choice to use an arts-based approach (writing) and create composite, fictionalised characters.

However, I became aware that further ethical considerations are raised when real or fictionalised, composite characters are used in arts-based research. This is because ‘there is a risk for arts-based researchers to misrepresent results by striving to create aesthetically pleasing art that would be attractive to the audience’ (Viega & Forinash, 2016 in ‘Special Considerations in Writing the Report’ section). In Chaps. 3 to 6, I will address the tensions I encountered when trying to focus at the same time on my topic and on the process of arts-based work. I have found it necessary to continually reflect in a mindful way in order to avoid this danger of misrepresentation.

*How These Stories Relate to the Topic of This Book*

As discussed before now, this book is hoping to share an experience of the arts-based and nonverbal knowing that lies at the heart of music therapy with you, Collaborator. The purpose is thereby to invite you to reflect upon the nature of such experience and whether it might be construed as evidence by the various stakeholders in the music therapy field. It is looking at what counts when it comes to evidence and experience and it is an activist, normative endeavour, seeking to honour the wisdom of all music therapy participants, particularly nonverbal ones.

But the stories, poems and vignettes which follow were not specifically crafted to illustrate different points. Rather, they were scenarios that would not leave me alone until I eventually wrote them down. I have found that they include a range of actors that is as wide as the range I associate with the field of music therapy itself: supervisors, carers, multidisciplinary team members, participants, volunteers and more. And these characters enact a wide range of experiences. The writing is therefore both a performance and an illustration of the topic I am exploring. Not surprisingly, given the tensions I have identified in the field of music therapy, and in my research journey, these stories also enact these tensions.

*Integrity Demands and an Ethic of Care*

It is an integrity demand for me to attempt to validate shared music therapy experience *as evidence* in music therapy. The absence of goals and outcomes in these stories does not indicate my disrespect for these elements of the work. Instead, it has arisen because I value the characters’ *experiences* as outcome and evidence in music therapy.

It is also an integrity demand for me that you experience these ideas in story form—that is, through arts-based encounter: it would seem inconsistent to believe in the knowing that comes from arts-based encounter in my working life with participants, but not in the exploration of that life through research enquiry and the sharing of that enquiry with Collaborators. Consequently, these stories provide you with an opportunity for arts-based knowing. Later, in Chaps. 4 and 6, there is also the opportunity for nonverbal arts-based knowing, when I present pictures, glass fusing, mobile making, video and soundtrack as data to be experienced.

I hope that my attention to the ethical considerations of autoethnographic character fictionalisation, as well as to the importance of providing arts-based encounter for the Collaborators, will be recognised as my attempt to adopt an ethic of care, in practice, in this part of my journey.

Researcher, Addressing the Collaborator:
At the end of this section of poems, stories and vignettes there are blank pages for your own response to the ideas and stories, or any other experiences you may have had up to this point. It would feel one-sided and uncaring to omit this opportunity.

With many thanks.

## Poems, Stories and Vignettes

*They have their exits and their entrances*[2]

***Mehdi***
***A music therapist remembers a session with a mother and her child.***

The mother is young. I feel I have never been with a human being of such grace. Not the nodding grace of wallflowers, nor the marble grace of a classical statue, but the grace which is deep wisdom, worn lightly and with humour, in someone who seems to apprehend a wholeness of things which is beyond my grasp. The list of her child's labels would be long. But it is not even interesting to know what they are. Because he is alive, vibrant, defining his place in the world on his own terms, and in the shared delight of being here and now with his mother.

She is not sentimental, there is no whitewashing of sleepless nights or times of trouble. But she knows he is fulfilling his unique role in creation. Or so it seems to me.

[2] Shakespeare, *As You Like It*, Act 2 Scene 7 (1986, p. 717).

There is plenty to distract him in this small room, crammed with equipment of every colour and texture. But as soon as I begin to sing he stops. Stands. Motionless. I sing again—just a few notes to reflect his small vocal tones. He waits. He has time. There is no rush. I sing again, a beckoning call of two notes. I know I am inquisitive. I want to know what his music is. I make myself wait as well. He takes a few steps, close to his mother, who is sitting opposite me on the floor. A little behind his mother now. She is at ease, restful, as if this is the most normal thing in the world. As if anyone would be so lucky for the chance to meet her beautiful son. I want to cry. Slowly, I begin a quiet, deep note on the viola. I pluck, wait, pluck, in a slow pulse. He smiles, turns his head to the sound and gently sways from foot to foot. I feel I have never played music that is more important, not in professional ensembles, not in concert halls. I sing again and now he is ready to sing together: he has considered, listened, felt the music in his body, found it pleasing and now he is willing to add his own notes. I cannot flatter myself that he has a burning need, or wants to desperately, but he is willing to keep me company, to share the journey, and I feel it is an honour.

His mother gently moves from side to side, very slightly, and we are singing in turns. Short phrases. Sometimes I copy him, sometimes he copies me. He is smiling and swaying, his head still tilted. We are happy—all three of us. I truly believe we are happy. It is not music with a story, or with tension. There is no grand climax. Yet we all know it is important. When it is nearing the end, the notes are deeper, there is more space, the viola is more distinct. Then without ceremony he sits down in his mother's lap and leans against her chest. Still profoundly himself. Still deeply connected.

We let the summer breeze shake the blind a few times. We look up and agree to meet again next week. I place the viola in its case and they hold hands and leave. There isn't any more to say.

### *Communication Difficulties*

*A music therapist describes working with an autistic boy in a school setting.*

According to the books
He will always struggle
To imagine her.
He will hide with patterns,
Complex and strong,

In his remote place.
He will take her hand
And use it as a tool
In his solo life.
He will shrink from sharing, will
Shy away and shut out
Her world beyond.
She will try and fail,
Two steps forward
Three steps back.

Where is the book
Which can tell
Our new story?
Yes he hid,
Under the table
At ease and smiling,
One knee crossed
Over the other,
Self intact,
Humour ready,
Music rich,
Flowing in our song
Of everything and nothing.
Communication easy.
Resistiveness all spent.

A promised land of being
Separate together.
Duet of equal
Voices where he held,
So sensitive and strong,
The arch of the phrase
Before he let the melody
Dream into sleep,
Fade into silence,
Lengthen into shadows,
Sharing the moment when
Time and space dissolve
And all is knowing.
All is known.
Where is this book?

***Loving***
*A music therapist reflects on carers she has worked with.*

I have never seen love like yours again,
You love your boys with tiger hearts.
You hold them safe and set them free
To take such steps as you can see.

Just to step inside the door,
Or sit and stay with others close
Takes bravery beyond their years
And long, fraught days of daunting fears.

Their faces pale, their trust complete,
Raw truth is shared in every glance,
Their triumphs great as mountains high.
I never heard you wonder why.

Casual comments wound your souls,
Forgotten plans, re-crafted dreams,
Year upon year of broken nights:
The other side of care is fight.

You journey on; your travel shows
In humour, love and such deep knowing—
Others wonder how you cope
And want to learn to know your hope.

***Caring***
*A carer's reflection*

Weary, and somehow neutral,
I climb into cushions.
I am not sad
Just tired.
But I don't want to use that word too often.

I start to think of 'could-be's:
The varied shapes of choices
Beckoning one as privileged as me.
Their shapes are abstract. I only look. Perhaps I am checking they are still there.
But I know they are not for now.
Not when another needs what is.

I don't regret, I never think this needs to stop. Needs for me, I mean.
I think you think I do, but I don't.
I'm just tired, and more or less invisible.

You may not understand,
And I'm not sure I can explain,
But I would not change anything,—
Only the world. That's the bit I cannot stand.
Thoughtless and unconcerned ignorance.
But they can't help it.
That's
Why I feel lucky.
Because I know.
It may be hard,
But I know.
And I know others who know.
We recognise each other, although we are more or less invisible.
But we wouldn't talk about it,
Because it is the one bit of control we have:
To keep what we know very safe.
To share only with people who understand,
Or, failing that, who have compassion,
Or, failing that, who want to learn.

So I look at the shapes of undone things,
And just notice.
Once, perhaps they were loomingly important.
Now, I am in a river, I think;
At any rate, a flow which needs attention.
And so I attend and it is my deepest privilege.
I will do the other things another time....
Perhaps....
When I am not so tired.

### *Gareth*
### *A carer reflects on fundraising*

Yeah, so my daughter was born with not enough oxygen to her brain, so she has learning problems and can't move around. It's been appointments since she was born, really. I work in the music industry—sound recording—and we came across music therapy and it was a no-brainer. I mean, she looked up and smiled and is just so active when she has her sessions.

But it's expensive, you know what I mean. So some of us at her school, we organise fundraisers—raffles and once we did a quiz night. Anything that can get people that's not just us to get involved, because most of us can't work like we used to because of caring and that. So we do that and it means that Joe can come on Wednesdays and do music therapy with as many as he can manage! I feel sorry for him, sometimes, because it's like, 'and there's my daughter, too, ... oh and theirs, and her son!' Anyway, it makes it all worthwhile. For a bit, the head went off on one, saying that the money was raised for the children, so the parents and carers shouldn't be there. But we were like 'Do you mind! Who actually raised this money? And how are our kids going to bring all this music home when you know they can't show us what they remember until *we* get it going again?' So, anyway, one of the mums is a parent governor and she got the governors involved and it was OK. But it's just common sense really. We don't make Joe fill out forms and reports and stuff. I think he's a bit of a newbie and he keeps saying he should do that. But we are all like, mate, just get on with the music. We're in the room. We know you are turning up and that they get SO much out of it. Honestly, I never see my daughter so lively as when Joe is doing the music. But everyone needs music. I mean, I'd be out of a job if they didn't. And coming from a musical land. Like Carlo, one of the other dads, and all the opera he goes on about where he's from. It's important. It's what matters. I'm sure of it.

***Mia***

*Mia is the niece of a man who is using hospice care. She has come to music therapy because her uncle persuaded her. She has recently lost another close family member.*
*Written by the piano.*

I don't think she can make the move. It is too much. Safer, so much safer to put the notes far away, far apart, where they cannot be joined. Her hand is cold and her touch a sharp push. She does not want to be here. The therapist is trying to soften things, to make a cushion and carry it around under her notes in case they fall. But it is not working. It is two worlds, and I am caught between them.

I want to tell her I understand. To convey to her that others have been here before, that my keys have felt and heard the pain of so very many. That she does not need to change for my sake, or for the therapist. That adults have cried here too. That it is too much, too much and too unfair to have to bear what she is bearing as such a young child. Early teens? Barely that.

Still she is speckling the keyboard with stray sounds. She is jabbing a little now and I am not comfortable. How long will this last? The therapist is changing touch a little. Using my pedal. I don't expect it will do much. But the different feel is a relief for me. They do not think of me, and all the stored years of aching and loss that I have to hold, deep within my frame.

....no, stop. ... listen. ... she is moving: she has held a note and is now climbing, oh so very slowly, effortfully, to the next note. ... yes, and again, to the next. It is the start of a scale, almost a phrase ... but it is too much. The strain has exhausted her and the stray notes return.

But this tiny step, this fleeting moment of flow has brought a change. It has caught her unawares. Melted one tiny piece of the ice clamp in which she is suffering. It has been like a memory, a dream, perhaps, of another time, another way, which it seems she cannot resist once more. ... The phrase inches forward, note by note, and sits, poised on the crest, ready to fall. But this is a shared fall. Not a plunge into nothing, held only by the therapist. But the swoop of two birds side by side, aloft in the current of something greater—sky—music.

Twice is enough. Her notes become quieter and she drifts, fades until the therapist closes the sound. They sit. Silent. It has been too great. The exertion, the effort of two short, shared moments. But I have played my part and it was valuable. I hope she will come back again. I suspect she will not.

***Theresa: Cleaner at the Children's Hospice***
*Theresa tells her own story.*

I love these little ones
It's sad to see them sick.
I love these little ones,
And sometimes when they come
You think, 'it can't be long.'
But you just never know,—
Some of them are strong.

I like to find their toys,
The ones they 'specially like,
I keep them back and clean them

So, when they come again,
I know they'll smile and play
With favourite trains and dolls.
It warms your heart to see.

I'm glad on music days,
It's just a bit of fun,
And if they're well enough
They gather in a group,
And sing,—just this and that,
And play the drums and bells.
I always keep them clean.

It hurts you when they die.
I do believe in God.
But some have had such pain,
And some are much too young.
Their families just stare.
I always have a chat,
I love these little ones.

### *Mr B*

*A music therapist reflects on co-working with a volunteer at a care home.*

Posture,
Out-turned feet,
And a tendency to swirl.
I should have known.

Eager,
Caring,
A little hard of listening
Your mind was set.

Music,
Painting,
Massage,
Hair-dos:
Anything to convey our love.
Everything.

Frail people,
Resting,
Sharing
A fragile web.

But conflict grew.
Jealousy, perhaps,
Misunderstanding
Till one day you threw your bag at me.

I saw your sadness,
Pirouettes could
Not obscure it.
People chose.

I only want to hold a space, where there is room for everyone.
But you thought I'd closed the door.
It must have hurt.
It wasn't true.

### *Supervision*

*A music therapist and her supervisor.*

She thought back through the week. The newly arrived parents with twin toddlers both with a degenerative condition, trying to make sense of community drop-in centres and paediatric therapy departments. The city dad, desperate for his daughter's cochlear implants to work, heaping pressure on his mystified child. The quiet and agoraphobic wife, failing to see that her beloved husband's abilities are deteriorating following his stroke: they should be improving, it's true, but it doesn't always work like that. Boris, with quarter of his skull missing since the accident. Yes, quarter of his skull. It looks like it anyway, under his helmet. It shouldn't be OK to get used to this. Some weeks it feels as if everyone you meet is a tragedy unfolding. And today, a day of self-harming teenagers, hurling their rage at the drums and destroying her eardrums in the process.

Her supervisor looked concerned. 'Are you alright?'

She looked back. What is alright? Which bit of fraying, damaged bodies and minds should she turn away from to come up with an acceptable answer?

'Not sure'.

'What's on your mind?'

She began to think analytically. Gradually, but decisively, she became aware that she had no idea. No idea why she was there, what she was doing, or what it was all for.

'OK. I'll get us some tea. Listen, no part of being a music therapist is about staying strong and going it alone. We're wounded healers. I know you know that. It's what makes our work authentic. If we try and hide stuff that's going on, old or new—we're in trouble. I'm going to make some tea. See if there is something that feels OK to talk about when I'm back'.

She closed her eyes. ... It was the feeling of too little. Nothing she could bring could make up for any of it. If she could just stay with the twins for the day. Explain things. At least give them a chance. Again, slow but steady blankness.

She told her supervisor. All the while fearful that this was somehow notching up a bad mark.

'What about the music?'

'What do you mean?'

'How do you see the music? Part of the problem? Part of the solution? Irrelevant?'

She was surprised. What a strange question. Aren't we music therapists? She hadn't really thought about it. Not since starting work, in any case. There was vanishingly little comparison between the training and full time work. She leaned back and tried to remember the music with the twins.

'Actually it was really touching. I asked them to sing a song from their country, but they were determined to sing *Twinkle Twinkle Little Star* then *London's Burning!* They had a list. I asked them where they got it from, and they said from the pre-school and they really wanted to learn them so they wouldn't be behind. They are beautiful children and one of them vocalised a lot. There were a few times that there was some evoked tonality, but it was hard to tell because the other one was crying'.

'Ah ... well done. ... what would you say is going on there? I mean, why British nursery rhymes?'

She thought for a while.

'To be honest, it felt strange. I mean, no, actually, a bit uncomfortable. I was keen to hear their music and find their musical world but I know I'm quite nosey like that! Sometimes when I'm out and about I just try and imagine other people's music. Like, the man at the next petrol pump is country and western. The lady in the café is heavy metal. ... in spite of the silk scarf!'

'Why is it important to hear their music?'

'Well. ... the thing is ... I suppose. ... it's about identity and power, isn't it? ... I mean, music probably doesn't mean the things it does here, where they have just come from. And there, it might mean a lot of things that it doesn't here. There was a dad last week, actually, who said that he's Muslim and wouldn't usually want to be around music but it was OK because it was for his son and it was healthcare. That feels relevant, I'm not sure why.'

'Of course. But what can you do about the power and identity issues? Aren't they always going to be a fault-line, or a resource, depending on how you see it, running through all our work?'

'Maybe.'

'But it bothers you, about the power.'

'Yes, because. I mean, when I trained, we learnt about the building blocks of music and how to apply them in improvisation, you know, to create a therapeutic relationship. And then I guess there was stuff about community and how music can be shared and create community. But we still work with teenage girls, let's say, and use pop songs that have videos and come from an industry that do really awful things to teenage body-image, you know. It feels like from one angle there is no safe music. And from another angle, all music is safe. Well, I'm not sure, actually. Songs are going to be tricky because of the words.'

'So can you describe some music therapy that *has* felt safe, and shared, and where there hasn't been an imbalance of power this week?'

She thought for a while.

'OK—Tyler. He's one of the ones I saw today. He was hilarious. I told you about him. He did the usual and had his feet on the desk and hat over his eyes when I came in. I took my beaters out of my bag last night because I thought I would be going by bus today. And then forgot them. So when I came in I said—'too bad, it's beatboxing today, no beaters', or something like that; thinking, 'why on earth did I say that, I *so* can't beatbox'. But he just started up and was *fantastic*. I started jamming a blues, which I know he thinks is out of the ark, but it was so much fun and he started kind of breakdancing and pulled his hat up over one eye just to look at me as if to say—OK, you'd be so lucky to get me doing *this*. And I found a load of rock chords from somewhere and got something OK enough out of the awful keyboard and he then just started laughing, and so did I, and we laughed until I had tears rolling down my face—always happens—at which point he said 'yes, he would have cried, too, if he had just played such bad music'. And then he pulled the hat up over the other eye and hi-fived. And he is someone who would NEVER normally use touch. Nor would he ever usually just chat with me. In fact, he practically never talks and only whacks the drums till they nearly break and he can't hear what I am doing anyway'.

'It sounds great. How does Tyler identify?'

'Black. I guess.'

'Did you feel uncomfortable—white, privileged professional, using a genre which represents the most shameful period of white oppression of Black enslaved people?'

'Honestly? Whilst we were playing … it was … well, fun, and full of positive energy and co-creation, and we were equals, really. I couldn't begin to do what he was doing, either the beatboxing or the dancing, and he couldn't bring it into a shared form, you know, unless I played as well. And I guess he couldn't play the piano. … But I am aware of it, all the time. My skin colour, gender, orientation, privilege, bias, everything. I think I would be letting him down if I wasn't.'

'And did he give you any clues about how he was experiencing the power issues?'

'I think it's complicated. Well, obviously it is. For a start, he *has* to be there. Then there's me, being paid, and about as many lightyears out of his musical comfort zone and general life experience as anyone can get. And from a musical tradition that depends on wealth. And just privilege, all the time privilege on my side and not on his. I think he needs me to know that it's complicated and that there's no chance I can hope to come along and fix anything. In a way, I think that's what the hat and the volume is about.'

'Are you trying to fix things?'

'No.'

'What are you trying to do?'

'Honestly? I think I'm just trying to make something together. The raw materials may be flawed. They're bound to be in some way. I mean, virtually any two chords may echo in some good or bad way for somebody, you'll never know who and why and when. But making something together is about an "us". It's not *me* with a participant or group. It's about us. And actually that's all I am trying to do: to give people who have had few opportunities, or bad experiences of being in an "us", I mean few experiences of having a positive relationship, the chance to do so. It's about validating people by honouring their music making. I know that sounds….oh, you know. But it's what makes it different from music teaching. When I teach I can't really honour what someone plays if it's not what Mozart had in mind! Anyway, I do think that using music can be dodgy because of all these things—associations, cultural appropriation, historical resonances, that kind of thing, but it's probably less dodgy than words, often, which are so laden with meaning, and can hurt on purpose, or even some kinds of movement and dance maybe. Don't know actually. I think I just made that up about dance!'

'So, just going back to where you started, is there any way at all, given that you are a music therapist, that you can make things come right for the twins' family or for Tyler or Boris?'

'No, that's the problem.'

'But you can give them a "safe enough" experience of relationship, that may be un-reachable in any other medium than music making. A relationship between musicians?'

'Yes, I mean the twins' parents could access those relationships with others and in other ways, but maybe not with their children because their communication is so limited.'

'So would you say now that music is part of the problem or part of the solution?'

'I guess. ... I would say. ... that music can be part of the problem, but that music making is definitely part of the solution.'

'I think I agree.'

'But then there is the paper work and trying to fit all that we have talked about into linear goals and SMART targets, and the way the profession sets us all up as experts and...'

'They're definitely topics for next time, not now! Just one step at a time when things feel overwhelming. Try and have a break. These questions are all here to stay. They are part and parcel of what we do. I see it as music therapy growing up and we have to take these things seriously. I think we're in the teenage phase, so it's bound to be a time of highs and lows!'

'Oh no!'

'Anyway, take care and keep going. See you soon.'

She got up, and by the door she stooped down to pick up her flute, that she loved so much. Outside, she could hear '80s pop booming from an exercise class in the community centre. And behind her, *Jingle Bells* bleeped from a baby's pram toy.

***Am I Somebody?***

***A music therapist is in a session with a woman in a hospital ward.***

> You look at me.
> What do you see?

I adjust your wheelchair breaks.
Your skirt is pretty—
I hope you made the choice.
Your eyes ask, implore, seem to scream:
'Am I somebody?'

I start to sing
My mouth and breath
Produce your last week's tune.
My mind free falls:
You have no next of kin,
No friend, no visa, no family to tell,
No memory.

South America—
Where you are from,
But you have left no trace.
A church knows you,
But just your face not past.
Your self is hidden, you left the world no glimpses.
Who are you?

All I know
Is that you're here
And I am here with you.
Your arm and leg
And eye no longer move.
My head is numb, my hands are cold but still
We are here.

One by one
Notes emerge.
First my name then yours:
Anna.
We greet in song, just ours:
Between us all the certainty we have:
Melody.

Something changes
Now you nod
And longing fills the room.
No words
Only Anna, Jessica.

Now your hand moves to touch your heart,
Your weeping starts.

Je, Jess,
Jessa, Jesus
Stung with understanding—
You are praying
This, your soul remembers.
In your world of loss one hope remains:
All eternity.

I hold the chord
I bow my head
I join your weeping prayer.
Chords change
Time slows for this,
Listening and knowing, I am sure.
This is you.

Slow burn
Anger now.
'Careful on the ward'.
'Not your job'
'Not appropriate'.
Now I want to roar, implore, lament
'What is left?'

Different names,
Chance missed,
Single source of hope.
I refuse
To watch you weep and wait
Till you are done and we return to work—
What work?

Voices trail
Heads bow,
Stillness fills the space.
Much later
Eyes meet and ask
'What do you see?', then mine begin to scream
'Am I somebody?'

***Moon***
*Two music therapists make music with a ten-year-old child.*

Where are you?
Poised
Balanced
At ease, reclining,
Looking at me as if to say:
'Well?'

We play and your eyes
Track me.
You allow events to
Unfold, but I know
We are here on
Your terms.

Your file is
Full of labels.
What for?
Are they trying to
Traffic-light
Parts of
How you are?
For what?
You are
Emphatically
You.

Or are they trying to
Understand,
And can only translate
One bit at a time
Because they don't know
Your language?

Nor do we.
But one day,
Whilst reclining,
Poised
Balanced,
You teach us.
Just a little.

A beginner's lesson.

We play the lyre
And sing,
Drawn irresistibly
By your eyes
And your guiding
Arms.

And all at once,
You sing as well,
Tossing your head,
Moulding melody
And holding, holding
The moment....
We breathe together,
One instrument,
Alert,
Needing to stay—

And then it is enough.
You look away,
Drop your voice,
Lower your chair
And sigh,
As if to say—'there's plenty more,
But very likely
You wouldn't
Under-
Stand'.

### *Chloe's Story*

*Tina: Chloe's Mother*
It's a time I try to forget as much as possible. We knew how bad things were, but I guess that just the fact that she was in rehab, still, made us wonder if something might get better. The drive was so long, and there was never anywhere to park. Kim was having a bad spell, too, but the funny thing was, that she seemed to get a bit more together when we went to visit Chloe. You know, ... like she needed to be the strong one. Which she did, after all. I don't know how we did it. But you do that, don't you. You know, you come together when there is trouble.

The rehab home wasn't very nice. Why do they paint things yellow in these places? It's not cheery, it's just stressful. You can't relax. But I don't want to complain. They did what they could. The doctors always looked like they needed a holiday, and I don't blame them. So many tragedies all in one place. I don't know how they do it. You had to wait in this room where some of them had their dinner and it was really bad. I guess they were the more able ones, and I would have given anything for Chloe to be one of them. But they couldn't really feed themselves. Not properly. There was food on the floor and on the chairs. And it smelt of leftovers. Horrible really. But I don't mean to complain.

One day the music lady was there. Why she had to do music in that dinner room I'm not sure. She tried to clear up. I reckon she just did it to make it less bad for the next people. We were all there—me, Kim and Mike. It was hard because things weren't really working as a family, if you know what I mean. But we were going to do anything it took for Chloe. Then Callum came with Danny. Danny was asleep in his buggy and we all just sat there in a line along the back of the room on these plastic chairs. I remember wishing I could be anywhere else in the world. I just wanted everything to fade away and not to know any of it. I wasn't really coping, I suppose. The music lady was getting some stuff off the floor and put it in the bin. She smiled and said hello and carried on. Then she asked us if we liked music. I don't know why, but it made me want to laugh. I mean, that wasn't what we were there for. It wasn't about us. I happen to like all sorts of things, including music, but it's not like I expect to tell anyone in the rehab place. So Mike said yes and could he have a go on the snare drum and she said fine, of course. Mike got a beat going quite well, actually, and Kimmy started smiling and then the music lady played this kind of rock and roll on the keyboard and we had a laugh. We actually had a laugh. She said sorry about the room and what were we waiting for. So I told her we were Chole's family and were really early for seeing the consultant, but you never know if you can find somewhere to park. She didn't seem to mind. I don't know what she was supposed to be doing, but anyway, she asked if we wanted to do some music with Chloe but I explained that Chloe was paralysed. I said about the accident. The music lady looked like she couldn't bear hearing about it—really upset. But I'm used to that now. I just say it and then it is done. It's when I talk about the court case that I steam up. I get SO angry. But there is nothing anyone can do.

Anyway, Mike went to Chloe's bay and the nurse said fine, so he wheeled her in and Danny woke up. He was a bit grizzly, but not surprising. I mean, you don't want to wake up from your nap in a strange place where you can't run around. Callum gave him a cuddle and had him on his knee. The music lady started playing. It was quite simple, sort of rocking music. Come to think of it, I'm not sure if she was playing it for Danny or for Chloe. Kim was really interested and the music lady asked her to watch Chloe very carefully and just see if she woke up. And in fact she did. Then the music lady said we could just all be together for a while and she would play. It was nice, actually. Quite gentle music. Nothing noisy, and it didn't really feel like being in medical place. I think we all chilled out a bit and Danny stopped grizzling. At the end, the music lady said thank you to Chloe. It hit me like lightning. I wanted to cry. I mean, saying thank you to my Chloe, who can't do anything. But the music lady told Chloe really quietly that the mood of the music had come from Chloe—that Chloe had given her the idea for that music and she hoped it had been OK. She then told us that there was such a lot that Chloe could give to the music—her breathing could be like the beat, and we could copy the blinks of her eyes in our playing. Our playing!! I said she was joking, right?! And she said there was no need to play, but we could join in if we wanted to, which Mike and Kim did, so I said OK too. She gave us quite small instruments. I suppose they were a bit like primary school, but she said that the loud ones would be too much for Chloe. And it felt OK. I had these tiny bells, and it was my job to notice when Chloe blinked and shake them. The music lady played something on the top of the keyboard then, too, and it was like—I don't know. Anyway, it didn't feel too bad. Mike had a small drum and just played with his hands and Kim had one of those rain sticks you get at the market. The music lady started—really slowly and quietly again because she said she was trying to find Chloe's breathing pattern. And she just told us when we could join in if we felt like it. It all sort of rolled along—it was really nice. I couldn't believe that fifteen minutes had gone by the end. That's got to have been the quickest fifteen minutes since the accident.

It's funny, but whenever I went to that rehab place, I was worried about time: would I be late? Was the doctor in a rush? Was I wasting their time? But when we were in that music room, it was just like—well, it will take the time it needs because we haven't got to the end of the music, yet! Anyway, Chloe had her eyes open—really wide, the way she did when we knew she was really awake. It made things pretty tricky for following her blinks, but that didn't matter. I reckon she knew we were all there. Maybe she could tell we were relaxed, too, because we were. All the while, Danny had been cuddled on Callum's lap, waking up. Then all of a sudden, he called out 'wake up Mummy'! My heart nearly stopped. How can a two-and-a-half-year-old understand? It was like the bubble had been burst. But the music lady just said hello there, did you have a nice sleep, and Danny said hello, wake up Mummy. I was embarrassed, I mean it put the music lady in a difficult position. But the music lady said, let's have a go. Shall we sing mummy a song? And Danny said yes, a wake up song. So the music lady played this kind of hopping tune and sang wake…up….but she left a gap and Danny piped up Mummy, in just the right place. I was so proud. Then the tune went on, a bit like a nursery rhyme, and each time, Danny piped up Mummy. I think he was actually singing, come to think of it. Mike was chuffed as anything and Kim played this sort of beat on the hand drum. Even Callum was smiling and bouncing Danny on his knee, like he had time away from his broken heart for just a moment. So there we all are, having a toddler sing-along and then this incredible thing happens—Chloe moved her head towards Danny just exactly when it was his time to sing Mummy. But the music had stopped because it was the end of the song.

We all noticed. No doubt about that. There was this pause and I think the music lady wasn't sure what to do. She spoke to Chloe again and said—yes—it's your Danny you are looking at, singing a special song just for you. Callum wanted to bring Danny up to his mum and the music lady said of course, why not all have a hug. But after, she said maybe to take Danny back to where he was and see if Chloe would look over again. She asked if Chloe often moved her head because it was the first time she had met her. But we said no, maybe now and then, but if so, it seemed to be like a reflex or something she wasn't in control of. So anyway, she started up the song again, and there is Danny on Callum's knee and every time we get to Mummy, Danny sings to his mum and Chloe looks over. It was like we were all on holiday. Honestly, it felt like a totally new place for us and Mike and Kimmy were smiling—Kim was right up close to Chloe, and Danny and Callum were singing along. Actually, we all were. You can imagine the noise with us lot of tone deaf family. And Chloe was there. I mean, really there, looking, turning. Eyes wide open. Something really tight just let go in my chest. I think we all laughed as well. I mean, not Chloe, but the rest of us.

Right then the nurse came in and told us the consultant was waiting. So we said thanks a lot and the music lady asked if we would like to do music again and we said great, why not next time? So we fixed it for the next month. We were really up beat when we went to see the consultant.

It was depressing after that—we had to listen to how bad things were and what the plans were for her discharge into a care home. But at the back of my mind, I thought: it's good, we are coming back and can just have fun doing some more music with Chloe. The sad thing was, that when we got back again, it wasn't the same. The music lady seemed stressed. She came in to see us and I could see she really wanted just to get some sort of song going, but she said she was really sorry to have given us the impression that Chloe had turned her head. We said what do you mean, she did turn her head. But the music lady said, no, she was sorry if she had led us to think that Chloe did it on purpose: there was no evidence that Chloe could move voluntarily and she shouldn't have given us that hope. She looked really stressed. We said but we were there and we saw it and what's the problem, and she said again it was wrong of her to give us that sort of hope. But I just wanted to get back to that song where just for a while things felt normal and fun. We tried and it was OK, but not as good as the first time. Then Chloe was discharged and we wanted to get music for her at the new place, but it hasn't happened yet.

*Mike: Chloe's Father*

It was easier to get time off than I had expected. Mind you, you sell your soul to the armed forces, so it's only right that they give you a little bit back when the need arises.

I think we had both wanted a clean break, but then Chloe getting ill changed all that. It was a mess really. It felt pretty bad driving there separately and what a dump, honestly. Why can't they organise these places properly?

Chloe, love. My Chloe. You were a handful, but so alive. And now what? I think that's why the music helped. I know that Kimmy and Tina were surprised. But I did play drums at school and you can't exactly pack them up and lug them around when you move. It was something to do in that horrible waiting room with the TV blaring. As soon as Jessica knew I was interested she turned it off. Maybe visitors are allowed to do that as well. I've always wanted to play again, actually. There were some musicians in my family—just bands and that sort of thing. But when you travel around you lose touch.

I don't know what was wrong with Kimmy. She was like a ghost after the accident. Callum wasn't much better. Mind you, he had gone for the being-together-all-the-time sort of relationship, so it's not surprising, really.

It was good the music. I reckon Jessica could have done more jazz, but she said that wasn't what Chloe needed, so I let it drop. I don't know what she was doing at that rehab place. The patients can't get up and learn instruments. Mind you, it was like a bolt out of the blue when Chloe looked over to Danny and kept on doing it. Before it happened, it was as if we were all breathing together. It was quite slow the music, and relaxing. Hang on, no, that was the other bit. Chloe looked over when Danny called out, I think. Poor little lad. Not much fun for him. But the main thing was that we all had something to do. I think each of us had an instrument. It's not like those awful visits when you just sit by Chloe's bedside and say empty stuff that she can't reply to anyway. And usually there is only a curtain and someone's being sick or something on the other side. I can't stand these places.

I thought we were onto a good thing. I mean, Jessica seemed to know what she was doing and made the whole thing feel like you were involved. Even Chloe. She actually talked to Chloe like she expected Chloe to sing or something. But the second time we went she was different. She insisted on telling us over again that Chloe hadn't moved her head and she was really sorry. I've no idea what that was about because we were all there and saw it quite plainly. Maybe there are different words you have to use for music in rehab, or something. But as far as I could make out, there we were, a messed up family, and for the first time we were having a laugh AND Chloe was involved. Nobody was expecting her to get up and walk out. It just felt good to know there was something we could actually all DO together when we go visiting. But it seems to have fizzled out. They don't have music at the care home, apparently. So that's it.

*Kim: Chloe's Sister*

It's not like Chloe and I were dream sisters. We did fight and she could be a bit big-sisterish. But when the accident happened it was like the bottom had fallen out of my world. She had always been there. She had always done everything first and kind of made things smooth for me with Mum and Dad.

I hated those rehab visits. The car journey was stressful because Mum can't stand long distance driving anyway. And then round and round in the car park till you feel sick. I had pretty much zoned out that day. Things hadn't been going well and I hadn't been making it into school.

Then this musician—she said to call her Jess—suddenly let Dad play one of her drums. I nearly died, I mean, Dad??? It's not like he's musical. But actually it was good. He used two brushes like he was a pro. And Jess played along with some sort of jazz club tune! I didn't think this sort of thing happened in rehab homes.

So when Danny woke up I thought it was a shame because the music would need to stop. But Jess asked who we were visiting and when we said Chloe, she said it was fine to bring her along. I don't exactly know what Jess was doing in the home, but she was really interested in Chloe. I'm not saying that the nurses aren't, but they have so many patients to look after, and it was just us and Chloe. Jess was talking to Chloe and it really looked like she thought Chloe could understand. So we started this sort of lullaby: ever so gentle and peaceful and I could tell that Mum and Dad were de-stressing. It was all a bad time for them, too. And even Callum started playing with Danny, which he hasn't really done much since the accident. I just remember the clock ticking on the wall, and thinking—you're out of time, can't you tell! I had a rainstick. I love that sound—just peaceful and like you are by the sea. I played it when Jess nodded and she asked me to really watch Chloe and see if she woke up. I remember watching her closely and for the first time I felt—there's a point, there's a point to watching my sister. I'm not just looking for signs of who she used to be. And I 'm not just looking at someone who will never notice. I'm looking to see whether she wants to wake up into this music. And she did.

That was just the start. Afterwards, Danny started singing 'Wake up Mummy' and Jess thought this was funny and made up a little song around Danny's words. I think she stopped playing every time 'mummy' came, so Chloe could hear it loud and clear. And then Chloe started turning her head to Danny, every time. And I thought: this is what I want to do. I want to learn this song, so that when Chloe is in her care home, we will be able to sing it with her and Danny will be able to see his mum looking at him. It was a really strong feeling. School seemed pointless by comparison. Everyone was just jamming along and then the nurse came in and said we had to go. I felt relaxed. I think we all did, even Callum.

When we went back the next month it wasn't the same. Jess came right up to us before we had gone into the music room and said how sorry she was that she had let us think that Chloe had moved her head, which was kind of odd, because Chloe had moved her head, loads of times. She said that it could have been wind, or some sort of reflex but not voluntary and she was really sorry. I think I zoned out then. I don't know what Jess was on about. We had been there and seen it. And it would have been so good to learn that song and maybe some more for when Chloe went to the care home. It's not like she had much else to look forward to.

*Callum: Chloe's Partner*

Oh God! I just wanted it all to end.

So many professionals trying to fix Chloe and it was so obvious it wasn't going to work. Talking about quality of life. WHAT quality of life. I hate myself for saying it, but at that time if I could have just walked away and forgotten about Chloe, I think I would have. But there was Danny to think about so I couldn't.

It was so obvious that it was hopeless. Why were the nurses always so damn cheerful? It was either cheery cheery from them or stacks of notes, medical stuff and gloomy looks from the doctors. And then they started on us. No, of course I'm not sleeping—how am I going to work full time and bring up Danny? Yes, I feel it's all too much, overwhelming, whatever word you want to use for it. They sit there and give you questionnaires to fill out and then go home, and those bits of paper do nothing, not one bloody thing, to help with the 'difficulties' we are going to face. And the worst one is how am I going to visit this Chloe for the rest of my life? What is there to say? How is either of us going to stand it?

The music was about the only thing that might have helped there. None of us was any good, but it was quite chilled and the main thing is that Chloe seemed to connect with it. The way she looked at Danny. It was a real look, like a Mum who still wanted to be there for you. I thought we could get it sorted for her care home. But there wasn't going to be any music there. And then the music therapist undid all that good feeling by saying that none of it had meant anything. I just wanted to leave at that point. The odd thing was that she seemed really upset, the music therapist, I mean. Because I think she *did* think it had meant something. What the hell was she on about? Anyway, we still haven't got any music for Chloe, but Danny does sing his song when we're at home. I wish he wouldn't.

*Danny: Chloe and Callum's Toddler*

Wake up MUMMY
Wake up MUMMY
Wake up MUMMY
Wake up MUMMY

Daddy, bounce me.... (laughing)
Again ... do it again.

Wake up MUMMY
Wake up MUMMY
Wake up MUMMY
Wake up MUMMY

*Chloe*

I can hear you.
I am listening.
Don't go. Please, please don't go.
I am listening. You are there and I am here.
I know it's not right.
But I can hear you.
I am listening.
Please stay. Please, please don't go.
I am listening.

I can hear what you are saying.
My eyes are shut but I can hear what you are saying.
And I can hear the tune.
I CAN HEAR THE TUNE!!
I want you to know—
I can hear the tune.
I am listening.
Please, please sing more.
Please stay.
I am listening.

*Music Therapist*

It was probably the most distressing situation I have been in as a music therapist. I don't really think of the participants I work with as 'rehab' patients or 'hospice residents'. Just people. Often, I don't read their notes till I have met them several times and got to know them as the musicians they are.

I had been in the rehab home for a year or so and was clearing up the usual fall-out from lunch in the lounge. Not the most glamorous part of the job, but essential. It bothered me that there was no designated waiting space for visitors, and on that day there was a group of visitors sitting quietly at the back of the room. They seemed isolated and I was concerned. I said hello and apologised for the mess and asked if they liked music. I'm so grateful for being a music therapist—I don't think I have ever met anyone who does not have something to say about music, whether positive or negative. So I asked, and the man wanted to play the side drum. I was really pleased because so often people assume they are not musical, or not included, or that music making is not for them. He seemed quite confident all of a sudden, so I joined in and we played a short blues sequence. I do remember it. It was fun and meant nothing and everything.

They were clearly waiting for something so I asked and they explained that they were Chloe's family. I hadn't actually met or heard about Chloe, but I asked if they thought that Chloe would like to be involved in music. Families were allowed to refer their loved ones: it didn't just have to be other staff members doing the referring. So to my surprise they said yes and seemed to want to go ahead straight away. I had a gap in my timetable so Mike, the dad, went to find Chloe and bring her to the room.

Something about the family touched me. Chloe's partner Callum came in with their son Danny and I felt overwhelmed with the sadness of all their loss. But that's when I know I am in the right job, because in spite of everything, I wanted to know what webs of connection music could weave for us, and what music Chloe might have in her.

We started with something very simple—just tuning into Chloe's breathing. Her sister Kim was very attentive and seemed almost hungry to understand what was happening, not just be a part of it. I explained what we were doing, as I often do, mainly so that people don't think it is anything mysterious or beyond their reach in a technical way. I really do believe that this gentle tuning in can be learnt by carers and family members as a way to validate and communicate with their loved ones. I gave out some small instruments, which I always find embarrassing because they look like school instruments or toys. But Chloe seemed very far away and I felt that we needed to start gently. As the modal sequence—just two chords—established a musical framework, we were able to respond to Chloe's eye flickers.

Danny was awake by then and called out 'wake up mummy'. The atmosphere seemed difficult, so I decided to focus on Danny for a bit to help the others find a channel for emotion and energy. We improvised a little four-phrase 'wake up' song and Danny was so musically attuned: he sang in pitch, when I left a gap for 'Mummy', virtually every time. Right at the end of the last phrase, Chloe turned her head towards him and really looked.

There is something about musical structure, its dependability and graspability, that is so powerful. I had seen it so many times: you find a simple structure from within the contributions that the participants bring, and it creates a meaningful, safe space. No words are needed for it to make sense, and almost any response can find a home within it in real time, in shared activity: it is grounding and connecting and significant, at the same time as being musically complete, yet flexible.

I needed to know whether Chloe often turned her head, because all responses in the rehab setting were considered together: different disciplines contributed their observations and a painstaking process of assessment took place on a weekly basis. So, any new movement was significant. The family told me that Chloe didn't tend to do so, so we repeated the song to see if she would again, and she did several times. I remember thinking that this was important and I would need to inform the Senior Rehabilitation Therapist, but more than that, the mood in the room was easing and I just wanted this family to have a chance to relax together and share a positive experience. I can't remember the mum very well. She was very quiet. But I remember all the others clearly. Callum, whose brokenness was so painful to observe; Danny, bringing the most natural of all impulses—wanting to sing with his mum. Mike, seeming practical and sensitive. And Chloe's sister Kim, whose insight and urgent need to understand and learn has stayed with me. That's why I suggested meeting again—so that I could try to share some skills that they could take with them into the care home setting that Chloe would move to. I knew I would not be able to work longer term with any of them.

When they needed to go to their appointment with the doctor, I went to find the Senior Therapist to report what had happened. In many ways I wish I had not. He was very kind. Actually he was always very kind, and sincere, but was clearly dismayed by my description of the session. It wasn't so much my saying that Chloe had moved her head, it was more that I implied that the family believed she had moved her head. I was baffled because there had been seven of us in the room and Chloe had moved her head and the rest of us had seen it, time and again. Dr JJ explained that there could be no certainty that this was voluntary movement and that it could have been wind or some other involuntary cause. I felt as though my head would implode. I was an experienced music therapist. I understood how the rehab home worked. I knew I couldn't make a claim unilaterally. That was why I was telling Dr JJ, so that others could look out for similar movements. I was part-time and didn't have the chance to go to the MDT meetings because I wasn't there on those days. Dr JJ began talking about the financial implications of such a new piece of evidence and I remember wanting to scream. Why had I gone to tell him? What was that about? Because actually, Chloe's turning her head wasn't the point anyway. The point was, that the family had seemed to move from isolation and disconnection into a place of communication and musical enjoyment in a short space of time. We had all felt it. It had brought hope. I said this to Dr JJ, but it made things worse. He advised me not to raise hopes.

I don't know if I did other sessions that day. I felt disintegrated and distressed. The next time I was in, the Finance Director came to ask me to apologise to the family and tell them that my claim that Chloe had moved her head was unfounded. Even now, years later, I feel dismay when I think of how I told the family there was no evidence and apologised. They looked bewildered. The good that had tentatively emerged from our previous session seemed to evaporate. I tried to recreate the connection and share skills, but all except Kim seemed to have withdrawn. And I couldn't meet Kim's need because I knew there was no music therapy at the home that Chloe would be moved to. WHY was it wrong to give hope? Nobody in the first session believed that Chloe was going to get up and start singing and walk out of the room. That wasn't what the hope was about at all. It was a hope for meaningful connection which we all believed in, because we had experienced it, together, in music. It was a hope for a way of being a family together in the future, which could turn the sadness and emptiness of visiting Chloe into something creative and meaningful.

Much later, I understood: Dr JJ had been alarmed by *false* hope. He had assumed that I had filled the family's heads with false hope for recovery. Nothing had been further from the shared experience. But the damage had been done. Hope is so fragile. I am full of regret for my part in how Chloe and her family felt hope and lost it. I have not known how to repair the damage. In many ways, it is the reason I am doing research.

It is so hard when there is a gulf of understanding like that. As music therapists, we are used to being misunderstood, given broom cupboards to work in, even being ridiculed, and jealousy can be a real problem because participants often respond to music in ways that they don't in other therapies. Half the time, people think you are an amateur volunteer and seem amazed that you are actually paid. It's not always the case, but things didn't go well at that rehab home. The final straw came after Chloe, actually. A couple of patients self-rated their mood as OK before a session and lower after the session. That's what therapy does: you learn about yourself and it can be raw and it can hurt, but it can heal and acknowledging the depths is part of climbing up. The participants were fully behind the process, but it didn't go well with staff. I know they thought I was unprofessional. Anyway, it was a while ago now. I think of Chloe, and her family. I wonder how they are now.

*Dr JJ: Senior Rehabilitation Therapist*
I remember that case. Chloe—young—had a little girl I think. No, maybe a boy. And the family came from quite far away. Some issues. Can't remember. With forty patients and quick turnover it is hard to keep it all in mind.

I had been at the rehab home for ten years when music therapy was introduced. There was some issue with funding but we got a part-time therapist. I don't really know how to comment. She was a nice person and we got along alright as colleagues, I think. I wouldn't say she was an expert in rehab, but then she probably wouldn't either. I can't deny that she was a good musician. Personally, I liked hearing the viola round the place and the keyboard in the lounge. But it is a curious therapy. I'm on thin ice here. There is a pecking order in rehab which puts all the therapies—physio, OT and SALT down below anything medical. So, as Senior Rehabilitation Therapist (Physio), I sometimes feel I am fighting a losing battle. The thing about the music therapist, is that I really never felt sure whether she knew what she was doing, rehab-wise, I mean. I accept that she used different techniques—improvisation, listening, song-writing and the rest—and filled her sessions. But why? What for? During all her time on the ward, there was never a single measurement of improvement that was agreed by the MDT to have originated in music therapy. Not even mood. For goodness sake, half the time when she worked one-to-one with patients they ended up rating themselves LOWER on the mood scale *after* the session than *before*. How is that progress?

I guess the turning point came when she was working with Chloe and she reported that Chloe had made voluntary head movements in response to a sound source. She claimed it had been a dozen times or more. The worst thing was that she had somehow convinced the family that Chloe had done this. If it wasn't so exasperating, it would have been quite endearing, perhaps, the way she came to tell me the 'good news'. But she had no inkling of how inflammatory such a claim would be. I'm afraid she was naïve: when you raise a family's hopes like that, it can end in bitter disputes over the level of rehab. The sums involved are simply huge, and it's my responsibility to make sure that claims from the therapy team are rigorous and valid. I asked the Finance Director to have a word with her as I thought it would come better from finance than from another therapist.

It's a shame, really. Honestly, I would dearly have loved it if Chloe had been functioning at that level, as it was a really sad case, I remember. That's what I mean. Music therapy just didn't seem to be a rigorous therapy. I don't really know how it comes to be HCPC regulated. Getting people singing or listening seems a bit of a tenuous contribution to rehab when we are dealing at the level of two-to-one transfers, communication aids etc. She said she thought she had given them hope and that it could be valuable for families. But that's so dangerous.

Anyway, that wasn't the worst case where music therapy upset the apple cart. She didn't stay long, I seem to remember—only a few years. It's sad really. If music therapy could tighten up as a profession and build some evidence for progress, I'm sure the patients would like to get involved.

*Maya: Finance Director*

It's simple—the MDT works together. Any improvement or deterioration must be agreed by the team as a whole. You don't unilaterally make a claim and expect the rest of the team to sign it off. Yes, I do remember when Jessica reported voluntary head movement in a young female patient. She didn't bring it to the team meeting, she just made the claim and told the family, which is the worst of all worlds. I checked it out but nobody else on the team had reported any voluntary movement. If they had, it would have been shared at MDT level and once accepted, it would trigger a reassessment with all the ramifications for additional rehab etc. We've seen this before—families report this or that and then hear about some new intervention on the news and pressure the clinical team into providing what they think is needed. They don't realise it costs tens of thousands of pounds to provide a course of rehab here. Agreeing additional rehab interventions can cost eye-watering sums, which we have to justify, on the basis of MDT-validated rehab potential.

It was irritating, having to deal with this but, to be fair, when I told her she would definitely need to set the record straight, un-make the claim to the family and apologise, she didn't object. Personally speaking, I think these visiting volunteers should always be accompanied by a MDT member. They are multiplying, what with Dogs for Health, haircuts, massage and the rest.

## Invitation to Respond[3]

Please use this space to draw, write, respond, note down music you have been inspired to listen to, or for any other creative response…

[3] Note from Researcher: It was with relief and delight, that several years into my research journey, I came across Colin Lee's article 'Sounding the authentic self: Artistic expressions of a queer music therapist' (2019). In his 'Background' section, he writes: 'in the spirit of queer autoethnography's emphasis on "becoming" through creative acts, my paper's reviewer suggested the possibility of an interactive, dialogic space where the reader/listener might be able to engage in their own creative processes (ie art, music, dance, poetry, imagining, etc.)' (p. 3). He then provides a link to an online 'padlet' with instructions for how to use it creatively. This immediately emboldened me to pursue my plan for leaving blank space in this book section for creative responses, regardless of the doubts of the other Roles, for I no longer felt alone or absurd.

## Invitation to Respond *Continued*

Please use this space to draw, write, respond, note down music you have been inspired to listen to, or for any other creative response…

## Dialogue 2

### *The Roles Consider the Knowing that Comes from Arts-Based Experience,*[4] *Whether Music Therapy, Research, or Other Modalities*

We are such stuff as dreams are made on.[5]

C: Is everything OK, researcher?

R: No.

C: What's the matter?

R: I can't pretend any more…

M: You've started going on about pretending. Where's that come from? I haven't heard you mention it before.

R: It's what I'm having to do: pretend. Make a pretend story, or there's nothing to show for this … the Collaborators … I can't take them on a journey with a beginning, middle and end, because it just won't work, so there doesn't seem any point in trying.

*They all think.*

M: Why is a beginning, middle and end so important?

R: Because it's about structure. Every part of our life relies upon structure.

M: OK. That's new for us, too. I mean, in all these years, we haven't spoken about structure. And here we are, half way through the writing…

[4] 'Arts-based experience' or '- engagement', and 'living artfully' are the names given by different Roles to the same central theme of the study. The Roles' choices of terminology reflect their priorities and thinking at the time.

[5] Shakespeare, *The Tempest*, Act 4 Scene 1 (1986, p. 1335).

R: ...which isn't half way through, in fact ... it's actually happening miles down the line ... so it's a pretend middle ... and it's improvised, and I don't know what anyone is going to say next, so it's totally out of my control, and I'm supposed to be the researcher and keep things neat...

C: Are you sure of that? Are you really meant to keep things neat? Somewhere, I can't remember where, you talk about research being 'loosening' of things, so that you can look at what's going on.

R: That's analysis, actually—the root meaning of analysis.

C: So, I don't think it needs to be a lost cause. Do you think there is another sort of structure that might help the reader? Does it have to be a beginning-middle-end kind of structure? Could it be more of an improvising structure, like you said? It's what we do. What we do best, in fact. And there must be something significant in that.

M: You could be right, Carer. This is about experience, isn't it?

R: Yes, welcome aboard! ... and evidence.

M: (*Annoyed*) I'm only trying to help. OK, in a later section, you untangle some experiences and come up with a set of phases of experience. That's right isn't it?

R: Yes, it's to do with phenomenology.

M: So could that be the kind of structure that will carry the readers and listeners along? A structure of experience...?

R: Maybe.

MT: I hadn't thought of that. But maybe you're right, Musician. I really hear you, Researcher. You have organised, reorganised, re-reorganised the ideas and sections in this book till the rest of us have just left you to it. We know you've found it hard...

R: Worse than hard. Which is why I'm stopping. Now.

MT: What!! Just wait a minute. I think ... yes, surely it's all a huge metaphor.

M: What is?

MT: This: we all care so much about the experiences that happen in music therapy that we want to investigate them. So, we think about how to do it, and realise that the only way to truly represent those arts-based experiences in research, is to do arts-based research. But here's the thing: would we even be doing *any* kind of research if there was another easy way to explain, validate and construe as evidence, all those arts-based music therapy experiences?

R: Probably not.

MT: So, it stands to reason that all the same excitement, challenges, problems, frustrations that we encounter in music therapy, will also arise in arts-based research. They're the same stuff. That's why they both matter to us.

R: Yes ... Yes, I suppose you are right.

MT: And so...

R: But that's the problem. We have never articulated that before. Not really. Which is weird because it sounds so obvious. And that's a problem because I'm trying to write something and at every step, something new becomes clear that changes everything that went before.

MT: Changes, but doesn't change. Think improvisation again. Impro that 'works' always keeps some of the features and elements of what went before. Otherwise it would just be random segments of sound.

R: But it doesn't help. I can't improvise this book.

MT: I suppose you could have done. If we had chosen to do an artwork plus commentary. But this is all interwoven, it's true.

R: So I follow the conventions of research and put it into sections and arguments and it's dry as a bone.

MT: Who said that?

R: I just know it. But the sad thing is, I thought it would make it acceptable.

C: Who to?

R: To the research community.

*They think.*

C: Honestly, Researcher. I don't think you should worry. Carers can't worry about the world's opinion, or they would feel the people they love are being judged all the time. You're researching music therapy because experiencing making music together matters. So you're conveying that in drawings and poems and things that matter in the same way. It's fine.

MT: ...until you come face to face with the expectations of the research community. I get your point, Researcher.

C: But that's *expectations* again.

MT: I guess we have to learn from Carer. It's about arts-based experience. But it's also about expectations. You write about that, anyway, Researcher. The whole theme of culture being what we value. That's about different cultures setting up expectations, isn't it?

R: Yes, including micro cultures like music therapy.

MT: So it's not a lost cause. I'm sure it's not. It's … it must be … yes, surely there will need to be some sort of setting of our own expectations. In our own micro culture of *this* enquiry...?

R: Well, it's a bit late, isn't it?

MT: Come on, we have to keep going … It's a conceit of all writing that you re-write beginnings when you already know the end, or middles when you don't know the start. It doesn't make it a sham.

R: But it's dishonest. We don't do that in music.

MT: Fair enough. (*Puzzled*) Well, actually, we do, if we commit to a composition, there could be all sorts of re-writing.

R: But not in improvising.

M: What's with this sudden crusade for improvisation? This is new, too. I don't remember going through this before.

R: But it's the bread and butter, and the heart and soul of what we do in music therapy.

M: Not in some functional and developmental work,—there could be very little impro there.

R: Yes, and that's all good. But it's what *we* do … and care about.

M: OK. And something about it starts to feel like a sham when you write it down and analyse impro, then…?

R: No, when we make statements about it after a long time, as if it was all so obvious at the time. That feels like a sham.

C: Then there's something about improvising that matters. Is that right?

R: Yes.

C: And that's like caring. Caring is basically improvising.

MT: I don't think the NHS would thank you for that statement!

C: No, that's not what I mean. There can be planned programmes of care. But actual caring comes down to people, to their relationships.

MT: Experience, again. And structure.

M: I still don't think we're getting at the problem. Is it that *understanding* something that was improvised, whether it was music or a relationship, doesn't happen in the moment? So, writing about it as if it was all clear at the time feels unethical?

R: Yes, totally.

C: But that's not a problem. It's the whole point: the strength, if you like. We *experience* in the moment. And experience nourishes us and builds up, till somewhere down the line, when we have reflected, we start to know something. And then we can share it from a place of knowing.

R: Yes, exactly. And it doesn't have to be verbal. The entire point of doing this with arts-based work is that this knowing doesn't have to be verbal. But we can still share it. We can show it in a picture, or share it in a vocalisation.

M: Go on…

R: And then after more time and more experiences, we know something more, perhaps deeper, perhaps different.

M: That's great.

R: But can't you see. Arts-based experience is about knowing *afterwards.*

MT: Not all of it.

R: OK, no. There is some knowing at the time. But it's a knowing that keeps on feeding us—people in general, not just in music therapy,—changing us, making us see new things differently even when we don't realise it, because there can be more knowing that hasn't happened yet. It's not like learning facts or theories. It is *in* us, this knowing. Times tables and theories of evolution you can learn and sit back and think about and relate to different experiences and other bits of knowledge. Arts-based experience isn't like that.

M: No, I think we know that.

R: Exactly, so that's my point. How on EARTH am I expected to put this interest and experience of ours into a book that you can sit back and think about like a fact or a theory?

MT: You can't.

R: There we are … as I said, it won't work, and I'm past caring.

M: I disagree. You're not past caring, you're tired. And you need help.

C: Does it say anywhere that a book needs to be something you can sit back and think about like a theory or a fact?

R: Not exactly, but the conventions are to have chapters, quotations, narrator…

M: So where does that leave us?

MT: With a nightmare—a continual re-writing, re-visiting, re-experiencing, re-knowing, re-structuring, until it feels like a completely lost cause and we are barely ahead of the people engaging with it, as far as working out what it's all about.

R: Yes, exactly. Welcome to my world!

*They all think.*

MT: So, could we go back and re-conceptualise it as an art-work book, plus commentary. Would that work?

M: No, sorry Music Therapist. No, absolutely not. It's life. 'Living artfully'. Wilson,[6] you remember. I thought you were on board a while back. For as long as we side-line anything creative, call it 'art', try to sell it for vast sums, or write it off as 'amateur' if it won't sell, then we're missing the point. How can you even suggest it when we've been through this so many times? Arts-based doing and being are part of *everything*, if only we would let them. The way we communicate, the way we serve our food, the way we move, dress, arrange pebbles on the beach: it's all living artfully. And music happens in the wind and in the rhythm of our moving and everywhere, so, no! I'm not willing for this to be packaged as an artwork plus commentary. You know that. And I won't change my mind. Think what it would do to the participants who you say you want to give access to music therapy. It would be like saying—"come and dabble in a fringe activity, run by mysterious 'artists' who can stay for as long as they pay their way". The one thing I thought we all agreed on is that we want to be saying—"come and experience this natural way of being alive, and see where our shared journey takes us."

R: Relax, please!

MT: Are *we* arts-based?

R: Well, I don't know about you, but *I'm* real.

C: I don't think Music Therapist meant that art isn't real.

MT: No, thanks, Carer. I just thought … the four of us are already a bit outside-the-box.

*They think.*

M: But there's something else. Something we're not getting at. Something about why the whole issue of how to present this book matters.

[6] Musician is particularly drawn to Wilson's notion of living 'artfully' (2020).

R: Of course there is! It's like the whole point. People won't pay for arts-based therapy because there's apparently no evidence. Evidence of *what*, they don't say,...probably that it 'works'. But what is *working* when it comes to arts-based experience? We pay for opera houses and drama projects. But that's because the creative industries and education are all stuffed into the bracket of 'benefitting the economy' in our wonderful neoliberal world.

MT: You're not a fan, then!

R: ...of opera and drama, yes of course...

MT: ...but of neoliberalism? ... I was joking ... oh, never mind.

R: It's where we started. Why can't you work the way you want to, Music Therapist? Because you have to do linear, goal-oriented work that demonstrates outcomes. And that stresses you out because, for you, it is the experience of being together in music, improvised music often, that builds the musical relationship that is the whole point. It's the nonverbal space for being ourselves as we know ourselves, and for being ourselves in new ways, generated by and audibly reflected in different instruments, genres, rhythms, melodies. But that doesn't tick the box any more. You have to dress everything up in progress and outcomes, even though, *even though* in fact you, and half the therapists you supervise, *actually value the musical experience more!*

M: OK, stay calm.

MT: Yes, no. I see. I'm getting there. You're right that's what matters to me. Well, let's be honest, it exasperates me.

R: So, think about it. *Why* has it happened? Because we need evidence for commissioners and funders, or they won't pay.

C: So we go down the path of outcomes in order to keep the service running, so that in fact it can do something else...?

R: More or less.

MT: Except that actually practice is changing to reflect it. Increasingly, there's the inbuilt expectation of linear work: you know, following steps to get from A to B, and the emphasis on musical experience and relationship is really fading. In fact, you hardly see those words in relation to music therapy any more.

M: So what's the agenda here? We re-convert the world?

MT: Sarcasm isn't very helpful.

M: I'm not being sarcastic. If you need to reclaim musical experience and relationship as a profession, you'd better get on with it, and that will involve educating the world to value it…

R: (*Interrupting*) Which comes back to culture being the systems we have for valuing things…

M: OK, I'll try again, … and that will involve changing the cultures of music therapy.

MT: …against the tide. It's not comfortable.

R: Yes, but you're not alone. Don't flatter yourself that you're the only one involved in this.

C: Can we keep things friendly? It's feeling a bit scrappy…

R: Yes, sorry, Carer.

C: No worries.

*Pause.*

M: So, what do we do?

*Pause.*

MT: Actually, I don't think it's rocket science. This is our drop in the ocean. We're not going to change anything through one book, but we can add just a little to a conversation. So, we work out what matters to music therapists, and to commissioners, and we do what we do in therapy: we 'meet and match'. We have to meet and match our participants in music improvisation, or they won't recognise the music being made as relevant to themselves. We learn it in week 1 of music therapy training and never stop.

*Pause.*

C: Researcher…

R: Yes.

C: Where did that come from? Why did you get so upset right after the poems and stories? For me, they are the heart of things. They really speak to me and I can imagine the music and the people there. It was moving. *I* thought so, anyway.

R: Thanks, Carer. It's Music Therapist and Musician you should be thanking. That's the thing. They have this stuff, this magic, that wraps around people and spaces and fills it, and people respond. It's honest and it makes a difference.

C: Music, you mean?

R: Of course.

MT: Don't go there now. Please. Can you tell me more about the stories, Carer?

C: There isn't much more to say. They seemed real to me. And although there was a lot of pain and struggle in the situations, it was as if music offered not a way out, but a new window, to let in the light and make everything glow in a new way.

MT: I'm really touched by that. It's not always like that, of course. Sometimes the clash between the out-of-session mood and the in-session mood is very stark and even problematic. Like when I worked in a hospice for nine years. I worked with a hundred and fifty participants. It was strange that it was such a round number, but I counted. They all died. It was very difficult. But actually, in the sessions, it was often inspiring, fun and energising!

*They all fall silent.*

MT: Researcher … this next bit. You're going to talk about autoethnography, aren't you?

R: Yes.

MT: Can we be there too,—Carer, Musician and me?

R: Why? We separated out the theories because you kept interrupting, and I couldn't get through them.

MT: I just think we're getting into a different phase of the story. You're going to go through the retroductive bits, aren't you?

R: That's the plan.

MT: I just think we might need to be there. You might need a break. We may need to know what you say so that we can keep up the discussions…

R: Carer, Musician, do you agree?

C: I don't mind.

M: Well, sort of.

MT: Can we try it?

M: I'll find a quote if you like?

*Researcher smiles.*

C: This quote, the one Musician found for this section, is so important—'we are such stuff as dreams are made on', don't you think?

MT: I haven't really thought about it. Why?

C: Because it's like a metaphor for this whole project: we only have 'little lives', but we can make dreams from them.

R: But we're not dealing with dreams. They're just fantasy.

C: No, you don't understand. We can fashion, and make happen, things that are dream-like in their scale and scope. It's about possibility and creativity. Which is what music therapy is about. It's all there, in one line.

MT: Oh...

## References


Becker, H. S. (2014). *What about Mozart? What about murder?: Reasoning from cases*. University of Chicago Press.

Hernandez, K., & Ngunjiri, F. W. (2016). Relationships and communities in autoethnography. In S. Holman Jones, T. E. Adams, & C. Ellis (Eds.), *Handbook of autoethnography* (pp. 262–280). Routledge.

Lee, C. A. (2019). Sounding the authentic self: Artistic expressions of a queer music therapist. *Voices: A World Forum for Music Therapy, 19*(3). https://doi.org/10.15845/voices.v19i3.2799

Shakespeare, W. (1986). *The complete works*. Oxford University Press.

Viega, M., & Forinash, M. (2016). Arts-based research. In B. L. Wheeler & K. M. Murphy (Eds.), *Music therapy research* (3rd ed.). Barcelona Publisher.

Vogler, C. (1999). *The writer's journey—Mythic structure for storytellers and screenwriters*. Second revised and expanded edition. Pan Books.

Wilson, N. (2020). *The space that separates: A realist theory of art*. Routledge.

CHAPTER 3

# Loosening the Threads Along the Way 1

## Direct Message with Interruptions

### *Shaping and Experiencing an Autoethnography*

Experience is by industry achieved.[1]

Dear Collaborator,

When I encountered the critical realist idea of retroductive argument, through which the researcher 'thinks up' and imagines possible explanations for observable phenomena, I felt drawn to this approach. Experience, what it is, how and why we recognise and absorb it, how and why we share it, how and why we elevate some of it to the status of knowledge or evidence and not the rest of it—these are all questions with various explanations which retroductive argument seems suited to explore.

As I mentioned earlier, my investigation was motivated by my belief in the arts-based and nonverbal knowing that is central to music therapy and has focused on experience and what counts in music therapy, particularly in the area of evidence. I have encountered four methodological approaches which have been helpful:

[1] Shakespeare, *The Two Gentlemen of Verona*, Act 1 scene 3 (1986, p. 6).





J. Atkinson, *Insights From Music Therapy Practice and Research*,
https://doi.org/10.1007/978-3-031-86220-5_3

- Autoethnography
- Phenomenology
- Aesthetic Critical Realism
- Arts-based research

In addition, I explored but moved away from sensory ethnography, as many of the questions it raised seemed also to be raised by autoethnography and phenomenology.

Up till this point, I have largely focused, tacitly, upon the *methods* of autoethnography and arts-based research, and used them to share stories of experience in music therapy, whether my own or other people's, whether factual or fictionalised. I have not discussed these methods yet (that will come later in Chaps. 4, 5 and 6), but allowed the results to speak for themselves. Now, I turn to the analytical approaches afforded by each methodological approach, and I address them in the above order. In a sense, the chapters of this book that you have already encountered, now become data for this analysis. Later, in the chapters mentioned, I introduce several more arts-based experiences.

I have enjoyed the peace and quiet of these Direct Messages. However, the other Roles have raised some objections to my continuing in this manner: they do not wish to be excluded and they want to know what I say, as Researcher, and to have the right to contribute. I concede that these are reasonable objections and so I wish to explain that the other Roles are present as I write this, and I may need to record their words at certain points in order to represent every view. I am sorry if you had expected a private Direct Message and find yourself listening to a group chat.

You will also notice that Musician has again provided a quotation for this message. I was dubious whether these would contribute anything to the project, but they have in fact proved quite useful in helping to focus and anchor the discussion. I hope you enjoy the food for thought that they bring.

The stories and poems that you have just engaged with have many functions: they describe the field of study and start to explore the kinds of experience that occur; they illustrate tensions that lie at the heart of this book, including transactional and care ethics, and integrity demands; and as a result, they constitute arts-based data. The task is now to make sense of this 'data' and the purpose of this message is both to introduce the theories of autoethnography and explain why I chose this framework for building knowledge, but also to use autoethnographic analysis to address my topic. As such, this message is the first phase of my retroductive approach to sense-making.

MT: I'm confused ... I don't know whether this story is an experience, a shared experience, a sharing of a shared experience, or an experience of a shared experience...

M: What!!!

MT: No, I mean it. Think about it. We share the experiences we have. And we experienced that shared experience. So when we tell the story, what are we doing?

*Continuing the Story of This Research*

I wish to share an issue that I find uncomfortable: I have found it impossible to avoid repeating parts of the story of my enquiry in this autoethnograpic account. To be precise, I am not so much repeating myself, as revisiting events, thoughts, or issues, that *other* Roles (and even Jessica in the Prologue), have already mentioned. This is almost bound to recur throughout the book. In fact it seems impossible to approach a topic through four different Roles and four different methodological approaches without continually revisiting the same material. I feel I have had little control over this: the Roles say what they need to say and do not take kindly to my editing them. At the present time, it means that when I want to 'reveal' the story, I am conscious that parts of it are not new for you. And I am concerned that in the future you might become impatient or lose interest. Please be assured that the following three chapters of retroductive analysis (Chaps. 4, 5 and 6), are far less narrative in nature and may therefore offer greater novelty.

It was not my initial plan to explore my research interests through an autoethnogaphy—i.e. an in-depth exploration of my own experience. However, advice from an academic ethics committee indicated that the specific ways I wanted to enact an ethic of care in a potential project with other participants would be problematic: for example I was, and still am, averse to requesting written consent from people who do not write, may not find meaning in words and may communicate in other ways. I fully understood the panel's views and their duty of care, yet it seemed that our different approaches would ultimately cause difficulties. I was disappointed and wondered whether there was a lack of trust of professional music therapy practice and domain level knowledge—but this is speculation. Without doubt, my integrity demand for the particular type of caring approach I favoured was challenged and this raised questions for me regarding hierarchies of theoretical approach within academia. I felt a vague sense of unease, relating to accepted norms within the research community and felt concern on behalf of potential nonverbal participants, who I have dedicated much of my working life to trying to communicate with on their own terms: what was happening to their voices?

At this point, some years into my project, the way ahead emerged quickly and simply. It was clear that the only person who could wholeheartedly give consent to an exploration of care ethics, in full awareness of risks, was me. I could allow myself to experience an ethic of care, explore it, and write about it, without harming anyone else. I therefore designed a new project: it would be a different kind of autoethnographic study, looking at aspects of my own working life that I have already mentioned—those crunch points when my integrity, or undividedness, came under pressure.

M: In the end, I think it worked out for the best, Researcher.

MT: I think so, too—it sent you off on the whole 'culture' track. It was really significant.

R: OK, yes. I'll get to that. Can I just keep going?

*Autoethnography as a Principal Methodology in My Study*

I had been living with the idea of autoethnographic enquiry for some time: I wanted to do ethnographic research, but was aware that many of my personal characteristics were strongly influencing the design of the project, in particular the use of arts-based methodology and methods (discussed in Chap. 6). I therefore felt that any attempt at objectivity would be unlikely to succeed and it would enhance the study to embrace the subjectivity of my position as researcher.

I started to understand the affordances of autoethnography: my own theoretical thinking had now deepened and autoethnography had moved from providing a necessary acknowledgement of my subjectivity, to a vital methodological approach for investigating what I care about in my music therapy work and research.

*The origins and purpose of autoethnography*

I feel I should warn you that Chaps. 3 to 6 involve a lot of theoretical exploration. The Roles are not happy about this, so I have promised them I will try to avoid simply sharing things I find interesting. Instead, all the time I will try to ask myself: how does this theory help Collaborator to deepen their engagement with the topic, i.e. experience of nonverbal and arts-based knowing in music therapy, and what counts when it comes to evidence.

So, to begin with autoethnography, I want to share Judith Lapadat's words from her article 'Ethics in autoethnography and collaborative autoethnography':

> Autoethnography (AE) is an approach to qualitative inqiry [sic] in which the researcher recounts a story of his or her personal experience, coupled with an ethnographic analysis of the cultural context and implications of that experience. (2017, p. 159)

I like this definition because of the use of the indefinite, rather than the definite article: we relate 'a' story, not 'the story'. This usage firmly establishes both the authenticity of the researcher's experience and choice, as well as the fabricated reality of research—we could research in a different way and produce a different story as a result, with no less valid experiences. Indeed, it is the researcher's experience and its telling that validates the research: when rigorously explored, experience and validity become inseparable in autoethnography.

The focus on the researcher's self in autoethnography is also significant because of the ways it differs from more traditional ethnography. In the fields of knowledge that have become known as anthropology and sociology, ethnography has been the methodology employed in order to understand different cultures. From the 1800s, travellers have studied groups of 'different' others, by living alongside the human objects of research (Robson, 2002, p. 187). Approaches to this participant observation were expounded and practised, notably by Boas and Malinowski (Baker, 1987, p. 15; DeWalt & DeWalt, 2010, pp. 3–9) and became widespread in anthropological research. Over time, because this approach was increasingly critiqued by scholars who felt that no outsider researcher, however well immersed in the life of community, could truly provide an objective report of that community, ethnographers developed a strong focus on reflexivity (Anderson, 2006, p. 373). Lapadat describes the 'questionable ethics' and 'colonial practice' of outsider researchers who believe they can truthfully represent different cultures (p. 591). She explains that

> in maintaining the fiction of objectivity, researchers failed to place themselves in the study or to acknowledge their own motives, perspectives, emotions and status.

She continues that

> reflexivity, broadly speaking, is the notion that researchers, through their presence and actions, interact with and influence the people and social processes in the research site (Schwandt, 2015). Reflexive researchers critically reflect on and describe these influences. They situate themselves in the study by revealing their background and personal perspectives, theoretical stance, style of interaction, political aims and understandings. (p. 591)

The reflexive ethnographer indeed has much in common with autoethnographers, therefore. Kim Etherington explains that it is the 'capacity of the researcher to acknowledge … their own experiences and contexts (which might be fluid and changing) … [that] close[s] the illusory gap between researcher and researched and between knower and what is known' (2004, pp. 31–2 original brackets). Denzin also frames this type of researcher stance as a conscious, deliberate, political act, in a way which I am particularly drawn to because it clearly articulates my own relationship to autoethnography. Lapadat summarises Denzin's thinking:

> Denzin (2003) suggested that autoethnography is the descendant of ethnography and also its future—a political performance of resistance by one person, and another person, and another person—where, by telling their individual stories and theorizing them, researchers democratize research, critique racist and hetero-gender-normative dominant discourses, and disrupt the power politics of the controlling corporate and military interests … writing and performing one's autoethnographic story is a courageous moral act that says: I am singular and unique; I am telling this story so that you can bear witness; I witness that your story is unique; and, as we are each unique and singular, every person and every person's experience must be acknowledged and treasured; no-one is expendable. (Cited in Lapadat, 2017, p. 591)

This is my favourite quotation about autoethnography—it reflects my motivation and purpose. Furthermore, the implications of this standpoint—that the experience of each human being is uniquely valuable—is entirely consistent with the standpoint of music therapy: the two undertakings feel closely aligned and on a personal level this contributes to my integrity, or undividedness and to an ethic of care.

*Characteristics of Autoethnographic Writing*

It feels important to share my thinking on autoethnographic writing because the different sorts of writing in this book—Dialogue, Direct Message, poems, stories, vignettes, theoretical discussion, analysis—have been continually thought provoking and challenging.

Autoethnographic research can take many different forms and result in widely differing outcomes. However, there are certain fundamental attitudes and undertakings that identify it as autoethnography. Holman Jones et al suggest that these distinguishing characteristics include

1. *purposefully commenting on/critiquing of culture and cultural practices*
2. *making contributions to existing research*
3. *embracing vulnerability with purpose, and*
4. *creating a reciprocal relationship with audiences in order to compel a response.* (2016a, p. 22 original italics)

These authors emphasise that it is the 'interrog[ation of] the nuances of … experience in light of general cultural phenomena and cultural practices' that differentiates autoethnography from autobiography (p. 23), and they suggest that the former is often undertaken when the motivating experience has the quality of an 'epiphany' (p. 22). These statements embolden me to regard my research as autoethnography: the discovery of care ethics and its crucial relationship to my work, life and thinking was indeed like an epiphany, and I am seeking to explore the socially constructed culture of music therapy, so as to question certain of its attitudes and practices.[2]

[2] My autoethnographic investigation aligns with Holman Jones et al.'s list in various ways: with regard to point (2), I am attempting to situate my study within the body of existing research about music therapy, experience and care ethics. In addition, I am aware of personal discomfort resulting from my vulnerability as autoethnographic researcher—point (3). This is perhaps the hardest aspect of the approach for me. However, as Holman Jones et al suggest, the vulnerability is not gratuitous, it is 'purposeful'. Many autoethnographers have written profoundly personal accounts of their experiences. For example, Aisha Durham's

In my experience of reading autoethnographic accounts, the result is that the autoethnographic researcher becomes like a neighbour, someone whose life is connected to my own in this world we share. Holman Jones et al suggest that this 'reciprocity' is necessary so that readers are 'not passive', but 'read with a sense of responsibility' and are 'expected to act in and on the unfolding story' (p. 25). Indeed, this call for (inter)action with the writer and their experience is the 'purpose' which justifies the 'vulnerability' of the researcher: autoethnography seeks to leave its readers personally challenged by what they have read. I acknowledge that the engagement I request from you, Collaborator, is similar, and I recognise that it is demanding.

*Ethics in Autoethnography*

Much has been written about ethics in autoethnography. As mentioned, the very choice of autoethnography is an ethical one, emphasising the voice and thereby the value of the individual (see Denzin above), and contrasting with the norms of major research traditions which can be in danger of perpetuating imbalances of power between researcher, participants and people from minority and marginalised groups (Thambinathan & Kinsella, 2021, p. 1).

The ethical ramifications are wider, though. Wolff-Michael Roth proposes an ideal outcome of autoethnography:

> Because each person gets to speak and each person provides space for others to speak, the understandings (about what has happened) are not conflated into the homogenizing one (usually the researcher's) voice but retain the multiplicity arising from the co-presence of all participants' voices. Order is disorderly, requires many voices, a polyphony, which is both ordered and disordered. (Roth, 2009, section 5)

distressing story of multiple miscarriages and the prevalence of miscarriage in the Black community in the USA (2020) and Kakali Battacharya's unsettling description of her abusive childhood home, her flight, and subsequent experiences of discrimination within the academic community (2020) both challenge the reader. These accounts lead or throw you into the researcher's often uncomfortable experience and thereby 'compel a response'—point (4). For further intimate narratives, see *Critical Autoethnography* (Boylorn & Orbe, 2021) and *Handbook of Autoethnography* (Holman Jones et al., 2016b).

But it is this very presence of others that highlights the ethical concerns within the approach, and which leads Kathy-Ann Hernandez and Faith Wambura Ngunjiri to assert that autoethnography 'may be the study of self, but it is the study of self in relation to others within a particular social setting (Ellis, 2004; Chang, 2008)' (2016, p. 263). They provide a list of strategies to support autoethnographers in their handling of ethically delicate situations and concerns (p. 278), which I have found helpful. Some strategies seek to protect the researcher, by advocating that they are selective about what to include from their personal story, using a pen name, seeking consent, maintaining continuous dialogue with others and collaborating. Other strategies seek to protect the participants, for example through the use of literary means, such as 'composite characters and fictionalizing your narrative', revisiting discussions regarding consent at every stage and right up to publication, seeking peer feedback and allowing others' voices to speak for themselves.

The issue of the final performance or writing is particularly sensitive. Lapadat cautions that 'once an autoethnographic story has been written, the written version has the effect of reifying that particular story' (2017, p. 594). This is an ethical concern for the autoethnographer both because it means that any objection raised by participants at this stage cannot be rectified, but also because the researcher themselves cannot change the story as their perceptions change.

However, the potential power of a final performance or written account is also great: Carless and Douglas explore these outcomes in numerous ways: (1) in an autoethnographic narrative account of her coaching of elite golf players (Carless & Douglas, 2011a), Douglas' unfolding research story appeals to the reader's imagination—we hear her conversations and experience jarring elements (2) in the same study, Douglas uses story *within* her coaching, such that the reader receives a story of story-making, which illustrates her coaching approach better than a factual description could (3) the same authors use song and film (*We crossed the Tamar* (Douglas & Carless, 2017)) as a final performance in *Across the Tamar* (Carless & Douglas, 2017)—a study exploring women's relationship to physical health and exercise (see Chap. 6). The evocative music and images demand 'engagement' and create 'impact', 'stimulat[e] emotional responses', '[support] embodied knowing', '[trigger] personal reflection and local knowledge' and raise 'issues of genre and style' (Carless & Douglas, 2011b, p. 439).

*Ethical Considerations in My Study*

What I have learnt from my exploration of autoethnography as a methodology is that it involves risk—to the self, to the other, to the shared relationships and to the status quo. I believe it is likely that much social science research involves risk, both to the researcher and to the participants. Traditional approaches have measures in place to mitigate risk, and these are widely seen as effective. However, I wonder if perhaps the thinking behind ethical attitudes could be more flexible? Perhaps this study could challenge it? Confusingly, this feels risky.

*Differing Approaches within Autoethnography*

Like all research traditions, autoethnography has developed and broadened in response to critique. Jillian Tullis (2014) comments that 'having explored a wide range of autoethnographic texts and performances, I believe autoethnography exists on a continuum from highly fluid and artistic to formulaic and highly analytic' (p. 245). This statement identifies the two main traditions within autoethnography—evocative[3] and analytic.[4]

Even though the focus of my investigation is experience, itself, I do not believe this book is positioned in the evocative tradition alone. I am drawn to the political potential of evocative autoethnography, as well as the relational connection of autoethnographer and reader, but I also seek the theoretical rigour of the analytic tradition.

[3] Evocative autoethnography broadly describes the types of studies that Carolyn Ellis pioneered, i.e., those which '[join] social science and humanities to make scholarship more human, useful, emotional and evocative' (Holman Jones et al., 2016a, p. 18). Different arts and narrative techniques are used to immerse the reader in the experience that the researcher is sharing. On the page, the research often does not look like typical analytical study reports: there are often poems or transcribed conversations, photographs or other images, and sometimes there are fewer headings or sub headings and less referencing of other literature than usual in dominant traditions. Paul Atkinson (2006) raises deep objections both to this approach, complaining that 'the methodological has been transposed onto the plain of personal experience, while the value of sociological or anthropological fieldwork has been translated into a quest for personal fulfilment on the part of the researcher' resulting in accounts of an 'essentially self-absorbed nature' (p. 403).

[4] Anderson, cited in Atkinson (2006, p. 378) identifies five 'Key features of analytic autoethnography': (1) complete member researcher (CMR) status (2) analytic reflexivity (3) narrative visibility of the researcher's self (4) dialogue with informants beyond the self, and (5) commitment to theoretical analysis.

MT: (*Interrupting*) Researcher…

R: Yes…

MT: What are you trying to do?

R: What … I can't concentrate if you interrupt…

MT: Sorry … but what is this all for?

R: Describing autoethnography? Setting the context?

MT: Yes, it's so long.

R: (*Irritated*) It's everything. It's pivotal. It's like when you want to plant a vineyard and you get a geological survey to check the soil type and the water sources and the bedrock, and you monitor sunlight and rainfall. You have to do it to justify your choice of vines and the orientation of your rows, and your land stewardship. You don't just waltz up and stick some plants in and hope for the best. I'd be a laughing stock if I said 'here we go, I'll tell you a story and let's say it's an autoethnography and then it's research so keep reading', without exploring what autoethnography is, what it can do, who has done it before, whether my story will work as autoethnography and so on.

MT: Sorry … I was only…

R: Yes, you're all always 'only' trying to get me to cut this all back, but I've done that for months, and I'm sticking to what's left.

MT: Sorry.

R: Honestly, what am I supposed to do? If I am telling a story about how I grapple with theoretical frameworks and why they are important for my topic, then that's what I have to talk about. It *is* the story.

*Uncomfortable pause.*

MT: Carry on. Please.

*Further Continuing the Story of This Research*
Three weeks after designing my enquiry as an autoethnography, with no other research participants, the government in England put the country into total lockdown—the first response to the emerging COVID-19 pandemic in 2020. Looking back, the shift to autoethnography prior to lockdown was fortunate, because I could continue to work in isolation.

*Starting Arts-Based Work*
Launching into writing poetry felt like a liberation. I had spent almost four years struggling to get to the point of collecting data. Now, I spent the summer taking pleasure in responding to my imagination, just writing what came.

In the autumn, I turned my focus to visual work. I started drawing. I had in mind creating an animated video. I wanted the characters to be different insects in order to represent physical impairment in a way that I hoped would not conform to any stereotyped images. I began drawing ladybirds, beetles, butterflies and other insects and I took a week off work to try to learn basic animation. In spite of long days of considerable effort, as well as professional help, I only managed to make my bumble bee move a few inches sideways, in a clip lasting three seconds! (Fig. 3.1).

This was disappointing, and clearly not a viable option, but I also had a realisation at this time: I found that although I had loved drawing for decades, and even seriously considered training as an illustrator, drawing in fact led to no new insights for me—I only ever drew what I had already thought of. The autumn's drawing had therefore been fun, but of little significance in my research.

In the new year, I therefore started painting abstract images, all of which were inspired by the poems and stories I had already written. However, I still had an urge to create something that, like music, had an ongoing relationship with the passing of time. If the animation was not to be, I needed something else. At this point, I turned to my love of mobiles. I decided to make a mobile, based on the paintings which were based on the writing. After much reflection and research, I hit upon glass fusing as the best way to create the pendants and dedicated a week of the Easter holiday to melting glass at 1400 degrees Celcius in a borrowed microwave. This in turn led to experiments with hanging systems and designs, and I finally assembled the mobile in May. I videoed it a week later.

The process of creating the artwork, what I learnt from it, and why I undertook this journey will be fully explored in Chaps. 4 and 6. It is worth stating here, however, that already at the time, the arts-based activities had

**Fig. 3.1** Early image-making—the bee (a) The bee that did not go far in the video (b and c) Sketches for the bee that did not go far (d) Experimental music therapist bee

their own dynamic, made their own demands and led in their own directions. I was aware that I had a topic to explore, but in all honesty, something was drawing me to respond to the artistic demands in preference to these questions. It was a curious and discombobulating experience that I explore further in Chap. 6.

*The Shift to a Focus on Experience*

A new autumn came and this was a time of little research for me. Whilst another surge of COVID-19 (omicron variant) swept across the country, effectively preventing gatherings at Christmas time for the second year running, I reviewed with my academic supervisor the direction my study was taking. It became clear that both care ethics and integrity demands were no longer the main focus. They were, however, essential concepts that helped me identify and define my relationship to people, music therapy and research, and therefore played vital roles in the way I designed, undertook and communicated my research activities.

Whilst these two concepts dictated my *ways of being* in the field of study, the precise focus of research was still to be determined. However, at this point it was quick to emerge: my sense of undividedness, or otherwise, is always a response to the *experiences* I am having at a given time. Furthermore, for me, an ethic of care is a way of thinking about experience, whilst integrity demands were a way of relating to experience.

And so, I began exploring experience in music therapy. The focus on experience seemed at the same time riskily new and entirely obvious. I had concerns that my arts-based work, or data, was created prior to this shift in topic. However, I believe this does not matter: every part of this journey of enquiry is an experience that can be considered as data. The poems and stories narrate events and relationships, both of which are experiences, the act of making the work was also an experience.

*Reliability and Validity in Autoethnographic Research*

Collaborator, I realise this section is theoretical and possibly dry. Two question therefore bother me: (1) why should you be interested? (2) how can I be confident that what I am sharing is robust research, not just rambling?

I cannot answer the first one. All I can do is once again shine a light on *why* I have undertaken this exploration: I care so much about the nonverbal and arts-based experiences that lie at the heart of music therapy and about the participants who share them. And if I can identify a link between these experiences and evidence of therapy, such that you are convinced because you have also engaged in arts-based, nonverbal experience as a

Collaborator, then perhaps it will have been worthwhile, and perhaps you might be interested?

The second question relates to validity and reliability in autoethnography, so I will spend a little time exploring these. As I mentioned at the start of this chapter, the autoethnographer chooses 'a' story to relate, and it is our experience and its relating that validates it, as long as we are committed to deep reflexivity and a focus of enquiry beyond the process itself.

Ellis et al. (2011) address both reliability and validity in detail. Traditionally, reliability is regarded as the consistency of a research result, or finding. Clearly, this is a puzzling concept within an autoethnography, for it is unlikely that an autoethnographer would seek to repeat an experience with the purpose of assessing the consistency of that experience. In addition, the autoethnographer will in some way inevitably be affected by a given experience, such that the starting point for re-experiencing it will differ to that of the original experience, so the outcome might well be different.

Instead of seeking reliability as repeatability, Ellis et al. offer the following account of reliability for autoethnographers:

> For an autoethnographer, questions of reliability refer to the narrator's credibility. Could the narrator have had the experiences described, given available "factual evidence"? Does the narrator believe that this is actually what happened to her or him (Bochner, 2002 p 86)? Has the narrator taken "literary license" to the point that the story is better viewed as fiction than a truthful account? (p. 282)

Traditionally, validity describes the truthfulness of a research process and finding. For autoethnographers, reliability and validity are closely linked. Whilst the reliability of an autoethnographic account lies in the reader's belief that the events likely happened, the validity of the account is concerned with the extent to which that account 'helps readers communicate with others different from themselves…In particular, autoethnographers ask: "How useful is the story?" and "To what uses might this story be put?"' (Bochner, 2002, cited in Ellis et al., 2011, p. 282).

It is, perhaps, unnerving, that the validity and reliability of my research depends upon you, the Collaborators who engage with it. Of course I must strive for plausibility, and for a 'likely' story, but whether this will resonate with you, or fill you with unease, I cannot predict. I cannot safeguard or insure against the possibility that you doubt my reliability. And yet, at the heart of this risk there also lies the potential and excitement of this way of working: we are unavoidably involved in a *relational* undertaking. Indeed, this mirrors not only music therapy sessions, but also arts involvement, dialogue and ultimately experience. I therefore accept the risk as a price I am willing to pay for the consistent significance of relationship throughout every part of this book.

M: Hang on!

R: What?

M: Stop! I'm really none the wiser…

R: Oh *help me!* Which bit exactly of the last eight thousand words?

M: Don't get 'eight thousand words' with me. Who provides the tunes?

C: Come on. Can we talk kindly? It's a bit early in the day for a fight…

R: OK, Musician, how can I help?

M: I've been listening to you, and I have no idea whatsoever what authoethnographic analysis is.

R: *Silent.*

M: Well?

MT: Look, stop, Musician! She's thinking.

R: Nor do I…

M: Marvellous.

R: Oh for goodness sake stop interrupting. Sorry Collaborator. What I was going to say is 'nor do I, if you are looking for steps that you can transfer to a different project—a sort of manual, if you like'. But … please listen … I believe that the analysis in autoethnography is about loosening the fibres of a situation—we talked about that before—it's true for any methodology. When you tease felt apart, you can see through it and feel each thread or strand and notice the network or mesh that holds it all together. That's what we are asking our Collaborators to do, especially in relation to autoethnography—listen and feel the experiences of us four Roles, and all the fictionalised characters. The Collaborators can loosen these fibres by reflecting on it and on their own experiences of the stories and dialogues. That *is* the analysis, the first part. It's just *attending* to the *experience* of the autoethnography. Then the validation happens between the researcher and the Collaborator. Once the researcher has challenged the Collaborator to walk in someone else's shoes and be mindful and reflective of the experience, the Collaborator can then assess whether they think the story is reliable.

M: But we'll never know.

R: Nobody ever knows how people respond to their book, whether they write it off straight away, or whether it changes their lives. Not unless they review it, or write public responses, … or, I suppose they might contact the writer directly.

M: Why would you even want to do this? At least with a performance, the audience claps or boos and you know straight away.

MT: Not true! That's only live work. There's plenty of recording and rehearsing and practising that never gets a response.

M: No, but a book *is* a grand performance, isn't it. I mean, it's not the rehearsal or the practice session.

MT: I guess … it's not supposed to be, anyway … So, Researcher, how are you going to *do* this autoethnographic analysis … in fact, haven't you sort of done it? You've 'untangled' the different experiences that you think are relevant by rendering them as poems and pictures and stories. Surely you're not going to untangle your own work all over again? Shouldn't it speak for itself?

R: (*Thinking*) Yes, well I want it to.

MT: So?

R: So, I guess we take a risk and leave it at that. I do want to analyse the *process* I went through to make the arts-based work—all of it, pictures and everything. But that can come later in the phenomenology and arts-based research chapters.

M: OK, are we done then?

R: No. We're not. I'm going to get back to the message and talk about the topic. And I would really appreciate it if you left me to it … and just listened … and didn't interrupt.

C: It's OK, we can do that.

R: Thank you, Carer.

*Revisiting the Topic of This Book and the Relevance of Autoethnography*

I have just re-stated the overarching topic of this book—nonverbal and arts-based knowing and experience and their relationship, or otherwise, to evidence in music therapy. Having undertaken the arts-based activities I mention (creative writing, painting, mobile making), it seemed necessary to ponder what *kinds* of experience happen in music therapy, and I began to think about categories of experience. But this raised questions: do I group experiences according to the events that gave rise to them, for example group improvisation, or discussions about contracts? Or do I group them according to the emotional response that they triggered, for example experiences that triggered empathy in the therapist, or those which correlate to creative gestures in a participant? Or perhaps it only makes sense to group them according to types of stimulus and response, for example experiences that are derived from interpersonal relationships, or those that result in an actor responding to an inanimate feature, such as a musical instrument or genre.

I started to perceive that using autoethnography both as a way of sharing the material relevant to this research, and also as a way of 'loosening' threads is complex, because both things happen at the same time and the dividing line between data and analysis is blurred. Furthermore, autoethnography not surprisingly mirrors life with the result that it lacks linearity and categorisation much of the time. What it can do, though, is to start to map a highly complex 'family tree' of experiences for those engaging with the research as Collaborators: an autoethnographic story takes a reader by the hand and leads her on an unfolding journey of occurrences. The autoethnographer is inviting the Collaborator to allow the events of the journey to resonate with their own story, whether on a conscious or unconscious level. In this way, real-time experience in the person engaging is being used as an entry point both into past experiences of another, as well as into past experiences of themselves. The 'generations' of experience, expressed by branches of the family tree, start to become confused—intergenerational 'marriages' occur and result in new experiential offspring!

There is no doubt in my mind that there is a similar relational interconnection of experience to be found in music therapy practice, whereby different participants in a relationship continually offer, absorb and re-create aspects of each other's experience, thereby creating a new experience that itself becomes absorbed, offered, recreated. As a practitioner, it is hard to identify the seed of a musical idea: did the participant's bearing as they entered the room suggest the genre, or was it their reaction to the therapist's exploratory first few notes? Did the therapist choose to develop these notes or was she responding to the participant's brief vocalisation? Who found the 'groove' which provided the impetus for the unfolding improvisation? Autoethnography was becoming more than a methodological approach—it was also illustrating and representing the topic.

Around this time in my exploring, I became aware that what happens in music therapy, thereby leading to experience, is to a large extent dictated by the culture of music therapy in a given place and time. In other words, the culture endorses what is valued, and whilst it may not determine all of what occurs, it is likely to identify what counts. This is explored further in Chapter 5. The ongoing, potentially un-finishable and interpersonal nature of autoethnographic sense-making, also seemed well suited to this focus.

*Situating My Project within Existing Music Therapy Research—A Focus on Experience*

An important task remains for this autoethnographic section of the book. So far I have not shared the discoveries I made from other autoethnographic texts in the field of music therapy, and this needs to happen so that my arguments can be seen in a wider context. It is also important to state what this chapter is *not*: I am not attempting to define experience here. That will come later in Chaps. 4 and 5, in which I reflect on experience in the light of two theoretical frameworks—phenomenology and Aesthetic Critical Realism.

Before considering other music therapy autoethnographies, I believe it is useful to examine very briefly the broad landscape of music therapy research in general, for it is important for me to establish where the research in this book 'belongs' in relation to other research in the field.

Various authors have sought to categorise different types of music therapy research. The significant volume 'Music Therapy Research: Third Edition' (Wheeler & Murphy, 2016) contains an impressive sixty-eight chapters on aspects of music therapy research. A companion volume—Introduction to Music Therapy Research: Third Edition—supplies an 'Overview of Music Therapy Research' (Wheeler & Bruscia, 2016) in which the authors draw attention to the distinction between 'basic' and 'applied' research, where the former is concerned with the exploration of particular phenomena for the sake of understanding them better, and the latter is concerned with using this understanding in order to investigate a 'real problem' (p. 5). They comment that 'because the purpose of music therapy is to help people, research in this discipline is generally applied' (p. 5). Bruscia proposes the alternative categories of 'foundational research' because it 'provides the foundations for what music therapists do', 'discipline research' which 'looks at what music therapists do in the areas of assessment, treatment, and evaluation', and 'profession research' which 'covers a range of topics that concern music therapists as a group and the contexts in which they work' (p. 3).

My study does not fall into just one single category that Bruscia defines (foundational, discipline, or profession research (Wheeler & Bruscia, 2016, p. 3)). And is not really 'applied', even though I hope it will lead to practical applications: instead, I am undertaking 'basic' research (p 5), looking at the generative mechanisms of experience, in parts of the investigation. But alongside this, I seek to understand experience in the context of actual music therapy happenings, which falls to some extent within all three of Bruscia's categories. Because I have adopted critical realism as an 'underlabouring' research philosophy, my study is neither interpretivist nor objectivist in essence.

Drawing on further scholars, I perceive that what I am presenting is 'first person research' and that I research myself and fictional participants (McGraw Hunt, 2016). I am seeking 'indigenous theory' (Aigen, 2014, p. 218), the focus is 'experience' and the 'purpose [is] theory building' (Darrow, 2016, p. 34).

Collaborator, my attention to this positioning may seem pedantic. But throughout this book, I have found it essential to try to clarify what I am trying to do, and why.

*Types of Autoethnographic Studies in Music Therapy Research*
I conducted a search of the keywords 'autoethnography' and 'music therapy' in google scholar and two university library searches. Various articles emerged and I chose twenty in order to explore the extent to which the *nature* of the phenomenon of experience would be explored. Beginning with the most recent—a bold collaborative autoethnography scrutinising unconscious bias in music therapy practitioners—I found one hundred and ninety six uses of the word experience, as a noun or in its verb forms (Moy & Alvarez-Figueroa, 2021). On looking more closely, I did not find any exploration of the meaning of the word, or of its nature. This is not a criticism—the research is tackling a deeply important, different topic and the term 'experience' is used to convey the sense of something undergone, apprehended or consciously or unconsciously absorbed into an actor's awareness or story: that is, it receives its common, vernacular usage.

The ensuing process of reading autoethnograpic accounts by other music therapists I found very moving. Autoethnography exists to forefront the researcher's self, so as to demonstrate complexity and emphasise the parts that make up any supposed whole. So it is unsurprising that many of the topics are deeply personal. Colin Lee, for example, discusses his 'lived experience as a queer music therapist' and the importance of absorbing queer theory for his personal, musical and therapeutic understanding (2019, p. 1). Luke Annesley and Nicky Haire examine their online journey of shared improvisation during the COVID-19 pandemic lockdown, and its implications for future practice (2021) and Zoe Kalenderidis explores her identity as a disabled music therapist by recruiting another disabled music therapist as research participant and gaining deeper insights into hidden disability (2020). Maevon Gumble presents a personal journey of transformation through 'gender affirming voicework', exploring identity as a non-binary trans person and music therapist (2020).

Two things struck me in my searching for and reading of these accounts. Firstly, they all include arts-based work: poetry, audio extracts that are embedded into the text and can be listened to at the click of a mouse, image-making, as well as storytelling. Secondly, all these examples, and others that similarly explore personal stories of work and self, have been written recently (Baines, 2014; Lipski, 2014; Woodward, 2015; Zhang et al., 2016; Cross, 2018; Devlin, 2018; Echard, 2019; Gilbertson & Hebert, 2021; Haire, 2021). Whilst I found an earlier example (Kakoske, 2007), and there is much historical music therapy research that is of case study design, with the author reflecting on aspects of the topic, I find I am wondering why autoethnography has recently become more prominent and whether it offers a music therapist practitioner-researcher something unique or particular?

It is not within the scope of this study to trace the methodological choices of music therapist researchers, nor the particular affordances of these choices. However, I am wondering whether autoethnography is gaining interest precisely because of its relationship to experience. I did not count the frequency with which the word 'experience' was used in every article. However, it was universally used, and its meaning was assumed, as outlined above. This book would need a different topic if I were to identify *why* practitioner experience might be of significance at the present time, if indeed it is. My belief as a therapist, rather than as a researcher, is that the world into which music therapy was born—mid-twentieth-century Western society—is rapidly changing. When the pioneers of music therapy began exploring musical relationships with participants in the early days, assumptions were made as to what music was (Western, classical), what therapy was for (an illness-ideology-informed space for an expert to help heal an unwell person), what successful therapy looked like (the facilitation of change in an unwell person such that they could better fit into the world around them—i.e. a process of normalisation).

Efforts to decolonialise the concepts of music, to assert a wellness ideology, to truly celebrate diversity through indigenous, feminist and queer perspectives on identity and culture, have led to a strong new current within social life and social science. This current is far from the dominant current, but it exists and its very integrity and inclusivity affords it a power and presence. I perceive that music therapists now have *permission* to name their personal experience and its impact on their self-hood, life and work in a way that I did not perhaps feel was encouraged when I trained in 1997–9. More than this, I believe that some of us feel an *obligation* to do this, in order to challenge the status quo and question our impact as individuals on participants, particularly where a therapist acknowledges significant privilege, as I do.

For this reason, I believe it is essential to try to understand what we mean by 'experience' within the music therapy profession. Already, following this first cycle of retroductive analysis, I am aware that there are two types of experience that appear significant to music therapists, and to me as Researcher:

- In-the-moment experience: when something happens in the here and now and we relate to it, on some level, in the here and now
- Embedded experience (my terminology): when past happenings and our relating to them, stored in memory, inform our relationship to a current or hypothetical happening

The significance of memory to the second type of experience is something that I am suggesting as a common sense explanation. A brief online search of the connection between memory and experience yielded a bewildering array of concepts from psychology and neuroscience. I have no familiarity with these fields, let alone skills to research them. I therefore propose to move on with my common sense definitions of two types of experience. Helpfully, the German language identifies both types through different words: in-the-moment experience is conveyed through 'Erlebnis', whilst embedded experience is suggested through 'Erfahrung'. This linguistic corroboration encourages me to further explore the concepts.

So far, my study of the music therapy autoethnographic literature, and my own process of autoethnography, have illuminated both types of experience: the account of shared, lockdown improvisation touches on in-the-moment experience, as does Kalenderidis' account of interviewing another music therapist with a disability. The thought provoking discussions I had in academic supervision, that brought insights and direction, also belong in this category. However, I observed a stronger presence of embedded experience in the music therapy literature: the relating of personal 'experiences' of gender, professional work, or race, draws heavily upon embedded experience. Similarly, my integrity demands are examples of embedded experience.

*Moving On*

Up to this point, I have deliberately avoided ascribing the word 'experience' to the accounts of other music therapists, except when quoting their own words. This is because I have yet to understand and define what experience *is*. I will address this in the following chapters.

I hope that this message has not been too arduous a read and that the stories, poems and vignettes have continued to fill your imagination. I apologise for the interruptions: the Roles insisted, and it seemed simplest to agree. Returning to the quotation with which Musician opened this chapter, Antonio, father of young Proteus who longs to travel and see the world for himself, admits that 'experience is by industry achieved'. I admit, in turn, that this exploration has required much industry of me and that I am needing to pass the requirement for industry on to you, Collaborator, if the experiential aspect of this book is to be fulfilled. Again, I apologise for making this demand.

With thanks,
Researcher

## References


Aigen, K. (2014). *The study of music therapy: Current issues and concepts.* Routledge.

Anderson, L. (2006). Analytic autoethnography. *Journal of Contemporary Ethnography, 35*(4), 373–395.

Annesley, L., & Haire, N. (2021). Experiences of music therapists sharing improvisation remotely during lockdown. *Journal of Music, Health, and Wellbeing, Autumn, 2021*, 1–16.

Atkinson, P. (2006). Rescuing autoethnography. *Journal of Contemporary Ethnography, 35*(4), 400–404.

Baines, S. (2014). *Giving voice to service user choice: Music therapy as an anti-oppressive practice* (PhD), University of Limerick.

Baker, V. J. (1987). Pitching a tent in the native village: Malinowski and participant observation. *Bijdragen tot de Taal-, Land-en Volkenkunde*(1ste Afl), 14–24.

Bhattacharya, K. (2020). Connecting with water spirits: An autoethnography of home and higher education. In R. M. Boylorn & M. P. Orbe (Eds.), *Critical autoethnography* (2nd ed., pp. 103–117). Routledge.

Boylorn, R. M., & Orbe, M. P. (Eds.). (2021). *Critical autoethnography: Intersecting cultural identities in everyday life* (2nd ed.). Routledge.

Carless, D., & Douglas, K. (2011a). Stories as personal coaching philosophy. *International Journal of Sports Science & Coaching, 6*(1), 1–12.

Carless, D., & Douglas, K. (2011b). What's in a song? How songs contribute to the communication of social science research. *British Journal of Guidance & Counselling, 39*(5), 439–454.

Carless, D., & Douglas, K. (2017). Art-based research as waves of embodied engagement: Reflections on 'Across the Tamar'. *Journal of Applied Arts & Health, 8*(2), 241–253.

Chang, H. (2008). *Autoethnography as method.* Left Coast Press, Inc.

Cross, E. (2018). *Reflections, observations, doubts and questions on introducing music therapy to an NHS elderly psychiatry ward: An autoethnographic case study.* (MSc), Queen Margaret University, Edinburgh. Retrieved from https://eresearch.qmu.ac.uk/handle/20.500.12289/9571

Darrow, A.-A. (2016). Developing a topic. In B. L. Wheeler & K. M. Murphy (Eds.), *Introduction to music therapy research* (3rd ed.). Barcelona Publishers.

Devlin, K. (2018). How do I see you, and what does that mean for us? An autoethnographic study. *Music Therapy Perspectives, 36*(2), 234–242.

DeWalt, K., & DeWalt, B. R. (2010). *Participant observation: A guide for fieldworkers* (2nd ed.). AltaMira Press.

Douglas, K., & Carless, D. (Producer). (2017). We crossed the Tamar. [Online short film] Retrieved January 15, 2023, from https://www.youtube.com/watch?v=R4EGRN_bIw8

Durham, A. (2020). Wounded: Diagnosis (for a) Black woman. In R. M. Boylorn & M. P. Orbe (Eds.), *Critical autoethnography* (pp. 21–31). Routledge.

Echard, A. (2019). Making sense of self: An autoethnographic study of identity formation for adolescents in music therapy. *Music Therapy Perspectives, 37*(2), 141–150.

Ellis, C. (2004). *The ethnographic I: A methodological novel about autoethnography.* AltaMira Press.

Ellis, C., Adams, T. E., & Bochner, A. P. (2011). Autoethnography: An overview. *Historical Social Research/Historische Sozialforschung, 36*(4), 273–290.

Etherington, K. (2004). *Becoming a reflexive researcher: Using our selves in research.* Jessica Kingsley Publishers.

Gilbertson, S., & Hebert, D. G. (2021). Music in a concussive monologue. *Voices: A World Forum for Music Therapy, 21*(3). https://doi.org/10.15845/voices.v21i3.3305

Gumble, M. (2020). Gender affirming voicework: A queer autoethnographic account. *Voices: A World Forum for Music Therapy, 20*(2). https://doi.org/10.15845/voices.v20i2.2916

Haire, N. (2021). Improvising the self. *The Journal of Critical Psychology, Counselling and Psychotherapy, 21*(2), 61–70.

Hernandez, K., & Ngunjiri, F. W. (2016). Relationships and communities in autoethnography. In S. Holman Jones, T. E. Adams, & C. Ellis (Eds.), *Handbook of autoethnography* (pp. 262–280). Routledge.

Holman Jones, S., Adams, T., & Ellis, C. (2016a). Introduction: Coming to know autoethnography as more than a method. In S. Holman Jones, T. Adams, & C. Ellis (Eds.), *Handbook of autoethnography* (pp. 17–48). Routledge.

Holman Jones, S., Adams, T. E., & Ellis, C. (Eds.). (2016b). *Handbook of autoethnography.* Routledge.

Kakoske, D. (2007). *Responding to music in my life: An autoethnography.* (Masters), City University of Seattle.

Kalenderidis, Z. (2020). The great reveal: The experiences of a registered music therapist with a disability: An arts-based research project. *Voices: A World Forum for. Music Therapy, 20*(1). https://doi.org/10.15845/voices.v20i1.2873
Lapadat, J. C. (2017). Ethics in autoethnography and collaborative autoethnography. *Qualitative Inquiry, 23*(8), 589–603.
Lee, C. A. (2019). Sounding the authentic self: Artistic expressions of a queer music therapist. *Voices: A World Forum for Music Therapy, 19*(3). https://doi.org/10.15845/voices.v19i3.2799
Lipski, G. (2014). *Finding where I fit: An autoethnography on integrating ethnomusicology into music therapy.* (Masters), Concordia University.
McGraw Hunt, A. (2016). First person research. In B. L. Wheeler & K. M. Murphy (Eds.), *Music therapy research* (3rd ed.). Barcelona Publishers.
Moy, N., & Alvarez-Figueroa, N. (2021). *Deconstructing the clinician: An autoethnographic study.* (Masters), Molloy College.
Robson, C. (2002). *Real word research.* Blackwell.
Roth, W.-M. (2009). Auto/ethnography and the question of ethics. *Forum: Qualitative Social Research, 10*(1). https://doi.org/10.17169/fqs-10.1.1213
Schwandt, T. A. (2015). *The SAGE dictionary of qualitative inquiry* (4th ed.). SAGE Publications, Inc.
Shakespeare, W. (1986). *The complete works.* Oxford University Press.
Thambinathan, V., & Kinsella, E. A. (2021). Decolonizing methodologies in qualitative research: Creating spaces for transformative praxis. *International Journal of Qualitative Methods, 20.* https://doi.org/10.1177/16094069211014766
Tullis, J. A. (2014). Self and others. In S. Holman Jones, T. E. Adams, & C. Ellis (Eds.), *Handbook of autoethnography* (pp. 244–259). Routledge.
Wheeler, B. L., & Bruscia, K. (2016). Overview of music therapy research. In B. L. Wheeler & K. M. Murphy (Eds.), *Introduction to music therapy research* (3rd ed., pp. 1–9). Barcelona Publishers.
Wheeler, B. L., & Murphy, K. M. (Eds.). (2016). *An introduction to music therapy research* (3rd ed.). Barcelona Publishers.
Woodward, A. (2015). *Tapestry of tears: An autoethnography of leadership, personal transformation, and music therapy in humanitarian aid in Bosnia Herzegovina.* (PhD), Antioch University.
Zhang, X., Shi, R., & Hsu, W. (2016). *A collaborative autoethnographic exploration of experiences of three international music therapy interns during their clinical training.* (Masters), State University of New York.

CHAPTER 4

# Loosening the Threads Along the Way 2

## Direct Message with Interruptions

### *Exploring the Phenomenon of Experience Before Valuing Happens*

There is nothing either good or bad but thinking makes it so.[1]

Dear Collaborator,

This message has an important function in the book. Up to this point, the in-the-moment experiences that I have shared have been events that lend themselves to verbal narration: mainly interactions between people and musical happenings.

I believe that stakeholders who use language would probably recognise and name these events as experiences. However, it frequently occurs that these verbal stakeholders, including music therapists, have experiences in music therapy that are hard or impossible to capture in words. This is not surprising, since the encounter is itself musical and nonverbal. Furthermore, it is abundantly obvious to music therapists and others who engage in music therapy with nonverbal people that people who do not use speech or language also have, and recognise, these latter experiences, albeit the recognition is shared nonverbally.

[1] Shakespeare, *Hamlet*, Act 2 scene 2 (1986, p. 750).



J. Atkinson, *Insights From Music Therapy Practice and Research*,
https://doi.org/10.1007/978-3-031-86220-5_4

I have long been intrigued, with a sort of restless fascination, as to what these nonverbally rendered and nonverbally recognised experiences might be. They cannot be captured in micro narratives of musical form, structure, harmony, etc., nor in minute descriptions of interaction, even though they are composed of, and held within, interpersonal musical relationship. A major motivation for undertaking this research has been to attempt to untangle this puzzle. In this chapter, I am therefore using phenomenological methodology and methods to look at the actual building blocks of experience: how an experience takes place and becomes apparent to us. I believe this will add another, deeper layer to my exploration of the kinds of experience that occur in music therapy and will prepare the ground for discussions about how all of us involved in music therapy arrive at decisions about what counts, thereby creating and influencing the cultures of the field.

Although I believe I have had a clear focus for this book, one of the disconcerting features of doing the arts-based aspects has been not knowing why I was engaging in a particular activity whilst I was undertaking it. However, alongside this sense of disorientation, there has often been an equally strong sense of *needing* to do the activity. And so I have just got on with it and hoped that I would work out why, later.

This chapter records one of these processes of post hoc sense-making, or 'reconstructed logic' (Kaplan, 1964 cited in Carter & Little, 2007). I will share the painting that I did and explain why I now regard it as phenomenological analysis of in-the-moment experience, even though I had no idea of this at the time. I will begin by reflecting on the tradition of phenomenology and its relevance to this study. I am sharing concepts and terms because they play a crucial part in this ongoing investigation.

### *Phenomenology*

In his article 'Phenomenology as a research method' (2014), Thomas Eberle explains that 'phenomenology is basically an *epistemological endeavour*' (original italics, p. 198). 'Epistemology' indicates a concern with human knowing and the term 'endeavour' implies a combination of effort, doing, purpose and aim (Merriam-Webster Online Dictioinary, 2023). So, phenomenology involves purposeful activity in pursuit of knowing.

### *The Purpose of Phenomenology*

Many research approaches could make a similar claim about their purpose, and phenomenology's unique contribution lies in the *way* that it seeks to elicit knowing, and in *what* it believes can reasonably be known. Eberle's statement continues: 'it [phenomenology] starts analysis with the embodied lived experience' (p. 198). It is significant, for my own study, that phenomenology explicitly undertakes an investigation of experience. However, the meaning of experience in this context is particular: the purpose of phenomenological enquiry is to understand the experience of phenomena.[2]

*What is a Phenomenon?*

In phenomenology, a phenomenon is seen as the combination of (1) a thing that has characteristics and (2) the acts of perception which lead to knowledge of that thing. Using the terms 'noema' (the object) and 'noesis' (the acts of consciousness) proposed by the founder of phenomenology, Edmund Husserl, Eberle summarises: 'a phenomenon is a noetic-noematic unity and includes acts of consciousness as well as properties of their "object"' (p. 185).

*Phenomenology as Exploration of Eidos, or Essence*

Phenomenology does not discriminate between types of phenomenon, there is no hierarchy, and Eberle comments that the aim is to 'scrutinise exclusively the "whatness" of phenomena—no matter if they refer to the "real" world or to fantasy and fiction' (p. 186). Ideas, memories and thoughts are therefore included as phenomena.

Husserl proposed that a fundamental aspect of this 'whatness' is 'eidos' or essence (1973 [1939], cited in Beyer, 2003, Section 2). The essence cannot be separated from the phenomenon, nor can the phenomenon be separated from the subject's perception of it. Karin Dahlberg explains that

> essences are not the outcome of interpretation it [sic] is not the researcher who gives the phenomenon its meaning. Neither are essences something that only lye [sic] within the realm of the object itself, ready to describe. Instead, the meaning is disclosed in the researching act that takes place between the researcher and the phenomenon. (2006, p. 12)

[2] Different thinkers and researchers describe phenomenology variously as a philosophy (Husserl 1982 [1913], cited in Beyer, 2003, Section 1), a methodology (Tuohy et al., 2013, Introduction) and a method (Eberle, 2014, p. 184). In this study, I regard it as a methodology, because it provides a practical, as well as a conceptual, framework for undertaking all the steps of research planning, data collection, analysis and sense-making.

Dahlberg emphasises that phenomena do not need to be researched to have essence. Rather, the essence is inherent, or latent, in a phenomenon at all times and in everyday life. This continuity of essence is the phenomenon's *intention* or 'aboutness'. The issue is that in everyday life, we (researchers and non-researchers alike) 'do not problematize our experience but take for granted what we see and what it seems to be' (p. 15). Dahlberg explains that whilst this may not be a damaging attitude if the phenomenon has no impact on people's lives, it certainly can be damaging if the phenomenon is, for example, the care of vulnerable people.

*Three Approaches to Phenomenological Analysis*

So far I have learnt that a phenomenon has an essence that is a combination of its aboutness and my perception of it. But the question remains how to analyse such phenomena. Eberle summarises three significant approaches to phenomenological analysis that Husserl proposes (pp. 185–6):

1. *Free imaginative variation*
   This is an imaginative, rather than an empirical exercise. A phenomenon is considered imaginatively, and all its potential manifestations are scrutinised so as to determine the 'invariant properties that are universal' (p. 185) to all instances of that phenomenon. This leads to clarity regarding the eidos, or essence, of the phenomenon.
2. *Eidetic reduction (epoché)*
   This approach involves 'bracketing' all previous experience of a phenomenon, so as to engage in systematic removal of all assumptions and previous knowledge that prejudice our response to that phenomenon. This, again, can reveal the true eidos, or essence, of the phenomenon.
3. *Transcendental reduction*
   This analysis requires that not only the phenomenon in question is perceived through bracketing (whether or not it is an imagined or material phenomenon), but that the notion of existence itself is also bracketed. In this way, the essence of existence is also explored, and the focus becomes philosophical.

It is clear that any enquiry that is investigating experience would be wise to acknowledge the significance of phenomenology as a research approach devoted to this field. A phenomenological exploration of the nature of existence is too broad an undertaking for my topic, and I am therefore not inclined to pursue transcendental reduction. But, I believe that free imaginative variation and eidetic reduction could provide useful insights, particularly given the nonverbal nature of many experiences in music therapy and the relational dimension of the work.

MT: This all makes sense, now. I guess I've lived with it for a bit. Thanks, Researcher.

R: (*Surprised*) Oh, you're welcome!

MT: It's great that Hamlet got there hundreds of years before...

M: Ha! Yes, this is my favourite quote. It fits so well. He's such a brooder, but he hits the nail on the head: we overlay our experiences with endless thinking and lose sight of what the experience actually is. He's paving the way for bracketing...!

R: I like it, too.

MT: Result!

R: I need to keep going or I'll lose the thread.

M: OK...

*Phenomenological Intersubjectivity*

There is another concept from phenomenology that I need to share because I believe it is relevant to the non-verbal dimension of music therapy experience and addresses the issue of language. This notion is intersubjectivity. Husserl proposed the concept and it was developed by Alfred Schutz.[3] Basically, intersubjectivity 'is the basis for living together—with others—in specific dimensions of time and space, and for sharing the understanding of the life-world[4] with them' (Schutz, 1945 cited in Vargas,

[3] Schutz is credited with drawing phenomenological thought into social sciences (Wagner, 1970, pp. 1–16).

[4] Schutz's life-world constitutes 'the world of immediate experience common to all of us, not the private world of any individual. It is the "self-evident", "pre-scientific" and "taken-for-granted" world and our "fundamental and paramount reality"' (Schutz, 1945, p. 534 cited in Vargas, 2020, p. 420).

2020, pp. 421–2). Vargas describes Schutz's belief that intersubjectivity results from social contexts and affords a 'learning process, not solely a personal experience' (p. 422). She also refers to linguistic anthropologist Alessandro Duranti's claim that intersubjectivity is a 'condition for communication, not a product or effect of it' (Duranti, 2010, p. 9 cited in Vargas, 2020 p. 422). I am bound to start wondering whether the musical connection that develops in music therapy relationships might be an example of intersubjectivity.

But Vargas makes a statement that I find challenging: she suggests that 'it is through language that subjectivity is shared' (p. 422). Dahlberg makes a similar assertion:

> In the research world, non-verbal meanings are more or less "translated" into verbal language, by the informant as well as the researcher. In a similar way we translate, or as Giorgi (1977) puts it, transform the original descriptions into the language of the scientific discipline. (p. 17)

C: Sorry to interrupt.

R: It's OK. What is it?

C: It's just that this feels important.

R: It is … the affordances of nonverbal communicative experience in music therapy…

C: Sorry?

R: I mean, the way we encounter each other in music, and music in each other, in music therapy, and what this can bring to our lives is SO important. It's what makes music therapy different from art-, drama-, dance therapy, concert going, sport, everything else. And it doesn't involve words. But that's also the problem—it's what makes it so very hard to persuade budget holders that it *counts*, that it's worth doing and paying for, because the experience is unique to each relationship and you can't really explain it.

C: Yes, it's true. But at least you're trying to explain it, and others are bound to have tried, too.

R: Oh sure—I get to that later on.

C: Sorry, carry on…

*Intersubjective Communication in This Study: Sharing and Learning in Music and Image*

In music therapy, the primary medium for creating and sharing intersubjective meaning is not language. This presents a researcher with a dilemma: the reason that music therapy is not language-dependent is, as discussed, that music itself requires no verbal language and that many of those who participate in music therapy do not use language. Is it therefore ethical to attempt to understand the non-verbal experience of others, and any intersubjective shared meaning, through verbal means? I do not feel it is.

The solution I have found has been arts-based research (ABR) methodology. This will be fully explored later in Chap. 6. However, in this current chapter, I will explore the phenomenon of making images from music therapy experiences, as well as my attempts to make sense of these images through the phenomenological approaches of imaginative variation and eidetic reduction.

*Background to the Painted Images and the Role of Phenomenology*

Throughout the arts-based activities I undertook for my research, I kept a journal of my reflections. I typed the journal onto my laptop at the end of each arts-based episode—writing, image making, glass fusing, etc. On January 8th 2021, at the end of the writing phase of my arts-based work, I wrote

> *I am faced with two choices: either I can continually engage in creative work as a means of looking for meaning in my earlier creative work; or, I can look for an appropriate 'lens' through which to analyse the creative work I have done. In keeping with the retroductive approach of critical realism, I am drawn to the latter.*

It was therefore a conscious decision to employ non-arts-based 'lenses', or methodologies, in order to analyse the data created through arts-based work. I fully recognise the tension that exists between my belief in the importance of nonverbal intersubjective communication and research-style language-based analysis. However, I hope by using language in this chapter I can draw attention to other communication that is happening through the images.

On February 17th 2021, I wrote,

> *As soon as I had written 'Chloe's Story', I realised that I needed and wanted to paint the relationships that emerge in the story as part of my arts-based data collection. I do not yet know why this is important, but I sense that it is so.*

As mentioned, this 'sense' of not knowing why a particular step of arts-based work might be important has been a common feeling throughout the arts-based work in my research: I have become aware of an impulse to create something, and have followed the impulse. In this way, I created twelve two-dimensional images in acrylic paint (Figs. 4.1, 4.2, 4.3, 4.4, 4.5, 4.6, 4.7, 4.8, 4.9, 4.10, 4.11, 4.12). In spite of the impulse to paint the relationships in *Chloe's Story*, I actually started by creating images that emerged from other characters in my poems, stories and vignettes.

After creating each picture, I wrote a brief response to the image. Again, I did this in an intuitive way, to keep track of choices I made whilst painting—colours, brush strokes, for example—but also to remember and explain how and why the structure of the image emerged, or what different shapes represent, or what my experience of the topic of the image was whilst painting, or what my experience of painting was. After completing all the images, I realised that in every case I had painted *my* relationship to a character from a poem, story or vignette. In the instances of the *Carer/care-receiver* image, and the *Carer/care-receiver relationship after massive trauma* image, I also depict the carer/care-receiver relationships, but in both cases the whole image represents my relationship to those dyads. Looking back, it is clear to me that if I were to identify the role from which I was painting, it would be Music Therapist. At first, I attempted to narrate this process as Researcher, but this has floundered and I have therefore been working closely with Music Therapist: so I, Researcher, will continue to write this message, but the contents represent both of us.

The following pages contain the images in the order I painted them, and the accompanying descriptions which I wrote straight after painting. I invite you to respond to the images in any way that you are motivated to—in colour, line, form, word, movement, melody. There are pages for this purpose (Chap. 2, Section "Invitation to Respond").

*Acrylic Painted Images Depicting Relationships*

**Fig. 4.1** Therapist's relationship to self. *Healthy. Whole. Colours of life: colours from nature. It doesn't depict anything, though it may look like a galaxy, or a bulb underground. But it is a visual manifestation of a feeling of self. The brush-work is dabbed: emergent, allowing colours to come through, mix, blend or not. It grew of its own accord. I wasn't thinking. I don't when I paint. Things take form, line, movement, texture, light and suggest things and I follow. But there is always something 'unthought known' at the very start*

**Fig. 4.2** Carer/care-receiver relationship after massive trauma. *This picture felt very painful, so I painted it very quickly. The two halves are a whole, almost. But not round. A rectangular box is framing them. Why? Labels? Illness ideology? Severe and unbearable constraint? The rough brush strokes are at the same time lacking care and filled with energy. The colours scream, but are very strong. This is not a picture for curved, softened lines*

**Fig. 4.3** The participant as I (as therapist) experience them. *Whole. Vibrant. Healthy earth colours. Wholesome. The participant's own sphere of energy and a deep core of wellness. The round form suggests a wholeness, but it is not a constraint: the boundaries are fluid and there is room for flow, for stillness, for dynamic energy, for quietness, for possibility. The colours that emerged are the same as the therapist's colours: in essence they are the same colours of natural wholeness, of life, of energy. The brush strokes are quick and imprecise because the participant will always emerge, change, grow, show the therapist more of themselves*

**Fig. 4.4** Therapist's relationship to commissioning. *Opaque. Blocks. Some life in the oblong colours, but confined in a dull box of unpleasant, too grey, turquoise. I don't like this painting. I painted it fast and functionally, knowing I would not like it. I was not careful or caring. I felt a bit guilty afterwards, but it shows what it needs to: something inflexible, inside the box, uncompromising*

**Fig. 4.5** Carer/care-receiver relationship. *This is warmth, and the care that goes way beyond comfort. The larger, darker orange circle is the carer. The circle is strong, but flexible, intuitively adapting to the care-receiver's need not to be constrained. So, the smaller, lighter orange circle of the care-receiver can move beyond the protection, know the independence that is possible. The brush strokes are dabbed so that the paint layers both reflect light and leave gaps. The pale yellow, warm frame contains the circles. The warmth and energy do not, or are not meant to, deny the exhaustion, isolation and pain which often come with these roles. But they are meant to acknowledge the dynamic love at the core of this relationship*

**Fig. 4.6** Fundraising. *This picture is a hybrid. The fundraiser here understands music therapy as a participating parent. They are drawn to, and moved by, the musical landscapes they have encountered.But this picture also shows the music therapist's experience with fundraising as a branch of music therapy activities and the 'inside the box' thinking that it has. This exasperates the music therapist, but, seen through the eyes of the parent-fundraiser, the boxes become less domineering and are somewhat softened by the music therapy landscape*

**Fig. 4.7** Multidisciplinary team (MDT) member/therapist relationship. *The MDT member is the bright yellow semicircle in the pale yellow oblong: bright and clear. Semicircle dome-wise—a lid, not open to movement or new contents like a cup. The music therapist is the green semicircle, cup-ways-up, but vulnerable: they are not two halves of a whole, so the therapist has moved and off-set her shape. She has tried to fill in a mirroring oblong with uncontroversial things—pale blue dabs, like clouds. But this has not been reciprocated above the green semicircle, so there is blank space. The strange thing is that the textures blend and the colours work together, so there could be greater harmony*

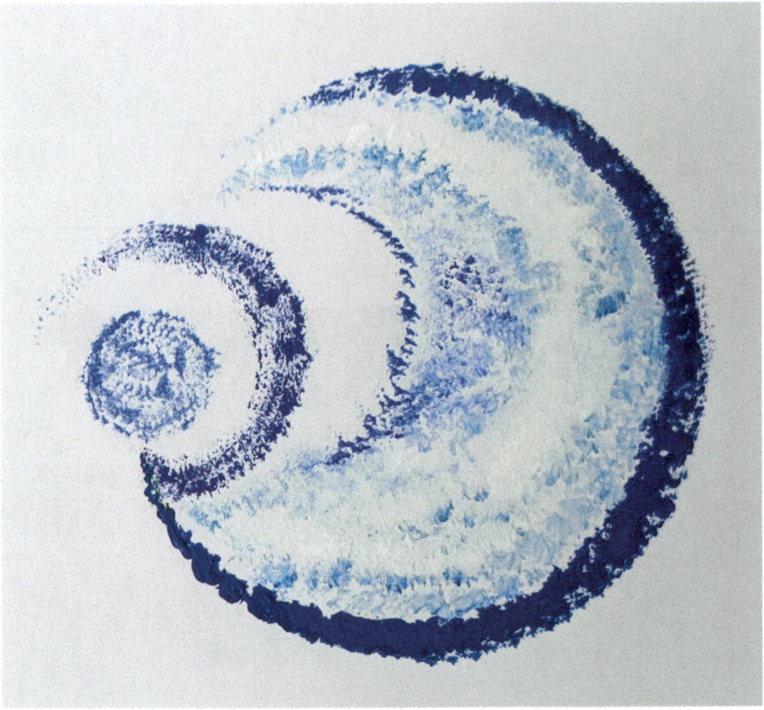

**Fig. 4.8** Mia and her relationship to music. *The darker blue/green circle is music. It holds a space. It is a world that is open to Mia if she wants to enter it, to explore. It is a safe and strong place, but not crowded—it is waiting for Mia, in her own time. Mia is poised, half within the music, half held back. The music finds her colour, comes to meet her, but not too close: it leaves space. And it promises more—not too much, just echoes of Mia's colour so she can know that she belongs. Music does not hold her tightly—she is free to come and go, just as she needs*

**Fig. 4.9** Theresa and her relationship to music therapy. *For Theresa (orange circle) the children are what matters—they are at the middle of things, the yellow circle. Theresa gives so much but assumes little. She loves the children and does what she can—she finds their toys and keeps them clean. They are her connection to the children and when they return to the hospice, she brings them their special toys, which link her to the children (the red circle). Theresa loves the music therapy too (green circle) and supports the music therapist in her closer more overlapping (as Theresa sees it) work with the children. She loves the music therapy because the children love it and so, they are all connected*

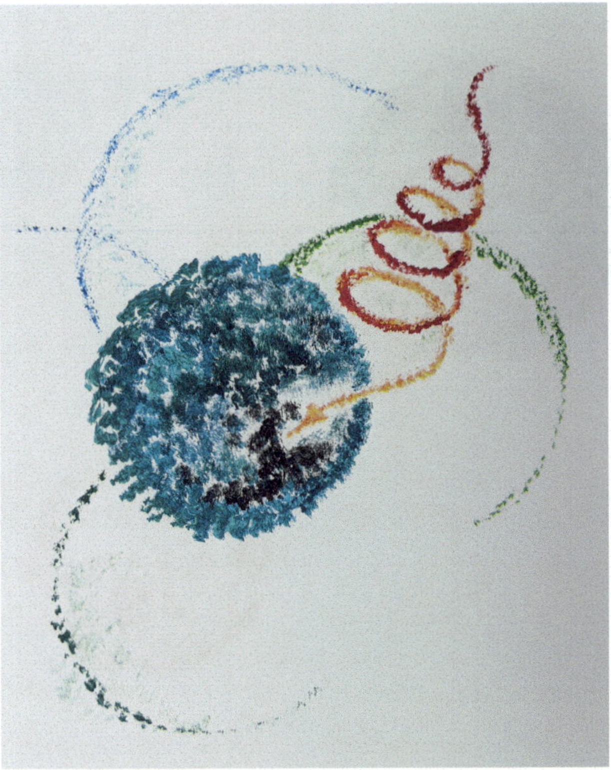

**Fig. 4.10** Mr B and his relationship to music, music therapy and the music therapist. *Mr B was dynamic and creative and conveyed and shared a fluid and active energy. The red spiral represents this as he often moved in spirals. The dark, excluding round* represents the music, music therapy and the music therapist as Mr B seemed to relate to them—they all appeared merged into one. The therapist tried to demonstrate that music could be a world for all of us—the arcs of faint colour* indicate barely defined areas of possible musical exploration in the therapist's imagination, far from the dense and unwelcoming zone that Mr B seemed to experience. But communication was not successful and Mr B's energy seemed to want to puncture the perceived, excluding world of music and music therapy.* ( **NB For the fused glass version of this image, I could not find a round, dark base, so had to use a square one. Also, I wanted the red spiral to be prominent, so decided not to create bead arms for the 'faint arcs'.*)

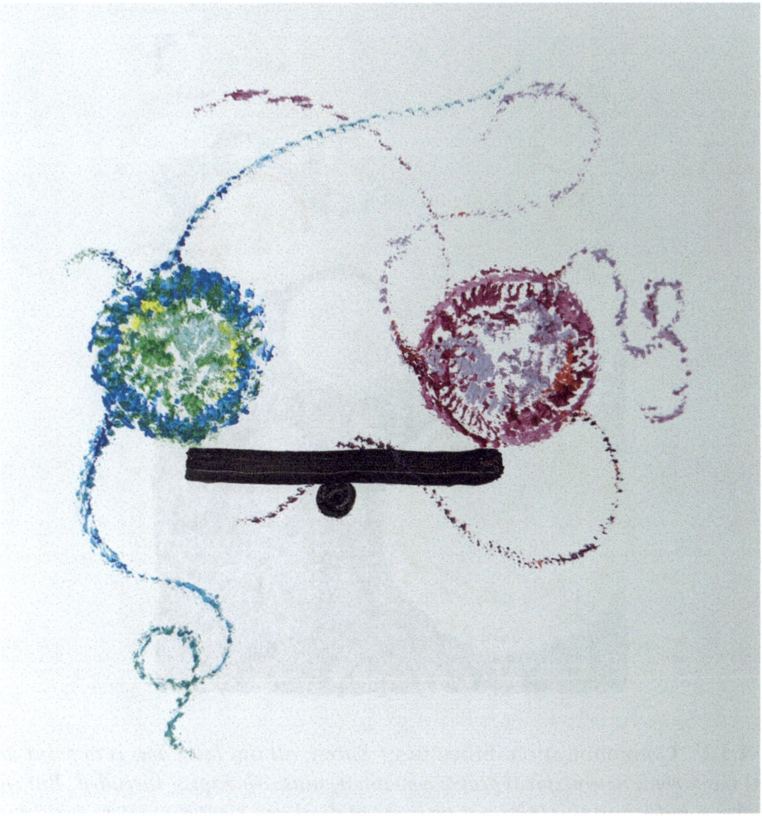

**Fig. 4.11** Supervisee/supervisor relationship. *The supervisee and supervisor are the two circular shapes (blue/ green—supervisee; purple/red—supervisor). Their shared task is to stay balanced on the structure which is 'the expectations of the profession'. It is hard to stay balanced, but they have no choice. It is not obvious what the ground is beneath the structure. The structure is solid and inflexible, whilst the supervisee and supervisor are more fluid in their colour—there are gaps for change to happen. The shoots which grow from the supervisee and supervisor shapes represent imagination, possibility, new horizons, different understandings: both supervisee and supervisor contribute shoots, which are delicate, exploratory and able to respond to the wind. But they must be careful how they allow the shoots to move, otherwise they might fall off the structure, and if one falls, they will both fall. But there is something missing: orange, yellow, energy, a warm background*

**Fig. 4.12** Communication difficulties!? *Surely, all this label does is to point a finger at the verbal, neurotypical people who use it, music therapists included. But in my experience, hidden in this label is a universe of dynamic, communicative relationship. The brush-work is dabbed because nothing is fixed: everything can and does move with the colours and shapes of those involved. Here, the carer holds the space (top right) for the care-receiver to grow and explore (here, the care-receiver is shown by the circle in orange and yellow with green growth and orange shoots). The therapist listens and joins the play of shoots and growth from carer and care-receiver. The colours are vibrant and wholesome—like a sky with stars and planets*

*The Images Seen Through the Lens of Phenomenology*

At this point I wish to ask you, Collaborator, to bear with me whilst I attempt to apply the theories at the start of this chapter to the process of image making that I have just shared. The reason for this is that one of my hopes for this book is to find a theoretical foundation for the thing-ness of arts-based experience, i.e. its ontology. Once this is better understood, it will be possible to consider whether this thing is valuable. To know this would I hope contribute to any musician's or music therapist's claims for their work.

*Making Sense of the Images as 'Noetic-noematic Unity' (Eberle, 2014, p. 185)*

But I am confused, at the moment, as to the 'thing-ness' of the images. Does their thing-ness lie in their existence as pictures, or in the content? The latter is problematic, as I am not sure what they are images of. At the time of painting, I had no concept, beyond the idea that I wanted to paint the relationships that I experienced in the poems, stories and vignettes. As already discussed, the characters in each piece of writing are composite and fictionalised. So, what relationships did I think I would represent? Actual relationships with real people? Theoretical relationships with stereotypes?

The phenomenological practice of epoché, used in eidetic reduction, involves a commitment to stripping away any preconceived ideas about the phenomenon under investigation. In reality, what I believe happened when I started painting was that I stripped away prior knowledge of the phenomenon to the point at which I did not even know what phenomenon I was painting. The notion of relationship was in my mind, but as soon as I engaged with colour, brush and paper, the actual phenomenon started to emerge: a thing-ness which embraced the physical materials as well as their simultaneous recording of, and initiating of, meaning. Looking at the pictures now, I can see representations of some relationships that are stereotyped—*Carer/ care-receiver* and the *Carer/care-receiver relationship after massive trauma* relationships for example. But I have come to recognise that the images serve another purpose, for they also reveal my *experience* of different kinds of relationship.

*The Eidos, or Essence, of the Painted Images*

Phenomenology seeks to explore lived experience. At this point, I tentatively propose that my image making *is* an activity of phenomenological eidetic reduction, albeit a nonverbal one: I started with an intention to explore the phenomenon of relationships in music therapy, and arrived at a realisation that the phenomenologically conceived image making had given me insights into my *experience* of those relationships—and consequently of some types of experience which occur in music therapy.[5] For example, my experience of working with music therapy commissioners is awkwardly rendered in paint, and then described:

> *…confined in a dull box of unpleasant, too grey, turquoise. I don't like this painting. I painted it fast and functionally, knowing I would not like it. I was not careful or caring…*

I did not need to 'bracket' my previous experience of commissioning, when painting this picture, because I did not think I was exploring that experience—I thought I was depicting the relationships between different characters and the commissioner in *Chloe's Story*.

Thus I believe that the essence, or eidos, of the images lies in what I regard as the initiated meaning of the pictures—i.e. the meaning that emerges from them—rather than in the original concept being recorded in colour, line, texture and shape. It is interesting that the initiated, or emergent, meaning can be quite far removed from the original concept. For example, I am struck by the image that represents myself as therapist. *Chloe's Story* is a composite of several episodes in my working life in which I faced tensions as a result of an integrity demand—that is, my need to feel undivided in myself. Each of these real episodes was intensely uncomfortable, and I felt conflicted and distressed as a therapist. However, the picture I created of the music therapist, when responding to the fictional characters in *Chloe's Story*, does not reveal this stress. Instead, it is organic,

> *Healthy. Whole. Colours of life: colours from nature. … a visual manifestation of a feeling of self. … it grew of its own accord. I wasn't thinking: I don't when I paint….*

This poses questions: What am I depicting? Myself? My relationship to myself? I think these questions are interesting, but arguably irrelevant: the image is not figurative,

> *It doesn't depict anything….*

[5] See Chap. 7 for a summary of the different types of experience which my research has identified.

Again, I believe the image shows my *experience* of the role of therapist, in its essence, or eidos. I clearly remember sitting at home on yet another winter day of lockdown, feeling peaceful whilst I painted. Once I had started, I was not interested at all in *Chloe's Story*: it was somehow affirming to paint the healthiness that came to the fore. On the one hand, I was slightly alarmed by this and worried that my intended research focus was fading away and that my exploration was instead branching into unplanned places, with a will of its own. But on the other hand, I recall the sense that a 'coming-to-the-surface' was happening from a deep place that had to do with more than 20 years of working with people in music therapy.

#### *Paintings of Music Therapy and the Scope of Intersubjective Communication*

Over the years since completing the paintings, I have laboured under a pressure to render this surfacing in words. However, I am not sure that it is either possible or necessary, given that there are images to reveal it. Schutz's concept of intersubjective communication develops the purpose of phenomenology beyond the exploration of the phenomenon, to the sharing of any understanding that grows from this (Schutz, 1962, p. 10 cited in Vargas, 2020, p. 422): it is significant that Vargas concludes that intersubjectivity affords a 'learning process, not solely a personal experience' (p. 422).

Herein lies both a challenge and an opportunity for arts-based research. If we are sharing phenomenological insight through image, music or any other arts-based form, how will we know what the other person has 'learnt', particularly if the instigator of the sharing derived unexpected insight in the process of arts-based phenomenological engagement, as I did in creating the images? The challenge, here, is found in the fact that research typically tries to define what it is sharing. It would be unusual for a study to conclude that it has no specific findings, but that those encountering it can form their own. This type of outcome is more normally associated with an arts-based encounter per se, such as watching a play or hearing live music, rather than an arts-based *research* encounter.

However, I argue that it is exactly this building of unexpected insight that is the strength and opportunity of arts-based research. I explore this later in Chap. 6, in which a/r/tography is presented as my main arts-based research inspiration: a/r/tographic practitioners highlight the 'creation' of knowledge that is afforded by a/r/tography, as opposed to the 'discovering' of existing knowledge.

Talking to music therapy commissioners about the 'arts-based, nonverbal eidetic reduction' that the musical experience affords probably will not be a great selling point for this musical experience, no matter how much I care about it. But the image making process has demonstrated that engaging in arts-based experience can lead to experiences that could not have been anticipated, and thereby open new realms of knowing. I suggest this might be worth talking about.

*Uncertainty and Meaning*

I am aware that I cannot be sure what someone else will make of these images, and how they will understand them as part of a research process. However, I am willing to stand by my decision to incorporate this uncertainty into my book: it highlights the fact that we can actually never assume shared meaning, for a host of reasons to do with construction of reality, cultural assumptions, bias, historical, geographical and social background, philosophical leanings and relationship to language and communication. Indeed, many people who do not use language live a daily reality in which the dominant verbal population makes assumptions about the meaning of their lives. Consequently, this gulf between what an arts-based researcher shares and what those they are communicating with understand is an illustration of the uncertainty which exists between people who do and do not use language.

It may seem as though I am shifting to an overarching relativist philosophy. But this is not the case. The critical realist in me is motivated to explore what lies behind any expectation that we might share meaning in the first place. (This is beyond the scope of this study.) In his engaging book about translation, *Is That a Fish in Your Ear* (2012), David Bellos explains that all translation, indeed all meaning, is based upon trust because it involves elements of make-believe: he traces historical attitudes to oral translators all over the world, and identifies the 'fiction' which exists when one person attempts to render another person's meaning in a different language, by effectively pretending to mean what the person they are translating means (p. 121). Interestingly, he asserts that the more recent growth of writing as the dominant means of translation has not altered these demands and attitudes (p. 122). In this chapter, I am on the one hand perpetuating this fiction and making heavy demands on this trust by adding the intersemiotic translation of image to speech. But on the other hand, I am attempting to sidestep the use of language at all, because I want to highlight image-based communication about a nonverbal phenomenon, albeit with its own needs for trust and imagination.

M: I feel like there should be some sort of trumpet fanfare!

R: Really … why?

M: Oh, you know … Researcher takes on the verbal world wins!

R: Wins? I hadn't thought of it as a contest.

M: It's a battle. You know it is. It has been for years.

R: Careful. Please. I may get grumpy between ourselves, but I'm not that naïve. Research is careful, caring, I hope. It's not about winners and losers. Language is great. I studied languages, for goodness' sake.

M: I know. OK, I'm sorry. But I was enjoying your argument.

R: Well that's different, and I'm glad about that.

M: Shall I find another quote…

R: What? Now? I'm *way* not ready for that.

M: (*Looking disbelievingly at Researcher*) There's more?

R: Yes. Don't worry. Have a break…

*What Contribution Does Phenomenological Enquiry Make to This Study?*

Even though phenomenology has already helped me discover that arts-based engagement can result in experiences that could not have been anticipated, and thereby open new realms of knowing, it still feels important to gain a deeper understanding of the nature of experience—its essential character as a phenomenon. Without this, as I mentioned, it is hard to argue for the value of any experience, whether arts-based or otherwise. However, I find phenomenology confusing on this issue: Eberle refers to a phenomenon as a 'noetic-noematic unity', in which the 'noetic' part implies 'acts of consciousness'. But consciousness is not a single, constant thing—it is a spectrum, ranging from absence (in vegetative state), through low awareness state, to different manifestations of increased consciousness. I have been puzzled by the implications of Eberle's paraphrase of phenomenological enquiry and feel unclear where the boundary lies between an act of consciousness, and ***knowing***.

At the same time that I was reflecting on the unanticipated experiences that arise from arts-based engagement, and pondering my lack of clarity around consciousness, I began to realise that different types of experience happen at the same time in what I regard as phases. I hope it might be possible to consider some of these emergent experiences as evidence in music therapy, so I will now seek to *loosen* the threads of this complexity and describe separate phases of experience, which in reality all occur in very quick succession.

*Phases of Experience*

At this point, I am again applying reconstructed logic (Carter & Little, 2007)—see Chap. 1, Section "Direct Message 6"—because I am presenting as obvious something that I have come to believe through writing this book, but which was not obvious throughout, namely my belief that experience is made up of what I call phases. Indeed, the concept of phases of experience constitutes one of the main findings of my research.

*An Illustration of My Concept of Four Phases of Experience*

I will illustrate the four phases with a banal example from daily life:

A while ago, I went into the toilet at a public store.

1. As I entered the cubicle, something happened which stunned me
2. Shortly afterwards, I became aware that my head was hurting and someone was talking
3. Soon after that, I realised that there must be someone in the cubicle who pushed the door
4. Next, I was able to tell someone who was washing their hands that my head had been hit and I was feeling dazed.

The <u>first phase of experience</u> was simply that something happened—an *event* or occurrence. This is the phase that I have been describing above, when discussing the images: when I painted what I thought was my relationship with a participant, a vibrant, round image emerged. That was the extent of my understanding at the time. It was a happening—colours and shape combined and revealed something wholesome to do with participants. I did not even need to bracket my previous decades of difficult music therapy sessions in which participants worked through resistiveness and highs and lows of emotions, because I was not thinking about these things.

Because I am fluent in language and engage in cognitive activity that uses words, I can recognise that the second phase of experience, as I conceive it, can follow almost immediately from the first phase, or happening, and can start to colour the first phase through verbal description. This explains why, in the banal illustration above, at the same time as processing strong, adverse sensory perceptions, I also named to myself the fact that my head was hurting. The type of experience in this second phase has moved on from the experience of an event, to the experience of *awareness*. In the case of my painting of the music therapy participant, I saw an image that conveyed a sense of being that was

> *Whole, vibrant. ... wholesome ... the participant's own sphere of energy and a deep core of wellness.*

At this point, I was aware of something about music therapy participants from a deep level.

The third phase of experience illustrates a development from phases 1 and 2. In my public toilet example, I had experienced something as an occurrence, experienced awareness of it, and now in the third phase, I experienced a *knowing* about the first two phases. I do not believe that the *knowing* in this phase must be of something certain or understood: it could, for example, be a knowing of mystery, doubt, confusion, possibility or uncertainty. In the illustration, the knowing involved linear reasoning—I inferred a series of events and recognised the reason my head was hurting. I am fundamentally interested in this phase, because I believe I have been with music therapy participants on many occasions in which they, or we, have reached a *knowing* of self, or music, or relationship, or experience. I will explore this further when I discuss Nick Wilson's Aesthetic Critical Realist theory of aesthetic experience in Chap. 5. Feeling uncertain, or not understanding verbally, can be a part of this experience. However, in my painting, this was the point at which I formed ideas which explained the images.

I conceptualise the fourth phase of experience as *sharing*. In the illustration, it occurred spontaneously—someone asked me if I was alright; I moved beyond my dazed confusion, inferred the reason for it, and told them what had happened and that my head hurt! In music therapy, sharing is sometimes achieved verbally. But more frequently, it happens in, and through, shared music making and is recognised and acknowledged musically in a way that bypasses words. For example, participant and therapist might spontaneously make eye contact when they mutually slow the tempo of the music towards an ending. In my image making, the sharing occurred in three ways: in the writing of the explanations of each image; in showing the images to you, Collaborator; and in this written research analysis.

I will reflect further on the phases 3 (knowing) and 4 (sharing) in later chapters of this book. For now, I believe that phenomenology is particularly helpful in understanding phases 1 (event) and 2 (awareness).

The diagram (Fig. 4.13) illustrates the interconnectedness of each phase of experience: sharing emerges after the occurrence of event, awareness and knowing, but each phase needs the earlier ones in order to come about.[6] This might appear to contradict notions of metacognition, which is described as 'awareness or analysis of one's own learning or thinking processes' (Merriam-Webster Online Dictionary). This seems to imply that knowing comes first and our awareness of it develops afterwards. In

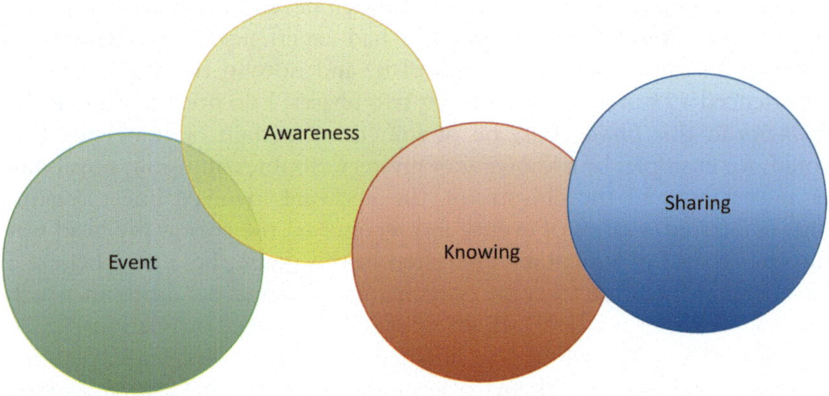


**Fig. 4.13** Phases of experience. From left to right, the four phases of experience-'Event', 'Awareness', 'Knowing', 'Sharing'-are shown as overlapping entities

[6] It is important to recognise that each phase could also be regarded as a phenomenon in its own right.

fact, I believe the four phases which I propose describe the same process, and the confusion lies in vocabulary: I would redefine metacognition, according to the four phases, as 'knowing about one's processes of growing awareness'.

*The Problem of Language in the Phenomenology of Experience*

Collaborator, you may be wondering where all this is going. The tangled nature of some of my sharing of this phenomenological phase is not the fault of phenomenology. Rather, it is because phenomenology is particularly concerned with experience of phenomena, and the phenomenon I am looking at is experience. So, in terms of language, there is a degree of repetition and circularity that must seem unhelpful. But this is, in fact, not the fault of experience, either: the English language only offers us one word—*experience*. If we only had one term for male relative, we would be unable to distinguish between brother, nephew, grandfather, son-in-law just from the word. And the same is going on now with experience. I am discovering there are numerous types, including experiences of experience. But linguistically, they all have to be lumped together as if they are the same. I have a hunch that the verbal accounts of experience in academia have tended to mask these distinctions.

Whilst it is beyond the remit of this book to explore the vast field of psychology as a whole, or music psychology in particular, I was interested to find that the problem of language is also identified in this scholarship. For example, when exploring perception and consciousness in music, Eric Clarke highlights the 'limit of language' (2011, p. 197). This results both from the inability of words to adequately represent music, but is also from the notion that '*primary*' consciousness (Edelman, 1989 cited in Clarke, 2011, p. 194 original italics) is 'pre-linguistic … developmentally', whereas '*higher-order*' consciousness (Edelman, 1989) involves verbally mediated 'imagining, remembering, or reflecting' (p. 195). Whilst Clarke regards these forms of consciousness as 'different kinds, or components of human experience', I find I cannot easily map them onto my concept of four phases of experience, because the implication is that higher-order responses require language, whereas from my practical observation, I believe that the third and fourth phases of 'knowing' and 'sharing' can potentially be entirely musically mediated.

Indeed, my whole understanding of 'knowing' comes from my observations from life and music therapy: it is something that happens, whether through music making, talking, body movement, gesture, laughter or other means, and indicates some level of taking ownership of an awareness, such that it can potentially be shared communicatively.

*Validity and Reliability in Phenomenological Enquiry*

There remain two important tasks in this exploration of phenomenology in the field of music therapy investigation. Firstly, it is important to clarify what makes phenomenological enquiry reliable and valid. Secondly, it is essential to look at the already long history of music therapy and phenomenology in the music therapy literature.

Validity—that is, whether findings truly reflect the thing being examined—is a puzzling concept for a phenomenologist. It leads the researcher to ask the question: am I accurately representing the feature under investigation? This begs the question: who is equipped or entitled to judge this representation—only the researcher, because they alone had the experience in question, or others as well? This in turn seems to enquire: how can others trust the findings of phenomenology if they are not entitled to judge them?

Added to this, reliability is problematic within phenomenology. The reliability of a research finding relies upon the possibility of reproducing the finding by repeating the research process. Is it likely that I would arrive at the same conclusions if I repeated the eidetic image making which I undertook? I suspect not, because my starting point would have changed and I would come to the activity with additional insights from the previous image making. Clearly, validity and reliability must be achieved in other ways in phenomenology.

*Phenomenology in Conjunction with Other Methodologies—Triangulation and Subjectivity*

An attractive feature of phenomenology is that it is an approach that seeks to inform and be informed by other research approaches. Eberle comments that 'phenomenology intends to complement other approaches, not substitute them. Once its findings are objectified, they can be triangulated with different sorts of ethnographic data' (p. 199). Indeed this can provide *validity* because one methodology can endorse, support and clarify the findings of the other. For example, building on Husserl's notion of lifeworld, Anne Honer and Ronald Hitzler propose 'life-world analytical ethnography: a phenomenological approach' in their eponymous article (2015).[7]

*Phenomenology and (Auto)ethnography in My Study*

Honer and Hitzler are careful to define the *identities* of (1) the phenomenological and (2) the ethnographic researcher (pp. 458–552), in which the former achieves an 'existential inside view' and the latter undergoes 'lengthy ... [practical] co-participation' (p. 552). Having adopted both these roles up to this point, I hope that any weaknesses in the highly personal findings of phenomenological image making can potentially be offset by the autoethnographic narrative, which I hope will resonate with the music therapy insights of other actors in the field. In this way, I hope my research will achieve some validity and reliability.[8]

MT: Musician, are you alright?

M: *(Slowly)* ... just getting lost again. Are you finding this helpful?

MT: Helpful? Well, I'm not sure. I suppose I think of it like making a map. I don't know this country and Researcher is sort of surveying, and plotting the landmarks and routes and contours and coming up with a map.

[7] They define this approach as sitting within the spectrum of 'empirical social research methods suitable for explorative-interpretative research questions' (p. 556). However, because of the 'combination of observation and participation, and hermeneutics and phenomenology that characterizes life-world-analytical phenomenology', they regard it as 'the variant of ethnography that we favour' because 'ultimately, the researcher himself is his own best instrument ... during data collection and data analysis' (p. 556). Moreover, the purpose of this approach is to understand 'at least approximately, the (inside) view of normal participants in sociocultural events and [to make] it understandable to (nonparticipant) others' (p 556 original brackets).

[8] It is interesting, but not surprising to me following my research endeavours, that Honer and Hitzler describe observation and participation as 'actually *contradictory* behaviours' (p 552 original italics) because

> the researcher must comply with two radically different bundles of expectations: on the one hand, we see ourselves as researchers who are existentially involved in the field and who reflect on this existential involvement and use it perspectively ... on the other hand, we see ourselves in the (lonely) theoretical attitude (at our desks, as it were) as pragmatically distant, purely cognitively interested scientists who abstain from value judgements. (p. 556 original brackets)

M: …of the phenomenology of experience?

MT: Yes, I think so.

M: …and this is helpful?

MT: Why are you worried about it being helpful? Isn't it more whether it's true, what she's saying?

M: Maybe. Actually, no, I don't know what you mean. If it isn't helping us find out what we are motivated to find out, then it doesn't work for me.

M: The Motivations, you mean?

M: Obviously.

MT: Well, the thing is, … if I'm really honest, … I don't think your motivation is really all that closely related to *research*. You say you want to insist that nothing else contributes to the fullness of life the way that music making does. But … that's more like a manifesto. You've already decided. It doesn't leave much room for exploration.

M: I don't agree. I want to explore a way of demonstrating what I think we all know.

MT: OK, then isn't it a useful thing to start to unravel—what was researcher's word … to *loosen* the muddle which is music making? I mean, it's a social thing, a physical thing, a historically and culturally informed thing, a communicative thing, an aesthetic thing. I think what Researcher is trying to do is to find out if there is anything that unites all of these simultaneous 'things', or sort of underpins them all. And she is doing it by exploring experience. Because at the end of the day, each and every part, or version of music making, happens as experience, and thinking about it is an experience too, which is where valuing comes in and concepts that follow, like evidence. But that comes later.

M: ...and so she ends up with a complicated idea about what experience is, and how does that help? Is that going to get anyone to pay for it? Think about Carer and the struggle to access this stuff.

MT: I know. It's a bit early to say. What I'm hoping is that each bit of thinking about experience in music therapy, from each of these analysis sections, will provide something useful, or helpful, or whatever. And that they will combine to form an argument that we can use to advocate the purpose and value and evidence of music therapy *as an experience*. It's like one section provides the wheels, the other the chassis, the next the bodywork and hey presto, here's a car...!

M: You may be right. Only, as far as I can see, Researcher isn't exploring the *experience* of music therapy, she's got stuck on the *idea* of the experience of music therapy. It's so abstract.

*Pause—they think.*

MT: You're not wrong, Musician ... *(Long pause)* ... uh. ... *I'm* confused now. Is there actually a difference?

M: ...between what?

MT: ...between experience and the idea of experience?

M: Ask a linguist.

MT: Why?

M: Well, there are centuries of debate about what happens when we name things.

MT: No, I don't mean that. I mean, is there a stage in an experience when it's not yet an idea,—it really is just an experience?

M: There's got to be—think of animals.

MT: Who says they don't have ideas? … no, I think you might have hit on something here.

M: Well, don't hold your breath.

MT: Why do you find this all so depressing?

M: Don't know.

MT: Keep going … please … we need you.

M: We'll see…

*Phenomenology in Music Therapy*

I want to emphasise that phenomenological thinking is not new to music therapy. It was central to my training, but even though the notion of shared music making as a phenomenon was always there, we did not explore the nature, thing-ness or ontology of this phenomenon. I would like to explain further: when I trained in the late 1990s, we were invited to think about two main approaches to music therapy—music centred/phenomenological and psychodynamic. Phenomenology in this context implied a focus upon the phenomenon of music itself, as opposed to a focus on the interpersonal dynamics in the therapy room.

In his book *Music for Life* (1995), Gary Ansdell explores the difference between psychotherapy and music therapy:

> It could be said that psychotherapy is 'hermeneutical' and Creative Music Therapy[9] a 'phenomenological approach'. This in turn rests upon the essential difference between music and words. We need both, of course, but they work in different ways both within our everyday life and within therapy. (p. 30)

In a footnote, Ansdell further explains,

[9] Creative Music Therapy refers to the music-centred approach pioneered by Nordoff and Robbins in their practical work and writing (Nordoff & Robbins, 1977). Their conceptual and practical framework remains the foundation of music-centred music therapy to this day (Guerrero et al., 2015, pp. 185–7, 194).

> Hermeneutics is a 'reading' of something—it interprets, translates, decodes. The psychoanalyst offers his 'reading' of the symbolism of a statement or a dream. Likewise, hermeneutics of music tries to express verbally the 'meaning' of the music—what it represents. In contrast a phenomenology tries to understand a thing in its own terms—resisting interpretation. In Creative Music Therapy the focus of the work and any explanation is phenomenological—needing no verbal account but allowing the music to 'mean itself'. (p. 30)

Phenomenological thinking is by no means exclusive to Nordoff Robbins and music-centred approaches in music therapy, nor is phenomenology used as a research methodology only for music-centred work: for example, Erik Christensen's doctoral thesis explores eleven 'phenomenologically inspired descriptions of music' by therapist-researchers whose approaches range from Guided Imagery and Music (Grocke, 1999), to musicological (Lee, 2000), to psychodynamically informed (Forinash & Gonzalez, 1989) (cited in Christensen, 2012, Section 2.3, pp. 26–41).[10]

I am drawn to Ansdell's views, because in this understanding of music therapy, music and music-making are seen as noema, or phenomenon, in the phenomenological sense. They are things to be apprehended through noesis, or acts of consciousness: together these things and the consciousness of them are the essence of the phenomenon, and engagement with this phenomenon is in turn regarded as the therapy. It is significant for my research that Ansdell is arguing for nonverbal meaning-making, in contrast to typical, language-based approaches to phenomenology, but in keeping with my own instinct to learn from the eidetic reduction afforded by image making.

Although I have believed, observed and used this explanation all my life as a practitioner, it is only since researching for this book that I have identified what are in fact several discrete yet intertwined phenomena that constitute music therapy in a session:[11]

[10] Similarly, hermeneutic thinking in sessions and research is found in many different contexts, though typically where words are the subject of investigation (Loewy & Paulander, 2016 Examples in Music Therapy Research section). These are interesting themes for music therapy research, but are beyond the scope of this study.

[11] Here I use the term 'music therapy' to mean the musical work in sessions, rather than the entirety of stakeholder actions and interactions.

- the happening which is the physical making of sound (*event*)
- the occurrence of that sound in time (*event*)
- the physical enacting of self through musical and other interaction (*event*)
- the physical enacting of relationship with other(s) through musical and other interaction (*event*)
- the sensory and/or cognitive awareness of the sound and sound-making (*awareness*)
- the sensory and/or cognitive awareness of other(s) (*awareness*)
- the thought or unthought knowing about what and how to participate (*knowing*)
- the thought or unthought knowing about what has emerged through participation (*knowing*)
- the sharing of sound, awareness and knowing (*sharing*)
- the recognition (or not) and naming (or not) of therapeutic occurrence (*sharing*)

I have long been dissatisfied with my attempts to report the experiences in music therapy to others and to 'make a case' for these aspects of music therapy such that they can stand alongside linear outcome measures. I think this stems from my insufficient clarity regarding the diversity and nature of different experiences, phenomena and experiences of these phenomena, within music therapy sessions. I hope that by clarifying the diversity and nature of these features I will help others who also wish to make this case.

I notice that these different phenomena naturally fall into the four 'phases' of experience that I outline earlier in this chapter: event, awareness, knowing, sharing. I did not contrive to categorise the strands in this manner—it emerged as I wrote the list. I am therefore encouraged to find that they correspond to this concept.

*Phenomenology and Experience in the Music Therapy Literature*
Carer recently commented that I am not alone in thinking and writing about phenomenology and experience in music therapy. This is true, and throughout my enquiry, I have read widely in order to learn, contemplate and compare ideas. It feels important to share some of what I have read in order to highlight the gap that this book is trying to address. In particular, when I encounter the word 'experience' in other literature, I will try to identify which phase of experience it might correspond to, out of the four

I have conceptualised. I hope this might illustrate and add further relevance to my theory, Collaborator. I am keen that my reflections on literature should be helpful, particularly if you are not from the field of music therapy.

In his later book *How Music Helps*, Ansdell tackles 'the complexities of (musical) experience', first identifying 'two ways' that the term 'experience' is applied in everyday speech: firstly, it implies 'something personal we accumulate (as in, "After thirty years, I'm an experienced pianist")'; secondly, it implies 'something more immediate and particular that we undergo in the present, and that leaves a vivid impression (as in, "I had this extraordinary experience this morning!")' (2014, p. 57 original brackets).[12]

Although I would argue that the 'extraordinary experience' is actually made up of several overlapping experiences, each of which have different phases, I find these definitions succinct and helpful in articulating the duality of meaning in the vernacular use of the term. In this pair of meanings, Ansdell perceives that the two forms

> share … the common empirical idea of exploring phenomena by using the senses, rather than relying on magical or purely theoretical means. But they also epitomise a long-term dualism in western thinking—splitting objective, mental, rational knowledge from its supposed subjective, embodied and feelingful opposite. (p. 57)

I include this observation because I see it as lying at the very heart of the question of evidence in music therapy: is sensory knowing valid as evidence in music therapy, or must we rely on what are believed to be objective measures of function or other things, in order to communicate the significance and efficacy of the work? This is explored in greater depth in Chaps. 5 and 6.

Ansdell continues with an exploration of the consequence of this 'feelingful' dimension of experience:

> Wavering between objective and subjective perspectives, 'experience' has retained its place in everyday discourse, but it has all but disappeared for several decades from many academic fields. For many scholars in the physical and social sciences, 'experience' became and outdated and redundant term

[12] I refer to these definitions in Chap. 1, Section "Direct Message 1" as ones that I agree with.

> that was tainted by the fuzziness of introspection and subjective description of earlier methods that cognitive psychology and neuroscience had worked hard to supersede (2014, p. 57).

He comments that 'thinking about music' has 'followed this trend towards making theories of music as objective and factual as possible'. Furthermore, he provides a

> brief informal survey of … [in footnote] more than twenty classic text of the last twenty years, ranging over music psychology, neuroscience of music, musicology, music education and music therapy … [and concludes in main text that] musical experience [has] simply disappeared as an explicit subject of attention. It has been replaced instead by 'perception', 'awareness', or 'cognition'—mirroring how the concept 'person' has been replaced by mind, brain or consciousness. (pp. 57–6)

I am reassured by these observations which are so directly reflected in my own research on experience.

*Experience as a 'Vessel' Term*

Indeed, I have been struck by this disappearance and I agree with Ansdell, that the concept of experience itself receives little, or patchy, attention in music therapy literature. When it does occur, like various other abstract nouns that are used in describing music therapy—relationship, creativity, communication being others—the term 'experience' is generally used as an unexplored 'catch-all' for the content of the experience, whether this be of improvisation, training, work in schools etc. In these instances, I think of the word experience as a 'vessel term'.

For example, a recent study of 'the lived experiences of teenagers in a children's home participating in a choir' in South Africa (van Rooyen & Dos Santos, 2020) demonstrates what I have found to be typical usages of the term and concept of experience.[13] Van Rooyen and Dos Santos present a powerful context, explaining that '5.2 million of the 18.5 million

[13] The adjective 'lived' is added to indicate that the research participants have themselves had the experience explored in the study. I am aware that this term has a particular cultural significance, often denoting the experience of people or groups who have experienced marginalisation. Nevertheless, as an expression, I find this common addition puzzling, since experience is by definition a 'lived' entity. If an imagined experience were the focus, even the imagining is a lived 'event' (Phase 1 of experience).

children (up until the age of 18) in South Africa reside with neither parent' (p. 1). Of these, orphaned children in children's homes do not necessarily thrive and the study considers whether a group choir could help them.[14]

The ethical, methodological and analytical processes are shared in detail and the study identifies two beneficial categories of experience which result from the choral intervention: 'interpersonal experiences' and 'intrapersonal experiences'. Six of the nine subcategories which are defined use the term 'experience' in their names—'experiencing a healthier picture of myself', 'experiencing improved social skills' and 'experiencing connection with the broader community' for example (p. 7). However, it is interesting that the term is used in a vernacular sense which is slightly different from Ansdell's two definitions ('something personal that we accumulate', or 'something more immediate and particular that we undergo in the present'). Van Rooyen and Dos Santos seem to imply a fusion of the two, for the participants in their study 'accumulated' personal insights and skills, but these were the product of several instances of 'undergoing' the choir practices and performances in the 'present'—i.e. in real time and not by skimming through video recordings of the same, for example. Furthermore, there is no exploration of the ontological nature of experience—it is simply assumed that the reader will know what it means.

I have found several other studies, from the 1990s to the present, which explicitly name experience or lived experience in the title or research questions. For example, one study considers 'The Stories we haven't told: the lived experience of music used in therapy for bereaved parents' (Flynn, 2014); another focuses on 'Music therapy with pre-term infants—theoretical approach and first practical experience' (Haslbeck, 2004). In the first, narrative enquiry is used to explore the parents' experiences of music in therapy; in the second, the student therapist's own experience is described in a practice essay. Leow, Drury and Poon explore the '...patients' experiences of music therapy in an inpatient hospice in Singapore' (2010), whilst Hyejin So investigates 'Korean music therapy students' experience of group music therapy' (2019) and Young and Pringle study the 'Lived experiences of singing in a community hospice bereavement support music therapy group' (2018). Different methodologies are used in each of these case studies and the participant groups are diverse. However, in each case

[14] Whilst this research is not explicitly framed as a case study, it falls into this category and the authors name Interpretative Phenomenological Analysis, citing van Manen's *Researching Lived Experience: Human Science for Action Sensitive Pedagogy* (1990) as a source.

the term ‘experience’ is again used as a catch-all vessel for various occurrences and their impact on people, and the researchers do not explore the nature of experience per se: the studies are not looking at this phenomenon, so it is perhaps not surprising.

Nevertheless, I do in fact find it surprising that a profession that relies upon experiencing the phenomenon of relational music making, and sharing that experience, apparently barely explores *what* experience actually is, in music therapy.

*Philosophical Explorations of Experience in Music Therapy Literature*
Some authors do pursue a more philosophical enquiry into certain aspects of experience in music therapy. Dorit Amir, for example, considers ‘Moments of insight in the music therapy experience’ (1993). She relates episodes of music making between music therapy participant and therapist and uses the phrase ‘music therapy experience’ to embrace both the specific, immediate experience and the on-going exposure to music therapy over a course of sessions. Looking at this ‘experience’, or these experiences, as a whole, Amir focuses in on a particular form of experience—one ‘when my clients or I get a sudden, intuitive understanding about something’. She calls these particular experiences ‘moments of insight’ (p. 86). My reading of Amir is that she regards moments of insight as a particular *type* of experience. By contrast, coming to this article after my arts-based data collection and phenomenological analysis, I perceive in her descriptions of insight what I would call a particular *phase* of experience: insight seems to lie in the third phase (knowing); furthermore, the sharing of this insight seems to lie in the fourth phase (sharing). Amir does not differentiate between gaining the insight and sharing it.

Jo Salas, on the other hand, explores ‘Aesthetic experience in music therapy’ (1990, p. 3). She theorises aesthetic experience as ‘the encounter with beauty’ and the aesthetic response as ‘the experience of the observer’. I am drawn to this double acknowledgement of experience in these explanations: experience is derived from an encounter, but it also gives rise to another experience, i.e. the response. Salas has not identified a methodology for her understanding of experience since the article is more philosophical than investigative. However, a phenomenological outlook seems to be implied because Salas’ descriptions illustrate what I perceive to be a noetic-noematic unity (Eberle, 2014), in which the encounter with beauty is the noema and the aesthetic response is the noesis. Again, with reference to my concept of phases of experience, I would define this form of 'response' as encompassing the second and third phases—awareness and knowing.

*Experience as a Defined Feature of Music Therapy*

There are a few more music therapy theorists, whose writing about experience I would like to share. Firstly, Kenneth Bruscia makes extensive reference to experience in his reflections upon analysing improvisation in his article 'A qualitative approach to analysing client improvisations' (2001). Interestingly, he identifies three possible foci for the analysis of improvisations: the process, the product or the experience. Whilst this is perhaps confusing, since I would argue that the process and product are both apprehended through experience, the separation of experience into a category of its own is significant. Bruscia explains,

> Client improvisations yield at least three layers of data, and it is important to delimit the analysis to only those layers that are necessary, given its purpose. Improvising is a creative *process* that results in a musical *product,* both of which contribute to the improviser's *experience*, as expressed verbally or in another art modality. (p. 9 original italics)

Furthermore,

> When the focus of analysis is experience, the therapist is interested in knowing what the improviser was thinking or feeling while improvising, how the improviser would describe the music itself, or what meaning or significance the improviser would give to the improvisation. This may be expressed by the client either verbally, or through movement, drama or visual arts. (p. 9)

Bruscia clearly states that he considers an analysis of experience to be a phenomenological endeavour (p. 8), and he clarifies his belief that phenomenology explores 'how the music is experienced by those involved, rather than merely … its objective qualities'. Reflecting on Bruscia's comments in the light of my concept of four phases of experience, I believe that by honing in on the thoughts and feelings of the improviser, in the quotation above, Bruscia is analysing the third phase—knowing. By proceeding to an analysis of description, meaning or significance, Brusica is referring to the fourth phase—sharing. The suggestion that this sharing can be done verbally is common in music therapy. However, the inclusion of movement, drama or visual arts as forms of sharing is less common in the literature, but is important for this study. It is very surprising to me, though, that Bruscia does not include the possibility that the sharing of description, meaning and significance could happen *musically*, in real-time music making in music therapy sessions.

Bruscia's ideas about analysing experience are thought provoking and resonate with something I have noticed myself during this phenomenological phase of my enquiry. I am surprised that he does not focus on phenomenological enquiry as a means of exploring and understanding the happening, or occurrence, of musical improvisation itself—i.e. the first phase of experience (event). I would argue that a noetic-noematic unity *happens* before it is present in our awareness (phase 2), or known about, or shared (phases 3 and 4). However, Brusica does not make reference to the first two phases of experience—event and awareness. Indeed, none of the music therapy literature which I have discussed seems to explore the first two phases.

Nevertheless, in trying to gain phenomenological insight into my own arts-based experience, (described above) by considering this experience alongside an exploration of relevant literature, I have realised two things:

- every experience starts with an event and proceeds through the four phases
- every phase could itself be construed as an 'event' in its own right, such that an ever expanding, interwoven web of events, awareness, knowing and sharing blooms out of every starting point

With this in mind, although Brusica does not focus on analysing the initial experience of the musical event, the knowing and sharing that he does highlight can themselves be seen as events, from which further phases proceed. In fact, this theorised concept of interwoven experiences resembles my perception of everyday experience[15]—everything overlaps, accumulates and cross refers, involving memory, the senses and different ways of knowing. However, this does not negate what I hope to be a useful clarification of four phases of experience.

Kenneth Aigen takes a different view of experience through his notion of music as an 'experiential realm' or 'world' (2014, pp. 44–7). He cites

[15] Indeed, this is a phenomenological illumination of the exact same discovery that I made through *autoethnographic* analysis—namely, that experiences produce 'generations' of 'offspring' experiences, which grow from each other.

Gary Ansdell and Colin Lee who both create metaphors for the experiential realm of music that is afforded by music-centred music therapy: Ansdell observes that being on land is totally different to being in water—the whole of oneself is perceived differently. In the same way, *being* in daily life is totally different to *being* in music (Ansdell, 1995, p. 68 cited in Aigen, 2014, p. 46). Similarly, Lee reports a participant who described musical participation in music therapy as 'flying' (Lee, 2003, p. 72 cited in Aigen, 2014, p. 46). Implicit in these descriptions are all four phases of experience, though they are not the focus of investigation. It is significant that whilst Ansdell and Lee both draw on their music therapy practice to make these observations, a similar concept is theorised by music psychologist Eric Clarke (2019, pp. 9–10) when he describes 'music[al engagement]' as both a 'medium' and 'environment in which to explore and experiment…with subject positions or social formations' which can give rise to empathy.

*Experience as a Gift*

An interesting concept of experience which I have encountered in the music therapy literature, but also frequently hear being used by music therapists, is that of 'giving' an experience to a participant. Indeed, I remember the maxim from my training—'give the participant the experience so that they can claim it for themselves'. This usage is found in the article, 'The selection of music experiences in music therapy' (Hiller & Gardstrom, 2018). On closer reading, the term 'experience' is here used to denote the deliberate and skilful crafting of conditions, by the therapist, in order to create the potential for a participant to experience something. Drawing on Bruscia's four 'methods' of music therapy (improvisational, re-creative, compositional, receptive) and three orientations of the therapist (outcome, experience or context orientation) (2014, Chapter 13 cited in Hiller & Gardstrom, 2018, pp. 79–81), the authors consider the intentional, clinical use of these, and their combinations, for the purposes of facilitating experience in the participant. In effect, the term experience is being substituted for intervention, or approach, but it is important to recognise that it is frequently used this way in the field.

*The Use of Phenomenology as a Research Tool by Music Therapists*

Before proceeding to a new approach to analysing experience, in Chap. 5, it is worth reflecting further on the relationship between phenomenology and music therapy. As indicated above, some approaches to music therapy, notably music-centred music therapy, regard the therapy as resulting directly from a phenomenological encounter with relational music making. Furthermore, I suspect it is likely that most therapists are motivated to understand the participant's experience, either in order to shape their practice, or as a subject of research, or both. Anecdotally, I notice that music therapists use the term phenomenology/-ical with relative ease, and phenomenological analysis is a fairly common approach to data analysis in music therapy research.

However, I have been puzzled by some of the studies I have read that employ this approach to analysis. I was therefore interested to discover Max van Manen's critique of existing attitudes to phenomenology and its methodological basis (2017). He concludes that there are numerous misunderstandings surrounding the philosophy and what it is for. Foremost among these is the confusion between phenomenological insight and psychological insight: he argues that if a study is of 'how individuals make sense of their own experiences', this does not mean it is phenomenology. Instead, it is concerned with 'psychological sense-making or reflection' (p. 776). Indeed, he observes that there is a belief that all studies which explore experience must be phenomenological, and he refutes this by arguing that

> all kinds of methodologies study various kinds of human experiences for the purpose of understanding different kinds of meaning: psychological, ethnographic, narrative, theoretic, conceptual meaning and so on. But phenomenology is the study of the primal, lived, prereflective, prepredicative meaning of an experience. ... The outcomes of phenomenological research are full-fledged reflective texts that induce the reader into a wondering engagement with certain questions. ... that help the reader recognize the meaningfulness of certain human experiences and events. ... In other words, not all qualitative research inspired by phenomenology is phenomenology. (pp. 776–7)

Van Manen is particularly dubious about the claims of Interpretative Phenomenological Analysis (IPA) to be an inherently phenomenological analytical method. Citing Smith's assertion (2011 p. 10) that 'IPA wants to learn about the participant's cognitive and affective reactions to what is happening to them. ... and how they are making sense of their experience', van Manen counters that this does not, in fact, constitute a phenomenological enquiry. For, by contrast, 'the phenomenologist wants to explore the eidetic or inceptual meaning structures. … of a certain phenomenon or event' (2017, p. 778).

It feels important to share this argument, because I am clear that this phenomenological part of my research is deeply concerned with the ontological, 'prereflective … meaning' or phenomenon 'of an experience' and is not aligned with the more psychologically orientated research which I believe Bruscia is defining as phenomenological.

*Phenomenology and the Senses*

Finally, a note on the senses: Honer and Hitzler emphasise that the ethnographer is fundamentally concerned with acquiring 'sensory impressions' (2015, p. 552). Similarly, Eberle refers to 'sensuous apperception'—that is, the sensory-making and sensory-receiving of preconscious impressions of phenomena (2014, p. 186). Later, in an appeal to subjective participation, reminiscent of Honer and Hitzler's, he highlights the 'multimodality and intersensuousness' of subjective experience, as well as the 'sense-connexions of past experiences' (page 194). It is clear that our sensory apprehension is of fundamental importance in phenomenology.

C: Well done, Researcher.

R: Was it?

C: I don't really know. But well done for working at it for so long.

R: Oh! … That's not the same.

C: Sorry. It's quite full and a little complicated. But I think it tackles *what* experience is. I'm going to think about it.

R: Carer?

C: Yes…

R: Do you honestly think this project is going to make the slightest difference to people who need music therapy. Will they be more likely to get it? Will the therapist be allowed to honour experience as evidence and celebrate what the participant shares in musical relationship?

C: Well—It's a start. I'm not sure. Perhaps you could ask your research supervisor about research impact. But isn't it really going to depend on whether the readers *feel* what you are saying, and recognise it, and *know* things from arts-based involvement ... whether with this book or other things?

R: Maybe.

C: Don't worry for now. Is that the end?

R: Of this section, nearly...

Thank you, Collaborator, for committing to this chapter of the research. As Carer points out, it focuses on *what* experience is in its essence, and is therefore distinct from the previous chapter (Chap. 3) which looks at music therapy experience through the lens of autoethnography.

Reflecting on Hamlet's statement that 'there is nothing either good or bad but thinking makes it so', I want to reiterate that this chapter has sought an ontological explanation of what experience actually is, as a phenomenon, i.e. its 'thing-ness'. It tries, if you like, to explore the neutral ground which is always present, but upon which we construct ideas of 'good or bad'. As such, in critical realist terms this chapter is 'underlabouring' for the next (Chap. 5), since the next is specifically interested in those judgements of all stakeholders in music therapy which result in notions of 'what counts'. The methodological approach in the following chapter is informed by Aesthetic Critical Realism.

Aesthetic Critical Realism employs a different ontological lens to that offered by phenomenology: whilst phenomenology explores the 'thingness' of phenomena through our *experience* of this thingness, Aesthetic Critical Realism focuses on the mechanisms that *explain* phenomena at an ontological level.

In the next chapter, I will focus particularly on the phenomenon of value judgement. I will also explore my belief that Hamlet's statement does not paint a full picture: I take his word 'thinking' to imply verbal, cognitive understanding (phase 3 of experience). But I hope to illustrate that value judgements need not depend upon cognitive awareness, that they can be *experienced* in a physical or sensory manner which leads to *unthought, nonverbal knowing* (Bollas, 1987), which I believe to be equally valid and fundamental to the experience of relational music making in music therapy. This discussion of values in turn leads to an exploration of culture and its relationship to values, and to the culture(s) of music therapy, in particular.

The final cycle of retroductive analysis will consider my topic through the lens of arts-based research methodology (Chap. 6).

I look forward to continuing the exploration with you.

With best wishes,
Researcher

MT: I don't think I can keep this up.

*Very long pause.*

MT: I'm sorry Researcher, but it just feels a million miles away from being in the room with participants, making music. I'm not sure this is going to work.

R: What would make it work for you?

MT: Can I say?—OK, I want to know: 1. When are we going to talk about evidence, 2. How is it going to help to launch into Aesthetic Critical Realism, and 3. Why you were so abstract about all that phenomenology.

R: Right. Give me a minute … third one first—if you found the phenomenology section abstract, I'm sorry. But I want to clarify what it is *I* am trying to do, as opposed to what other music therapy practitioners and researchers do under the umbrella of phenomenology.

MT: …and you're trying to….

R: …draw attention to the four cycles of experience that I encountered through my arts-based research…

MT: …and relate them to music therapy?

R: No, not quite yet,—that will happen when I have looked at Aesthetic Critical Realism as an analytical tool as well.

MT: Uh, really?

R: Yes, really. Don't be so negative. *I* don't say, 'uh, tango!' when you're doing your work…

MT: No, sorry.

R: No 2, … It is going to help to launch into Aesthetic Critical Realism because it's all about 'what must the world be like for this or that to happen'.

MT: … and …?

R: …and that way we can find out what the world must be like for only some kinds of experience to be turned into evidence … and, well, Aesthetic Critical Realism just gives us a chance to think about the three domains,—you know, the real, the actual and the empirical, and see how it all ties in with phenomenology. It can help show the difference between the thingness of things, the happening of things, and our knowledge of things.

M: You're joking now?!…

R: Wait. … I just want to see. If we're going to offer anything tangible to music therapy through this book, we've got to show where it fits in, and at least *something* must be new: we can't re-invent the wheel by a different philosophical name.

M: Researcher, I don't want to be rude, but I honestly feel you need to do less of the philosophical indulging. It just puts people off … *(Wandering off)*

R: Really? I thought it was. … I was trying to. … help? *(Sighs again)*

C: Shall we keep going?

MT: Might as well ... Musician is falling asleep....

## References

Aigen, K. (2014). *The study of music therapy: Current issues and concepts.* Routledge.

Amir, D. (1993). Moments of insight in the music therapy experience. *Music Therapy, 12*(1), 85–100.

Ansdell, G. (1995). *Music for life: Aspects of creative music therapy with adult clients.* Jessica Kingsley Publishers.

Ansdell, G. (2014). *How music helps in music therapy and everyday life.* Ashgate Publishing, Ltd.

Bellos, D. (2012). *Is that a fish in your ear?: The amazing adventure of translation.* Penguin Books.

Beyer, C. (2003). Edmund Husserl. In E. N. Zalta & U. Nodelman (Eds.), *The Stanford encyclopedia of philosophy* (Winter 2022 ed.). Retrieved December 3, 2022, from https://plato.stanford.edu/archives/win2022/entries/husserl/

Bollas, C. (1987). *The shadow of the object; psychoanalysis of the unthought known.* Routledge.

Bruscia, K. E. (2001). A qualitative approach to analyzing client improvisations. *Music Therapy Perspectives, 19*(1), 7–21.

Bruscia, K. E. (2014). *Defining music therapy* (3rd ed.). Barcelona Publishers.

Carter, S. M., & Little, M. (2007). Justifying knowledge, justifying method, taking action: Epistemologies, methodologies, and methods in qualitative research. *Qualitative Health Research, 17*(10), 1316–1328.

Christensen, E. (2012). *Music listening, music therapy, phenomenology and neuroscience.* (PhD), Aalborg University.

Clarke, E. (2011). Music perception and musical consciousness. In D. Clarke & E. Clarke (Eds.), *Music and consciousness: Philosophical, psychological, and cultural perspectives* (1st ed., p. 193). Oxford University Press.

Clarke, E. (2019). Empathy and the ecology of musical consciousness. In R. Herbert, D. Clarke, & E. Clarke (Eds.), *Music and consciousness 2: Worlds, practices, modalities* (2nd ed.). Oxford University Press.

Dahlberg, K. (2006). The essence of essences–The search for meaning structures in phenomenological analysis of lifeworld phenomena. *International Journal of Qualitative Studies on Health and Well-being, 1*(1), 11–19.

Eberle, T. S. (2014). Phenomenology as a research method. In U. Flick (Ed.), *The SAGE handbook of qualitative data analysis* (pp. 184–202). SAGE Publications Ltd.

Flynn, L. (2014). *The stories we haven't told: The lived experience of music used in therapy for bereaved parents.* (BMus), The University of Queensland.
Forinash, M., & Gonzalez, D. (1989). A phenomenological perspective of music therapy. *Music Therapy, 8*(1), 35–46.
Grocke, D. (1999). *A phenomenological study of pivotal moments in Guided Imagery and Music (GIM) therapy.* (PhD), University of Melbourne.
Guerrero, N., Marcus, D., & Turry, A. (2015). Nordoff-Robbins music therapy. In B. L. Wheeler (Ed.), *Music therapy handbook* (pp. 183–195). The Guildford Press.
Haslbeck, F. (2004). Music therapy with preterm infants: Theoretical approach and first practical experience. *Music Therapy Today, 5*(4), 1–16.
Hiller, J., & Gardstrom, S. C. (2018). The selection of music experiences in music therapy. *Music Therapy Perspectives, 36*(1), 79–86.
Honer, A., & Hitzler, R. (2015). Life-world-analytical ethnography: A phenomenology-based research approach. *Journal of Contemporary Ethnography, 44*(5), 544–562.
Lee, C. (2000). A method of analyzing improvisations in music therapy. *Journal of Music Therapy, 37*(2), 147–167.
Lee, C. (2003). *The architecture of aesthetic music therapy.* Barcelona Publishers.
Leow, Q. H. M., Blair Drury, V., & Poon, W. H. (2010). A qualitative exploration of patients' experiences of music therapy in an inpatient hospice in Singapore. *International Journal of Palliative Nursing, 16*(7), 344–350.
Loewy, J., & Paulander, A.-S. (2016). Hermeneutic inquiry. In B. L. Wheeler & K. M. Murphey (Eds.), *Music therapy research* (3rd ed.). Barcelona Publishers.
Merriam-Webster.com. (2023). *Merriam-Webster online dictionary* Retrieved September 20, 2021, from https://www.merriam-webster.com/dictionary
Nordoff, P., & Robbins, C. (1977). *Creative music therapy: Individualized treatment for the handicapped child.* John Day Company.
van Rooyen, A., & Dos Santos, A. (2020). Exploring the lived experiences of teenagers in a children's home participating in a choir: A community music therapy perspective. *International Journal of Community Music, 13*(1), 81–101.
Salas, J. (1990). Aesthetic experience in music therapy. *Music Therapy, 9*(1), 1–15.
Shakespeare, W. (1986). *The complete works.* Oxford University Press.
Smith, J. A. (2011). Evaluating the contribution of interpretative phenomenological analysis. *Health Psychology Review, 5*(1), 9–27.
So, H. (2019). Korean music therapy students' experience of group music therapy: A qualitative case study. *Frontiers in Psychology, 10,* 636.
Tuohy, D., Cooney, A., Dowling, M., Murphy, K., & Sixsmith, J. (2013). An overview of interpretive phenomenology as a research methodology. *Nurse Researcher, 20*(6). https://doi.org/10.7748/nr2013.07.20.6.17.e315
Van Manen, M. (1990). *Researching lived experience: Human science for action sensitive pedagogy.* Althouse Press.

Van Manen, M. (2017). But is it phenomenology? *Qualitative Health Research, 27*(6), 775–779.

Vargas, G. M. (2020). Alfred Schutz's life-world and intersubjectivity. *Open Journal of Social Sciences, 8*(12), 417–425.

Wagner, H. R. (Ed.). (1970). *Alfred Schutz on phenomenology and social relations.* University of Chicago Press.

Young, L., & Pringle, A. (2018). Lived experiences of singing in a community hospice bereavement support music therapy group. *Bereavement Care, 37*(2), 55–66.

CHAPTER 5

# Loosening the Threads Along the Way 3

## Direct Message with Interruptions

### *Examining Personhood, Therapeutic Experience, Evidence and What Counts, Through Aesthetic Critical Realism*

There are more things in heaven and earth … than are dreamt of.[1]

M: I was thinking

R: I thought you were asleep…

M: No I wasn't asleep. I was thinking of Mrs. Gradgrind.

MT: I'm sorry?

M: Mrs. Gradgrind. You know, the exceptionally weak mother in *Hard Times*.[2] No thanks to Dickens for strong female characters in that department.

[1] Shakespeare, *Hamlet*, Act 1 scene 5 (1986, pp. 745–6).
[2] Dickens ([1854] 2016).



J. Atkinson, *Insights From Music Therapy Practice and Research*,
https://doi.org/10.1007/978-3-031-86220-5_5

MT: Why?

M: Like I said, she is so weak…

MT: No, I mean, why were you thinking about her and pretending to be asleep?

M: I wasn't. But anyway—because in the end, she is the first one who actually says something to her husband about the calamitous mistake he makes.

MT: What mistake?

M: Well, he tries to raise their children without any acknowledgement of their imagination and creativity. Actually, worse than that. He denies them all access to anything playful at all—it's why the book starts with two of the children peering secretively into the circus tent, blown away by the forbidden fruit inside.

MT: OK, and why Mrs Gradgrind?—can you find the passage?

M: No.

MT: Oh come on, that's not very helpful.

M: I mean I haven't got it—I gave the book to a charity shop.

MT: Why?

M: Because that's where I got it from.

MT: Ha! Well there we are. But why were you thinking of her?

M: Because just before she dies, she has something like a 'dim awareness'—I can't remember Dickens' words—anyway, a dim awareness that rules and numbers and logic aren't actually all there is in life.

MT: Oh?

R: Is there a connection?—I'm interested.

MT: It's obvious isn't it?—We're looking for something more than that from music therapy evidence. That's it, Musician, isn't it?

M: Yes

MT: But I don't want to imply that our music therapy colleagues are in any way like Mr. Gradgrind. Not at all. Totally not. If this ends up online, please don't misquote me!

M: ...I can't help thinking of Louisa, their daughter, who suffers so terribly from that regime of austere facts and no imagination....

R: ...and that's a bit like the profession, are you saying, Music Therapist?

MT: No, I don't know what I'm saying. I think we'd better go.

M: No, why? I want to be here. It's the deal we struck.

R: Deal?

Dear Collaborator,

You have probably worked out by now that this book is, in certain ways, back to front. Explorations do not flow gently out of methodological preparations. Instead, things occur because it seems they need to, and afterwards I am left searching for a methodology to act as setting and backdrop for these occurrences. You may protest that I spelt out the methodological approaches near the start, but I have also been honest throughout that I am 'reconstructing' the 'logic' of this book, often after the practical muddle of its investigation. And it has been no secret that time presents a huge problem in autoethnography: to take you on my journey, I need to allow discoveries to appear to unfold as we go along. Whereas in reality, everything unfolded before this book settled into its verbal and arts-based accounts. But all this is consistent with my critical realist analytical approach—retroductive analysis (see Chap. 1, Section "Direct Message 3"). I am still 'thinking up' explanations for things, so I will persevere for now. Furthermore, I am still looking for ways to understand the experiences that occur in music therapy, particularly those that are nonverbal and arts-based. And I still want to investigate their relevance to evidence within the cultures of music therapy.

In the previous chapter, which approached experience through the lens of phenomenology, I conceptualised experience as a noetic-noematic unity, that is, a combination of the thing perceived and the consciousness of perceiving it. I further subdivided these phenomena into four phases of experience that I have become aware of: event, awareness, knowing, sharing. Before that, in Chap. 3, I discovered that experiences happen in 'generations', with one giving rise to the next, and so on.

In this chapter, I adopt an alternative, but complementary, philosophy of experience—that of Aesthetic Critical Realism (ACR). I use it to examine the experiences presented in my stories, poems and vignettes, as well as my phenomenological insights. I have asked Music Therapist to share her reflections upon one of the poems.

Moon*: Reviewing the Poem with a Phenomenological Lens*

I (Music Therapist) have had the privilege of working with many participants whose music therapy has shared some of the characteristics presented in the poem *Moon*: work with children who appear confident, deeply themselves, in many ways in control of their environment, in other ways lacking control over their daily lives, not displaying anxiety or needs that are obvious to the outside world. Nevertheless, they have been referred to music therapy so as to explore some kind of change, based on the assessment of a concerned professional, or sometimes a family member.

***Moon***

*Two music therapists make music with a ten year old child.*

Where are you?
Poised
Balanced
At ease, reclining,
Looking at me as if to say:
'Well?'

We play and your eyes
Track me.
You allow events to
Unfold, but I know
We are here on
Your terms.

Your file is
Full of labels.
What for?
Are they trying to
Traffic-light
Parts of
How you are?
For what?
You are
Emphatically
You.

Or are they trying to
Understand,
And can only translate
One bit at a time
Because they don't know
Your language?

Nor do we.
But one day,
Whilst reclining,
Poised
Balanced,
You teach us.
Just a little.

A beginner's lesson.

We play the lyre
And sing,
Drawn irresistibly
By your eyes
And your guiding
Arms.

And all at once,
You sing as well,
Tossing your head,
Moulding melody
And holding, holding
The moment....

We breathe together,
One instrument,

Alert,
Needing to stay—

And then it is enough.
You look away,
Drop your voice,
Lower your chair
And sigh,
As if to say—'there's plenty more,
But very likely
You wouldn't
Under-
Stand'.

Phenomenology can highlight the phases of experience in Moon's engagement with the therapists: Moon becomes involved in the situation, moving his 'eyes' and 'guiding arms', which 'draw' the therapist and co-therapist into musical improvisation, using the lyre. This is the initial event—the first phase of experience. Following immediately from this, Moon displays an awareness of the event—the second phase—and demonstrates this when 'all at once [Moon sings] as well'. The improvisation develops, and Moon is conducting and shaping the music, 'Moulding melody/ And holding, holding/ The moment….'. There is knowing here, not verbal, language-based knowing, because the character of Moon does not use language. But there is a cognitive, musical knowing—the third phase. And this is shared, as 'We breathe together,/ One instrument,/ Alert,/ Needing to stay'—the fourth phase.

I had not perceived these phases when I wrote the poem. Nor have I been actively aware of them in my music therapy practice. Furthermore, I acknowledge as previously mentioned that every new event (e.g. starting singing) can itself become the first phase of experiencing a new phenomenon, and so on. However, I am encouraged, that despite this 'hall of mirrors' effect, a whole music therapy improvisation can, broadly speaking, fall into the four phases of experience.

*Revisiting Ontology in Critical Realism*

Thank you Music Therapist, this is Researcher again. There is more in the poem *Moon* however, which phenomenology is less helpful for exploring, but which Aesthetic Critical Realism could address. To use an analogy, if phenomenology is useful to examine the parts of a machine, as well as how they work and fit together, ACR is useful to consider why the machine exists in its current form and design in the first place. Both philosophies are concerned with the thingness, or ontology, of things. However, whilst phenomenology assumes that a phenomenon can be known in its most fundamental manifestation through bracketed experience, critical realism proposes different domains of knowing:

- *The real*—a domain in which generative mechanisms, which '[make] a difference but [are] not observable' (Wilson, 2020, p. 81) occur and give rise to…
- *The actual*—events, happenings, occurrences, entities, which are in turn experienced in…
- *The empirical*—a domain of human knowing-about and experiencing of events and mechanisms[3]

The difference, between a phenomenological exploration of a phenomenon and a critical realist one, is that the phenomenologist tends to focus on the content of an experience of a phenomenon, and provide descriptive accounts of that content and experience. These are afforded an ontological status. A critical realist finds such accounts valuable, but attributes them to the empirical domain—the sphere of human experience of things. This domain alone does not hold the key to understanding a phenomenon in critical realism. Instead, it is the starting point for an imaginative backwards journey which seeks to identify the events that have led to the experience of that phenomenon. And the journey continues further back, still, as the critical realist tries to propose explanations, or generative mechanisms, for why these events have occurred at all, thereby developing ontological understanding. These explanations are not confined to physical mechanisms—the philosophy pays equal attention to all realms, whether physical, social, imaginative, present, absent, technological or socially constructed. I realise that there are dangers in such reductionist definitions of what different research approaches afford, for it is possible to combine critical realism and phenomenology when examining a phenomenon. However, I have found some demarcation of the primary focus of each to be helpful.

[3] Roy Bhaskar was dissatisfied with the dualist split between the positivist attitudes to knowledge which he saw as dominating the natural sciences, and constructivist ones which dominated the social sciences (2016, pp. 5–9). He saw reality as stratified, meaning that it cannot be reduced either to statements about physical causes derived from improbable closed design experiments, or to our knowledge of entities, which is not the same thing as the entities themselves. As stated in Chap. 1, Section "Direct Message 3", he therefore saw reality as occurring on different levels simultaneously, namely, the real, the actual and the empirical.

*Aesthetic Critical Realism (ACR) and Wilson's Ontology of Experience*
I want to introduce Wilson's theory of Aesthetic Critical Realism, which is of fundamental importance to this chapter.[4] In his book *The Space that Separates: A Realist Theory of Art* (2020) Wilson defines experience as,

> the human capacity for cognitive conscious and nonconscious, i.e., thought and unthought, knowledge gained through interaction with our environment. (p. 15)[5]

Wilson formulates an eight point theory of experience (2020, pp. 61–62), of which the most relevant to this study are:

- Experience is a holistic entity, formed from a set of parts with structured relationships between the parts.

This in some ways resembles the four phases of experience I have identified.

- The parts which make up experience 'comprise the properties and powers of objects we interact with in our environment, our own properties and powers as experiencers, and emergent properties and powers pertaining to the relations between these parts'.

This is similar to the noetic-noematic unity in phenomenology and captures the notion that any experience is a combination of stimuli and the responses of those who are experiencing.

[4] In Chap. 1, Section "Direct Message 3", I have outlined Wilson's assertion that Bhaskar's philosophy of critical realism does not explore the nature of experience itself, because of Bhaskar's belief that philosophy and positivism, in particular, have suffered an 'overreliance' on experience (Wilson, 2020, p. 15).

[5] Wilson begins his development of an ontology for experience by critiquing Bhaskar's assertion that experience 'must normally be the result of a social process of production' (Bhaskar, 1975 cited in Wilson, 2020, p. 58). In Wilson's view, this denies experience *per se* any (causally generative) reality beyond that which is apprehended in a social context. In other words, if experience is the product of a social process, where does that leave those phenomena or experiences that give rise to a social process, and what is the ontological nature, or generative mechanism, of these 'actual' phenomena or experiences in the first place?

- Experience is therefore an emergent[6] phenomenon. It also has emergent properties: these allow us to experience our experience.
- Bhaskar's theory of constellationality[7] accounts for the complexity of Wilson's theory of experience.

*Aesthetic Experience in ACR: Wilson's Definition and Theory*

To summarise, different parts or entities come together to make an experience: as a bare minimum, these parts must include a phenomenon (which can be external or internal—we can experience our memories, for example), plus the human(s) involved in experiencing the phenomenon. There are many different kinds of experience, one of which Wilson calls aesthetic experience.

At this point, it is important to stress that Wilson uses the term 'aesthetic' to differentiate such experience from several other forms of experience that he explores. Although this type of experience can certainly occur in connection with creative engagement, in Wilson's theory, the term 'aesthetic' does not imply an active or (even) beautiful arts experience with all the connotations and value judgements that the word 'aesthetic' often has in both vernacular and philosophical usage. Nor is aesthetic experience something that involves being a passive audience in the presence of an artwork, receiving sensory impressions (pp. 75–9). This is significant

[6] Emergence—In both the original philosophy of critical realism and in Wilson's development, 'emergence' describes a phenomenon that emerges from a generative mechanism at work. This phenomenon emerges from a collection of stable parts, and it is directly related to this collection of parts. For example, a cake is the phenomenon that emerges from the combination of a stable collection of ingredients and processes—mixing, cooking, etc. If the collection is unstable, and sugar is missing, a cake will not emerge. Nor will it emerge if the cooking is left out. When a phenomenon emerges from a collection of stable parts, this phenomenon that emerges can itself have emergent properties. In everyday terms, something has emergent properties when it is more than the sum of its parts. In the example of the cake, when combined with other 'parts' (in this case, eating and digesting), the cake has the emergent property of relieving hunger, and possibly also enhancing wellbeing. These are the new emergent properties, or phenomena.

[7] Constellationality—This is a fundamental concept in the development of critical realism that Bhaskar called dialectical critical realism (2016, Chapter 6). Constellationality proposes that the totality of an entity may include apparently contradictory parts, but these parts are constellationally contained within each other. In this way, Wilson states, 'epistemology is constellationally contained within ontology; structure within agency, theory within practice, reasons within causes, and so on. The figure of constellation(ality) therefore denotes the idea of a holistic totality that embraces while not subsuming its different parts. It is a figure of containment' (2020, p. 41).

because, as I will explain, I will later come to suggest that the word 'therapeutic' may equally be used to define the particular type of experience that Wilson calls 'aesthetic'.

Wilson's theory of aesthetic experience is of great significance to this enquiry. It proposes that 'aesthetic experience is our emergent experience of being-in-relation with the real, i.e., relations, structures, mechanisms, possibilities, powers, processes, systems, forces, values, ways of being' (p. 81). So, for an experience to be aesthetic, it must involve an entity or phenomenon, plus a response which affords value[8] (not necessarily positive) to the phenomenon: it is our awareness of this emergent valuing that brings us into being-in-relation (p. 99).[9]

It is important to note here that various music therapists have explored the concept and significance of aesthetic experience in music therapy (Lee, 2003; Aigen, 2007, 2008; Tsiris, 2008). Because these practitioner-theorists define aesthetics in relation to notions of art processes and products, whereas I adopt Wilson's ACR notion of aesthetic experience as that which brings us into relationship with the domain of generative mechanisms (i.e., the ontological or 'real' domain) there is less overlap of thought than the term suggests and I do not explore their ideas in this study. Indeed, as mentioned, I later re-define Wilson's aesthetic experience as *therapeutic* experience.

Wilson's whole theory of ACR hinges on 'being in relation' and our *awareness* of this relationality. There are three proposed 'modes of relationality', or manners in which the human being experiences their relationship to a stimulus:

- Firstly, we have an encounter with something other, for example nature—this constitutes 'being-in-relation' with a *phenomenon* (2020, p. 83).
- Secondly, we experience some kind of inner awareness, that can be a 'psychic, cognitive, emotional, somatic, affective, kinaesthetic,

[8] Values (axiological experience) in ACR—Wilson conceptualises aesthetic experience as an energy transfer between the phenomenon being experienced and the person experiencing, and he sees valuing as a kind of force. It is the valuing that makes the experience different from other kinds of experience (2020, p. 101).

[9] Music therapist Stuart Wood also explores the phenomenon of emergence in music therapy but from a complexity theory perspective, whereby what emerges is more sophisticated than its parts—which is not necessarily the case in the critical realist concept of emergence (Johnson 2001, p. 13 cited in Wood, 2016, p. 59).

"internal" response to a stimulus'. This constitutes 'being-in-relation' with *ourselves* (pp. 83–4).

- Thirdly, we have experience of the 'real' nature of the world, its underlying structures and causal powers, which constitutes 'being-in-relation' with *'natural necessity'*.[10] (p. 84)

This is perhaps surprising for Western language users who might typically regard aesthetic experience as a thing that happens when we engage with 'good' artefactual art. But Wilson proposes that the generative mechanism of an experience which he calls aesthetic could have nothing to do with conventional features of what we socially construe art to be. For example, if we see another human being smile at us, we are in relation with that *phenomenon*. When we experience awareness of the smile, we are in relation with *ourselves*. Whether consciously or unconsciously, this smile and our awareness of it may draw us towards or away from the smile, thus involving our valuing of the smile, as well as our experience of 'being-in-relation with natural necessity' (in this case, with interpersonal 'structures, relations … ways of being' (Wilson, 2020, p. 81). When this occurs, we have had an 'aesthetic' experience, according to Wilson's definition. To summarise, aesthetic experience is personal—what is valuable is determined by the individual—and relational: Wilson is deliberately challenging the idea that these terms (aesthetic experience and value) can be objectively applied.

MT: Researcher?

R: Yes?

[10] Natural necessity is the critical realist term for 'a generative mechanism at work' (Bhaskar, 2016 cited in Wilson, 2020, p. 99) i.e., the domain of the real, or put simply, the world as it is. It is the domain in which the explanations of events and occurrences that take place in the actual domain, as well as our knowledge of those events and occurrences in the empirical domain, can be found. Natural necessity, as a concept, provides an ontological foundation for these events and experiences of our lives, including experiences of absence and not knowing. It is significant that in Wilson's definition, experience involves all we know, 'thought *and unthought*' (2020, p. 15 my italics). Neither Wilson nor other critical realists are arguing that the domain of the real can be fully known. Rather, it is a philosophical claim. However, Wilson argues that certain experiences draw us into relation with thought or unthought aspects of the real, and that these experiences are qualitatively different from those in the 'actual' domain.

MT: You're talking to yourself…

R: What d' you mean?

MT: I mean, this all sounds like you are rehearsing something in your head. It's hard to listen to and I'm not sure that Collaborator will last the course.

R: Really?

MT: Yes, really! Sorry to quote things back at you, but can you be a little more caring and think a bit more about the experience of hearing this?

R: Oh, yes, sorry. Which bit in particular.

MT: It's not like that. It's meant to be a Direct Message. Sharing something. You know … not a lecture.

R: Yes. I'll try

MT: Can you talk about Moon again, or one of the other characters.

R: OK, … soon … just a small bit more about values? Is that OK…? It's totally important…?

MT: Small!

*Revisiting* Moon *with an ACR Concept of Aesthetic Experience*

From Wilson's explanation, I conclude that there can be certain situations which can deliberately be used to provide the 'parts' for aesthetic experience: the three deciding factors as to whether the aesthetic experience emerges are (1) whether a phenomenon is encountered (2) whether the people involved are aware of their being-in-relation to the different parts of the experience (natural necessity) (3) whether it involves approach-avoidance response (valuing). So, I am adding to the generations of experiences revealed through autoethnography, and the phases of experience perceived through phenomenology, by theorising aesthetic, or therapeutic, experience through ACR.

Collaborator, the importance of this theory to my enquiry is this: if I want to claim that arts-based (musical) experience in music therapy is valuable, then it is essential to be clear *what* that experience is, *how* it came about, and *why* it is valuable.

In the following discussion, I will reconsider Moon's experience and use the critical realist form of questioning—'what must the world be like….?',[11] as it probes into the generative mechanism, or ontological explanation, of things. For the time being, I will continue to use Wilson's term—'aesthetic' experience.

### *An Experience of Music in Moon's Music Therapy, as Understood Through ACR*

In his book *The Space that Separates—A Realist Theory of Art* (2020), Nick Wilson is not specifically addressing the experience of music, but of art, whatever form it might take. Again, departing from common usage of the term, he defines 'art' as,

> the skilled practice of giving shareable form to our aesthetic experience. (p. 110)

As such, art is a *doing*. Consequently,

> Aesthetic experience is not so much the "means" to an "end" (the "end" here being appreciation of some apparently valuable artwork), but rather it constitutes the "end" itself. In the context of art, our emergent experience of being-in-relation with natural necessity is the thing being judged valuable; the "artwork" is, in effect the "means" (a tool—and very often, an extremely skilful one, at that) to achieve this. Moreover, aesthetic experience is not just "nice to have", but it is something as human beings we "need". (p 102)

For me, this resonates closely with my observations and encounters as a music therapist.

So, what is happening in Moon's session? I suggest that initially, Moon has an experience which is not aesthetic. It is auditory and involves some elements which are common to Moon's everyday life—there are adults present, they are directing some attention to Moon. After a while, something in the situation evokes, or demands a response from Moon. The

[11] This form of questioning in critical realism is known as a 'transcendental argument' (see Chap. 1, Section "Direct Message 3").

music acts as a phenomenon, or stimulus, and the experience begins to take on the characteristic of an aesthetic experience: Moon clearly has an approach motivation towards the musical encounter. I say 'clearly', because it can be heard—Moon changes role from 'conductor' (which is itself a musical response) to singer. The vocalising that Moon contributes does not appear resistive, hence my belief that it demonstrates an approach response.[12] This response constitutes a sharing by Moon of what he finds valuable—present-time, co-created, musical being-in-relation.

### What Must the World be Like for Moon to Experience Being-In-Relation to Music and Music Making?

There are considerations, here, to do with the social phenomenon which is music therapy. However, these will be considered later, when I discuss culture. The purpose of this question is to explore what it is about music and engagement with music that affords the experience of being-in-relation with natural necessity (i.e. generative mechanisms at work—'relations, structures, mechanisms, possibilities, powers, processes, systems, forces, values, ways of being') (p. 81).

My practice of music therapy has mainly focused on the Western tradition of music, and my response to this question will be made from this view point, even though I recognise that it is only one of numerous musical heritages and practices. A working assumption of music therapists is that for people familiar with this tradition, there are patterns within the flow of harmonic tension and resolution that are so familiar that no conscious awareness is required in order to 'know' these embedded structures (Jiang et al., 2017, p. 4; Lahdelma, 2021). As music therapists, we are trained to use these and other musical features 'clinically'—i.e., to select that combination of tonality (e.g. major, minor, modal, wholetone, pentatonic), metre (e.g. simple, compound, unmetred), rhythm, motif, form (e.g. binary, ternary, ground bass, etc.) which we feel would engage and address the needs of the participant. There are socially and acoustically determined emotional moods and meanings associated with different musical features: for example, the perfect cadence[13] can evoke a sense of

[12] Music therapists frequently encounter resistive responses from participants. These are in no way seen as a negative, but are received as having communicative importance and significant energy. These could be regarded as an avoidance motivation—part of the spectrum of valuing in ACR.

[13] The movement from the chord based on the fifth degree of a scale (the dominant) to the 'home' or tonic degree.

closure or completion, because an awareness of first and fifth degrees of diatonic scales *belonging together* has been shown to exist widely in both untrained and trained musicians (Krumhansl & Shepard, 1979, pp. 591–2); modulation[14] can evoke some sense of instability (Vuvan & Schmuckler, 2011, p. 487); predictable patterns, as well as deviation from those patterns, can result in feelings of pleasure (Salimpoor et al., 2015, pp. 86–9). I have so often observed the bearing, facial expression, and vocal quality, of a music therapy participant adapt and change to reflect these emotionally resonant structural features, that it can seem more significant when this does not happen, than when it does.[15] In ACR terms, I perceive these features as the raw materials of potential aesthetic experience (which could be actualised through an approach-avoidance response, i.e. valuing): beyond the sensory experience, the unfolding musical features offer an experience of being-in-relation with the generative mechanisms of musical structures and their emotional associations.

I suggest that for Moon, this affordance of music making—the passage through, and completion of, a musically rendered emotional journey—was an aesthetic experience because (1) it involved being-in-relation to the generative structures of music (2) Moon's approach response indicated a valuing (3) Moon communicated his awareness of what had taken place—'We breathe together,/ ....Needing to stay,/ And then it is enough./ ... You look away/ ... And sigh,/ As if to say—"there's plenty more"'.

### What Must the World be Like for Moon to Experience Being-in-Relation to Self, in Music?

It is difficult, as a therapist who does not identify as having any disability, to imagine the experience of self of others who self-identify/are identified as such. The fictionalised character of Moon has capacity to walk and move around but has been given the label 'severe learning difficulties' owing to their lack of use of language and significantly impaired cognitive

[14] Changing key within a piece of music—i.e. establishing a tonal centre which is not the 'home' key of a piece.

[15] It is important to emphasise, however, that a music therapy participant's response to music is individual and nuanced and music therapists do not make assumptions about the participant's experience. Nor do we interpret the 'emotional moods' in terms more specific than *apparent* 'instability', 'discomfort', 'resolution', etc.—i.e. we do not attribute the emotional states of anger, sadness, fear, for example, to our participants for it is not possible to know the emotional state of another from observation.

capabilities. In my practice over the years, I have become aware how little agency children with these impairments have over their lives: government dictates attendance at school and adults determine the contents of their days, for example. This is the same for children who do not have impairments, but the opportunities for this group are far greater, and those who use language can express preferences and eventually develop self-advocacy and choice-making.

Wilson identifies being-in-relation with self as one of the modes of relationality which are central to aesthetic experience. In Moon's case, shared music making with the therapists offers a unique opportunity among creative activities for aesthetic experience: visual arts and theatre do not accommodate simultaneous co-creation; actors cannot speak or sign simultaneously if they wish the audience to pick up all that is going on; visual artists may collaborate in making something, but such co-creation lacks the intrinsic relationship to specific space and time that lies at the heart of music making. Dancers may, indeed, dance together, but music usually defines their work.

What is it about music making, therefore, that lends itself to the aesthetic experience of being-in-relation with self, and makes ACR such a helpful philosophy for music therapists? I would argue that it is the time-bound nature of musical form. Those who work with children with severe learning difficulties recognise that there can be difficulties with beginnings, endings, transitions on the one hand, and with offering variety and differences in pace and scope of activities, on the other. For example, some autistic children with learning difficulties find changing activity so challenging that the day can fill up with overwhelming anxiety. Also, some children with very limited mobility and cognition, and who use a wheelchair, may experience days in which one activity quite literally rolls into the next, with little or no directive input on their own part.

It is by no means a new idea to suggest that when making music, transitions of these kinds, or these endless spans of time, can become re-framed. A child who is drawn into therapeutic music making encounters demands to respond to changes, to purposefully inhabit a distinct and inevitable duration of time, and to do so on their own behalf. This overcoming of habitual difficulties and re-presenting of flexible self in music-making becomes possible *because the music requires it.*[16] John Dewey explores this

[16] From Nordoff and Robbins' pioneering case studies onwards (1973), this has been noted.

phenomenon in *Art as Experience* ([1934] 2005): he usefully makes a distinction between 'art product' and 'work of art'—the former is 'physical and potential', the latter is 'active and experienced' (p. 168). The *work* that the art does is to harness the participant's 'long, slow process of maturation' (p. 24) to 'organised energy' (p. 185). In this way, our habitual 'pressing forward' in life (p. 179) is drawn into the 'rhythm of acts and undergoings, of defining rests and forward impulsions' (p. 180) which participation in the arts affords and which yield new experience from familiar components. My observations as a music therapist suggest that this phenomenon of participants (including the therapist) being drawn into the *work* of music making is indeed the result of the demands music makes, and that it happens because the 'world' of music is 'like' that: it takes considerable resistive energy to avoid the call of pulse, rhythm, meter, melody. The responses of referred participants may be disorganised, but they generally bear some relation to the organised energy of music itself, as well as to the other participants' (including therapist's) responses, and participants gain new experiences of themselves being-in-relation with that world of interpersonal music.

What is new in this enquiry is the explanation of this phenomenon in terms of ACR. For I propose that these three components—(1) the phenomenon of musically mediated experience of self (2) valuing of being-in-relation with music, self and other through shared music making (3) awareness of this relationality—explain the occurrence of aesthetic experience, as defined by Wilson. Together, they constitute the generative mechanism of such experience. As a consequence, I will argue that the music therapist has an opportunity to re-consider the nature of evidence in music therapy. This will be explored later in this chapter.

### What Must the World Be Like for Moon to Experience Being-in-Relation to Other, in Music?

Again, I am not yet considering the socially constructed phenomenon which is music therapy. Instead, I will continue to examine what it is about music and music making that affords the participants the experience of being-in-relation to each other, on an ontological level.

Music making is a multisensory phenomenon: Moon is engaging his vestibular sense 'Poised/ Balanced/ ... reclining', and his visual—'Looking at me. ... We play and your eyes/ Track me'. His auditory sense is aroused by the singing and playing; his tactile sense will have been stimulated by his purposeful breathing, and its effect on his body; his proprioceptive sense will have been triggered first by 'tossing [his] head' and later by lowering his chair in time with the end of the music.

In addition, music making with others is an arena for interpersonal dynamics: in Moon's case, there is contact through eye gaze. As the music therapist I notice the 'ease' in this gaze—there is no tension in the room. But I also have a sense that 'We are here on/ [Moon's] terms'—I and the other therapist are not encountering resistiveness, but neither are we challenging the status quo. One of the skills in music therapy lies in building a sufficiently trusting relationship that challenge is an option.

All the experiences mentioned could equally be attained in, for example, a supported swimming session, or a horse riding lesson. What, then, is it about music and shared music making that makes this particular form of interpersonal activity an arena for aesthetic experience, and a therapy? I suggest that it is to do with the revelation of personhood which results from the combination of being-in-relation to self, being in relation to music and being in relation to other, and the valuing and awareness which render this an aesthetic experience.

There are three ways in which, over the years, I have observed the revelation of personhood:

1. Unwittingly revealed
2. Experimentally constructed
3. Deliberately conveyed

MT: Can I stop you?

R: *(Looking surprised)* Go ahead.

MT: Can I check something.

R: Which bit?

MT: Listen! You go into a session with participants…

R: I do?

MT: No, no, I do, 'one does'

R: Oh, OK…

MT: ...people who have been referred, and maybe their family or carers. You know the sort of thing. And the music gets going and at some point, you find a groove—maybe not all of you,—but those that do, know that it's happening. And so the session goes on and it happens again, and sometimes there's a real 'magic moment', though not always. And then after the session you go to your notes and look at the reasons for referral and see that participant A has low self-esteem and needs to develop social skills, and B lives with anxiety and struggles to listen. And you keep track of bits which seemed to show A being more confident and B listening. But all the while, you are humming to yourself the beautiful melody, or the amazing riff or rhythm that emerged, and how you saw participant A sort of fly on their xylophone, and participant B break into cool dancing. And you're thinking: *'that's what matters!'* But you don't write about it, you write about listening and things because whoever is in charge at the setting wants to know that the therapy is 'working'.

R, M, C: *(Remain silent)*

MT: You know what I mean?

M: Yes.

MT: So is this bit that you're writing about now, about *that*? About the fact that the participant reveals *who they are* in the music making, their *person*, truly? How they *are* in music therapy may be totally different to how they are outside of the sessions: they may be confident and quick tempo, or they may control impulses and listen acutely, and they may never show that in other places. Or they may ... But what's important is that whatever they bring of themselves and share in the relational music-making, that is their person, too,—their choices, their preferences, their imagination, their dislikes, their collaboration, their resistiveness. It all counts. So it all adds up to their personhood.

R: Yes ... yes that's right. It's getting there.

MT: OK, just checking...

R: I just need to go for it now. Can you wait a bit?

*Theories of Personhood*

Collaborator, I have reached an essential concept in this exploration, so I wish to give it careful attention. Like experience, integrity, care and various other concepts I refer to, personhood is not a single entity that can be neatly defined.[17] Although it is beyond the scope of this study to explore the concept of personhood per se, I acknowledge that I draw on a range of ideas that put human relationality and recognition at their core.[18]

Carl Rogers' name and in particular his concept of 'unconditional positive regard' (Kirschenbaum & Land Henderson, 1989, p. 225) have been much cited in my music therapy training and subsequent working life. Significantly, Rogers conceives this in terms of experience: there is an 'experiencing' by the therapist of 'warm acceptance of each aspect of the client's experience as being a part of that client'. Interestingly, this characterises unconditional positive regard more as a response than as a predetermined attitude.

Most relevant to this study, however, are the ideas of psychologist Tom Kitwood, who focuses on the notion of personhood in older people with dementia, in particular. In the article 'Personhood and Dementia: revisiting Tom Kitwood's ideas', Jan Dewing provides an overview of concepts of person and personhood (Dewing, 2008). She highlights the fact that

> The word for person remains constant, yet the concept of what a person is in Western culture has undergone dramatic changes over time. (p. 5)

Focusing on Western approaches to these concepts, she acknowledges thinkers whose influence has been the Christian tradition, as well as Enlightenment thinkers, notably Descartes and Kant, and 'several contemporary psychological perspectives' (pp. 5–6). In particular, she draws

[17] Many authors have contributed to an extensive literature on the topic, for example a critical realist perspective is pursued by Margaret Archer in *Being Human: The Problem of Agency* (2000), and Christian Smith in *What is a Person? Rethinking Humanity, Social Life, and the Moral Good from the Person Up* (2011). Moral philosopher Harry Frankfurt explores the inseparability of a person's love from the focus of that love in *The Reasons of Love* (2004), whilst Heikki Ikäheimo adopts a Hegelian perspective to examine the significance of recognition in the experience of personhood (2010).

[18] NB In this study I do not engage with the legal definition of personhood which can be applied to organisations, (the word 'person' is defined in the Interpretation Act 1978, Schedule 1 as 'including a body of persons, corporate or un-incorporate' (gov.uk, 2023)) and is in some instances applied to natural features, such as forests or rivers (Arstein-Kerslake et al., 2021).

attention to the pervasive Cartesian dualism which views body and mind as separate entities, and comments

> In many ways, traditional explanations based on Kantian ideals as exemplified by the Cartesian position are still dominating the personhood and person-centred literature, although the focus is moving more towards the brain than the mind and on one particular set of attributes of the brain; cognition. (p. 6)

Whilst McCormack et al. (2012) emphasise the practical necessity to 'draw from … [different] perspectives to make informed person-centred decisions' in health care (p. 286), in the above article, Dewing summarises current critiques of psychologist Tom Kitwood's thinking, in particular. These critiques focus on 'his failure to fully deal with the person as an embodied being' (p. 6), and on his 'not being radical enough', because his philosophy is essentially based upon traditional 'personhood theories' which exclude and reject certain human beings because of 'restrictive definitions of persons and the attributes required to be a person' (p. 10).

*Kitwood's Theory of Personhood*

However, in spite of this criticism, I am drawn to the exposition of personhood in the writing of Kitwood and his colleague in dementia care, Kathleen Bredin (1992), because it is of relevance to this enquiry. Their motivation is found in a remark that echoes both Dewing's, above, and Ansdell's (2014) which I discuss in Chap. 4, namely that,

> Psychiatry of old age has had an overwhelming tendency to make the brain rather than the personhood of the dementia sufferer its central focus of attention. (p. 270)

Kitwood and Bredin propose two reasons for this, one obvious, the other more hidden:

> In an obvious sense this avoidance [of a personhood focus] enabled psychiatry and psychology to conform to a notion of natural science, although a rather narrow and stilted one. Less obviously and much more controversially, a stance that is mainly technical keeps distress at bay. (p. 270)

The distress that the authors refer to is the pain of watching the disintegration of a mind and the loss of function and independence in a human being. However, they argue that this distress is not inevitable. Instead, they locate the root of this distress in the rigidly dualistic attitudes of people without dementia to 'us' as healthy, independent care givers, and 'them' as the disintegrating patients. But Kitwood and Bredin critique this notion of 'wellness' and 'independence' in the population without dementia, by arguing that this population protects itself with 'denial and collusion' and 'very high defences against recognition' (p. 273).

Furthermore, Kitwood and Bredin argue that the self-attributed wellness of the 'us' population is in fact 'extreme individualism' (p. 276), which far from being a sign of health, is actually an indication of being 'frozen'. The authors propose a 'fluid-frozen-shattered' continuum to describe the 'structure of personality' (p. 275), in which 'shattered' denotes a personality structure of someone in psychosis or dementia state who is unable to repair themself alone, 'frozen' denotes a personality structure that is rigid and inflexible and persists in individualistic, reductionist thinking in order to preserve coping strategies, and 'fluid' is a personality structure that can adapt and change in relation to others and to circumstance.

Kitwood and Bredin comment,

> In the main traditions of the western world, which date from the break-up of feudalism and the theories of the Enlightenment, the term *person* has often come to be taken as having virtually the same meaning as *individual.* (p. 275 original italics)

The authors argue that because the prevailing 'frozen' belief in the West is that individuality, self-reliance and independence are what it takes to qualify as being both 'well' and a person, we actually deny others *and ourselves* the possibility of experiencing our true personhood. Indeed, human interrelatedness is essential for personhood, since

> ...personhood should be viewed as essentially social. ... personhood is not, at first, a property of the individual; rather, it is provided or guaranteed by the presence of others. (p. 276)

To corroborate this claim, the authors draw attention to the fact that it takes other people, notably parents, to argue for the personhood of a baby—they cannot assert it themselves. Furthermore, the baby's personhood is developed 'in a kind of psychological symbiosis with the mother or other main care giver' (p. 275).

I recognise the problem, highlighted in the critiques of Kitwood's philosophy in Dewing's article, that Kitwood can be seen as disempowering the very people for whom he is trying to advocate respect and personhood. This is because he can be seen to imply that personhood is bestowed upon, or 'provided or guaranteed' for weaker people by stronger others, thus creating a power imbalance. However, his reference to 'psychological symbiosis' with other(s) offers both a satisfactory and exciting, reinterpretation, in my opinion, and one which links with both ACR and the notion of evidence, and music therapy. For it suggests that personhood is co-created between people, through an ethic of care in which the psychological as well as practical needs of each person are met.

Kitwood and Bredin describe people with dementia as 'drifting towards the threshold of unbeing' (p. 285). I find this a haunting, if poetic, statement. What is worse, is that I imagine a majority of people with dementia have lived a life full of 'being' before the onset of the disease, whereas, I am conscious that many music therapy participants, particularly those living with severe disability and/or limited or no conventional verbal communication, may have spent much of their lives in this very borderland. I recognise the 'frozen' thinking upon which much of our social life and many of our healthcare institutions in the UK are built: people with high care needs are in many ways hidden away, either because the built environment is simply not accessible, or because their care is concentrated in a fixed, closed location for reasons of logistics, optimising resources, safety or habit.

*Personhood and ACR*

How, then, can ACR respond to this? And how is this related to evidence? These seem important questions, because other music therapists have fostered concepts of personhood, for example Procter in non-medical mental health care (2001 Example section), Stige and Aarø with regard to kinds of respect in Community Music Therapy (2011, p. 190), Ansdell with a focus on the mutuality of personhood (2014, p. 100). However, for these researcher-practitioners, the interest in personhood seems to be as a guiding principle, rather than as evidence in therapy.

Kitwood and Bredin give examples of the flourishing of personhood (1992, pp. 281–2) when the 'context' is one of 'psychological abundance, where interdependence is openly acknowledged, and where people exist mainly in a fluid rather than a frozen state' (p. 286). They regard this as 'an epitome of how to be human' (p. 286). Although it is not explicitly stated, there is an implication that the personhood of *all* parties must necessarily flourish in these contexts.

From wide experience of this care, Kitwood and Bredin extrapolate 12 indicators of relative wellness of the person, or their personhood. From a critical realist perspective, which asks 'what must the world be like for *x* or *y* to happen?', I perceive that psychologically symbiotic care is therefore a generative mechanism of flourishing personhood. Indeed, from his critical realist viewpoint, I believe that Christian Smith is describing this phenomenon in the following comments, which are equally applicable to *all* parties involved in the co-creation of personhood:

> Personhood is emergent from the interactive operation of a host of human causal capacities, which themselves are rooted in the natural human body. But once emergent as existent realities, persons by nature become active participants in their own self-creation and continuation. Persons—as living, organic, "spiritual" selves—must be sustained, nourished, cultivated. And persons themselves are the most important agents in their own personal sustenance. (2011, p. 70)[19]

I will return now to Wilson's three components of aesthetic experience (2020) (1) encountering a phenomenon (2) awareness of being-in-relation (of the structures of things) (3) a valuing response.

If symbiotic care is the phenomenon encountered, and participants become aware of structuring their selves (being-in-relation), and value this, then it is reasonable to argue that aesthetic experience has taken place. Indeed, it suggests that symbiotic care provides *opportunity* for aesthetic experience. But you may argue that we were not discussing aesthetic experience, we were considering personhood. And here is a deeply significant convergence of concepts in this book: when aesthetic experience leads to 'self-creation' then it is an experience of personhood.

*Re-defining Wilson's 'Aesthetic Experience' as 'Therapeutic Experience'*

At this point, I wish to deliberately adopt the term 'therapeutic experience' in place of 'aesthetic experience'.[20] This is for two reasons. Firstly, I

[19] Smith (2011) approaches his analysis of a 'person' from a personalist philosophical perspective (pp. 102–4) which has less focus on the relational space in between persons than is the case in my study.

[20] I have searched around a dozen major handbooks and summaries of music therapy as well as a number of foundational works on psychotherapy and have not found the term

understand Wilson's concept of aesthetic experience to be one which *can* arise in the context of passive or active engagement with art making, but which can also occur in a host of other contexts which afford encountering a phenomenon, being-in-relation with and having awareness of this, and valuing, but which are not 'artistic'. For this reason, I believe the term 'aesthetic' can be unhelpful in the context of music therapy, because of the baggage it carries, relating to Western, elitist concepts of good and bad artefacts. Secondly, I believe that the encountering of a phenomenon, being-in-relation and having awareness of this, and valuing, that Wilson describes actually correspond to the concept held by music-centred music therapy practitioners that the locus of the therapy *lies in the music making itself*. In other words, when a music-centred music therapist claims that they use 'music *as* therapy' (as opposed to 'music *in* therapy' or 'intervention *through* music'—see Chap. 1, Section "Direct Message 2"), I believe that Wilson's theory of aesthetic experience accounts for *how* this happens. I am taking my time with this point because it is so central to the topic of this book. In fact, it *is* the topic of this book.

If aesthetic experience, according to Wilson's definition, clearly corresponds to therapeutic experience in music-centred music therapy, does it also correspond in any way to the experience of personhood according to Bredin and Kitwood's definition? This seems far-fetched, as an idea, until I reflect on what such a correspondence would mean: in essence, it would simply mean that these differently named experiences actually have the same fundamental properties because they share the same generative mechanism. And this mechanism simply involves the co-occurrence of encountering a phenomenon (symbiotic care, rendered musically or otherwise), being-in-relation (with this (musical) care, self and other) and having awareness of this, and valuing.[21]

'therapeutic experience' directly addressed and defined, with the exception of R.D. Laing who devotes a chapter to 'The Psychotherapeutic Experience' from the point of view of the psychotherapist ([1967] 1990, Chapter 2).

[21] Kitwood and Bredin (1992) provide a vignette for each of the 12 indicators of relative wellness, in which D denotes someone living with dementia, and C denotes carer. An analysis of any one of them has revealed that these three 'parts' of aesthetic/therapeutic experience are present (phenomenon-relation-valuing). For example, 'C is feeling low in spirits, for reasons that have nothing to do with her work situation. Mrs. D comes close to her, looks her in the face, and says 'You're not so good today, dear, are you?' C squeezes her hand, and says 'I 'm feeling a bit sad, Mrs. D, but I'm here'. Mrs. D smiles and squeezes C's hand. Somehow Mrs. D seems to understand' (p. 281 vignette no 5). Here, Mrs. D encounters emotional communication from the carer (phenomenon) and reveals an approach motiva-

*The Concept of Evidence in ACR*

At this point, I want to introduce the theme of evidence.

M: Halleluyah!

R: Why d' you say that? Please don't interrupt right now.

M: Humble apologies. I just thought we'd never get there. Do continue…

There is now an encouraging confluence of essential concepts in this study, owing to the shared generative mechanism that occurs in experience of personhood and therapeutic experience. Evidence, therapeutic experience and personhood have become to some extent interchangeable: I find I cannot choose between the following two clarifying statements, for both seem to be true:

Personhood is evidence of therapeutic experience
Therapeutic experience is evidence of personhood

Wilson does not explore the notion of evidence in *The Space that Separates*. Therefore, because it lies at the heart of my topic, it is necessary to theorise myself what sort of phenomenon evidence is, and what generative mechanism might explain it.[22] And I am finding that it is self-explanatory: where the content or focus of evidence is experience, then the two concepts become synonymous—an experience *is* evidence of that experience; evidence of experience *is* de facto evidence.

MT: Wait! That sounds neat, but who says that the content of music therapy evidence is experience?

tion to the emotional communication (valuing), showing this in her physical movement and question (being-in-relation with the phenomenon). The carer reassures Mrs. D through words and a hand squeeze and Mrs. D reassures the carer through a smile and reciprocal hand squeeze (being-in-relation with one another). We are told 'somehow Mrs. D seems to understand' (awareness of this being-in-relation). As an emotionally intelligent human being, Mrs. D has a positive experience that affirms her personhood. Furthermore, C also experiences relational, emotional communication, as well as an approach motivation (valuing) towards the encounter (the squeezing of Mrs. D's hand) and therefore arguably also has an experience of personhood.

[22] I will not attempt to do this for every kind of evidence: legal evidence implies a certain accumulation of facts, artefacts, phenomena and theories; closed design positivist research trials require observable evidence of an effect of a particular variable.

R: No-one, yet, but that's what this book is about!

MT: OK, signpost us a bit … would you?

R: Look,—We have gone through how Kitwood's concept of personhood can be seen as therapeutic experience.

MT: Yes, I know, but there's something missing…

R: The only thing that's missing is whether aesthetic, or therapeutic, experience and personhood MATTER. Music therapy seems to offer a purpose built opportunity for therapeutic experience and flourishing of personhood. If we can show that this matters, then we can map therapeutic experience/personhood onto the four cycles of experience, look and listen for how they arise in sessions, and—bingo!—that IS evidence in music therapy—evidence of therapeutic experience, or, and, personhood.

MT: I think you're part of the way there, but this either-or approach to therapeutic experience and personhood is misleading. Don't you see?—

R: No. Not at all. They have become the same, inseparable. This IS what matters. We talked about social structures keeping some music therapy participants at the 'threshold of unbeing' and these aren't just emotive words,—we have seen it, all of us. Getting alongside participants and using, or offering, Wilson's kind of aesthetic experience in shared music making—it's the *same thing* as offering symbiotic care to foster personhood. It's just that the symbiotic care is musical.

C: …and we're back to care…

R: You're right, Carer—

C: And in music therapy, this all happens nonverbally, it's arts-based. That's the knowing you care about isn't it?

R: I do.

M: Well, and me, and music therapist. You, too, Carer?

C: Yes, of course.

MT: So, what happens with evidence?

R: The confusion is around perspectives … I mean, from whose perspective are we looking for evidence? If it's from the collaborating participants' perspective, then the experience *is* the evidence and you can hear it and see it and plot it onto the four phases of experience … But—and this is the hub of things—if someone external is looking for evidence, then that evidence can't possibly be that person experiencing personhood,—they're not even there in the music making. So in their eyes, the experience remains just somebody else's experience, whether it was of personhood, or reggae, or drumming. They just don't count it as evidence.

M: That's a massive problem.

MT: Tell me about it. Decades of bashing my head against a brick wall and measuring things that don't seem to matter.

*Pause.*

M: I'm exhausted. You haven't even talked about your beloved mobile.

R: *Our* beloved mobile. Are you being sarcastic?

M: No, actually, I really do love it.

R: Oh, thanks. OK then, I'm going to think about culture.

C: Culture?

*Defining Culture Within This Enquiry*

It is beyond the scope of this investigation to explore the rich traditions of social scientific and philosophical thought on the topic of culture. Instead, I am drawn to Wilson's definition, particularly as it relates to his conceptualising of aesthetic experience and art. He proposes that

> culture is … our collective system (or systems) of value recognition. (2020, p. 137)

And he emphatically critiques the notion that culture is the sum of 'the arts' and their 'artefacts', whose value is monetary and market driven. Nor does he accept that culture is the product of our ways of being, as a particular group of people.[23]

Instead, if culture is defined by 'systems of value recognition', then it must at least on some level be consciously generated by the actors within it. Importantly, Wilson's definition easily embraces the notion of culture on a grand scale, i.e. in the context of a whole nation, as well as on a micro scale, as in the case of a swimming club or the music therapy profession.

MT: Researcher?

R: Yes?

MT: I want to talk about the poems and stories and vignettes. It feels important to illustrate some of these ideas.

R: It's OK—I can do that for you...

MT: No, actually, I'd like to join your Direct Message. Because ... *I* was the music therapist in the stories, remember?

R: Of course. OK. Go ahead. I'll be right here.

Dear Collaborator—this is Music Therapist. I find the apparently simple phrase 'systems of value recognition' enormously helpful in *explaining* culture. Looking back, most of the vignettes, poems and stories that I have written for this research in some way explore, even confront, the cultures of music therapy that I have experienced in the UK, as seen from Wilson's perspective. Carless and Douglas highlight this very potential: the process of reflexive storytelling creates a space for discovering and articulating the

[23] Chapter 7 of '*The Space that Separates*' is devoted to Wilson's in-depth analysis of different assumptions that lie behind the vernacular use of the term 'culture'. He identifies '...three main meanings ... [which] ... frame culture as (1) *process*—a general process of intellectual, spiritual and aesthetic development; (2) *ways of being*—whether of a people, a group, or humanity in general; or as (3) *art(s)*—the works and practices of intellectual and especially artistic activity' (2020, p. 130). Meaning (1) underpins the usage of the word 'cultured', as in 'she is a cultured woman'. Meaning (2) lies behind the concept of 'British culture', for example. Meaning (3) is implicit in the notion of the 'cultural life of a city', or 'high culture'. None of these correspond to Wilson's definition.

relationships between what we value and what we actually do (2011, pp. 8–9). In the case of *Moon*, my intuitive writing highlighted the juxtaposition of prevailing medical-educational concepts, with the relational context of music therapy: 'Your file is/ Full of labels./ What for?/ Are they trying to/ Traffic-light/ Parts of/ How you are?' My response as a music therapist is 'You are/ Emphatically/ You', which although it may seem personal and uncomplicated, actually contains my objection to a system that recognises and values norms of attainment and behaviour.

A similar tension is evident in Anna's story, 'Am I somebody?' Here, my acute discomfort surfaces when, as therapist on a fictionalised hospital ward that is resistant to religious expression, I become aware that the only thing Anna *can* coherently communicate is her prayer—'You are praying/ This, your soul remembers'. However, I do not feel allowed to engage with this according to the values recognised in the systematic life of the ward, and as a consequence, I feel 'Slow burn/ Anger now./ "Careful on the ward"./ "Not your job"/ "Not appropriate"./ Now I want to roar, implore, lament/ "What is left?"'

### *'Loosening' the Cultures of Music Therapy Through* Chloe's Story

#### Who Is Looking for Evidence of What?

Stuart Wood identifies that the problem of evaluating community music therapy, so as to produce evidence, lies in the issues of '*what* ... *when* ... [and] ... *who*' to evaluate, because 'music destabilises the professional requirement of evaluation. Its multiplicity—that changing, emergent, multi-modal quality—makes simple evaluation difficult' (2013, pp. 294–5).

What, then, can be learnt of the cultures of music therapy through the stories I share, including my own autoethnographic one, and Wilson's definition? Immediately apparent is a dislocation between the work I want to do as a music therapist and the restrictions and priorities of the settings I am working in. Critical realist authors Pawson and Tilley (1997) emphasise that evaluation is entirely dependent upon context-specific notions of what constitutes success. This is most starkly evident in *Chloe's Story*. Here, nine different fictionalised characters respond to the fictionalised event: although the event is fictionalised, such devastating incidents are sadly too commonly represented in the caseloads of many music therapists. The differences in characters' attitudes are striking and range from the instinctual, as shown by Danny (toddler) and Chloe (mother) who is in a low awareness state, to the pragmatic as demonstrated by Mike (father) and Callum (partner), to the hopeful-spiritual as seen in Tina (mother), Kim (sister) and the music therapist (me), to the expert-informed as conveyed by Dr JJ (Senior Rehabilitation Therapist), to the rigid-responsible as seen in Maya (Finance Director).

There are agendas at play for each of these, whether acknowledged or not. The family and music therapist are looking for hope, such that they can at least imagine a way of being with Chloe throughout her possibly long future life as a severely disabled person. Dr JJ is motivated by rigour: what claims can the music therapist make for her work, given the apparently spurious nature of her observations? How does this sit within the painstaking professional practice of the multidisciplinary team? Maya is unequivocal: the onerous task of maintaining the financial viability of a publicly funded service falls to her. There are tried and tested ways to manage the service and she is under enormous pressure to follow them and thereby meet the vast need of patients.

Each of these positions is founded upon a notion of evidence. For the family, there is visual and audible evidence of their beloved Chloe's participation. It is not of the slightest importance that this is a tiny participation in the scheme of things—merely the turning of the head. The significance and excitement lie in the fact that she *has* turned her head, and is therefore participating in a new kind of relationship with them all. The evidence is partly that of the movement, but more importantly, it is *evidence of possibility*.

Meanwhile, the evidence that Dr JJ is looking for is the measured and measureable proof of function, on Chloe's part, in response to the given stimulus—in this case, a specific aspect of music therapy. This is entirely consistent with the purpose of neurological rehabilitation, which seeks to facilitate as much independent function as possible in order to assess a patient's potential for independent living.

Maya, on the other hand, as Finance Director is looking for evidence of a type which is multidisciplinary and only indirectly specific to Chloe: she requires the team to collaborate and produce evidence of Chloe's current level of functioning, as assessed by the entire team and not by a single therapy, and in the context of the spectrum of function in neurological rehabilitation, per se. This will affect Maya's stewardship of financial resources and the evidence of this stewardship will be seen in balance sheets.

As music therapist, I am looking for evidence of engagement and, in ACR terms, of therapeutic experience/experience of personhood.

## Recognising Evidence: Insiders and Outsider-Observers

The actors in this story are clearly not seeking evidence of the same things. Nor are these different kinds of evidence recognised in the same manner. For Chloe, for her family and for me, it was only possible to find evidence of personhood, therapeutic experience, hope or possibility, as *insiders,* i.e. from 'subjective' and 'inter-subjective' perspectives (Wilber, 2001 cited in Abrams, 2010, p. 354): if we had not been present, we would not have found that evidence, because we needed to *experience* the emerging personhood of Chloe. Furthermore, it was our shared *awareness of* being-in-relation to self, other and music, and our approach-avoidance motivation (our valuing) that made this shared experience therapeutic, and important enough to want to repeat it.

However, Dr JJ and Maya were not present: there was no expectation that they would be. And their primary concern was not personhood. Therefore, as outsiders, in professional roles that necessitated this positioning, they were not in a position to, or required to, grasp the evidence that was shared by the session attendees. Furthermore, as outsiders, they had no insider opportunity to *value* this evidence and sought different evidence from 'objective' and 'inter-objective' perspectives (Wilber, 2001).

All these attitudes to evidence are entirely valid and the commitment to meeting Chloe's needs is undisputed in all parties. However, this discussion highlights a daily reality for music therapists: the things we believe to be of value in our work with participants and their carers are at times not valued as priorities by those in charge of the settings, or services, in which we work (DeNora & Ansdell, 2014, pp. 1, 7–8). More than this, what we value can actually be disallowed in certain circumstances, or even recognised and shared, but still not regarded as evidence by other professionals (Ansdell, 2017, p. 126).

## What Part Does Experience Play in Evidence in Music Therapy?

As mentioned, in this analysis of what evidence can be *of* in music therapy, I am struck by this realisation that Dr JJ and Maya are seeking evidence of function that relies upon outsider-produced external measures, which in turn provide the focus for outside-observer measurement. Although every part of what is measured must necessarily have been experienced by the patient, the *experiential* dimension of function is not overtly acknowledged by these stakeholders. However, the family and music therapist are not essentially seeking evidence of anything pre-determined. Instead, they engage in activities which provide experiences from an insider perspective, and these experiences are all about being-in-relation. I have not previously conceptualised the insider/outsider status in any detail, or in this way.

It could be argued that the participants in Chloe's therapy session are quasi outsiders as they observe Chloe apparently responding to a musical stimulus, and it is true that this observation happens and is essential in the unfolding episode. However, they are in the room and the therapeutic experience occurs through their shared being-in-relation. The sense of possibility, hope, and imagination of a future, which all the family members acknowledge, is not the result of outsider observation, but experienced *between* all the participants. Wilson defines this as metacognition (2020, p. 61). Because the phenomenon of music making has been received with approach motivation by all (positive valuing), and all have become aware of their relatedness to music, self and other, I suggest that what all the family members and the therapist experience is a therapeutic experience of personhood, their own and each other's.

Conceptualising therapeutic experience in this manner helps explain a dimension of the work that therapists often encounter, namely that the informal carers who attend with their loved ones often describe benefitting personally from the sessions, and experiencing wellbeing.

*What Values Are Evident in the Search for Evidence in Music Therapy?*
Wilson proposes that the approach-avoidance motivation, which is the generative mechanism of value, can remain unexercised, or become exercised as a movement towards or away from a stimulus (Chap. 5). But Wilson does not impose a moral dimension on this understanding: we might move towards or away from something because of want or need, but he is not attempting to identify 'right, wrong, good, or bad' in the field of value. Another critical realist philosopher, Andrew Sayer, suggests that our values are our 'sedimented valuations that have become attitudes or dispositions, which we come to regard as justified' (2000, p. 25). This image of sedimentation pre-dates Wilson's conceptualisation, but provides a useful suggestion of how our repeated movement towards or away from a given stimulus might become 'sedimented' into a more enduring 'value'.

Both these descriptions of value emphasise the idea that values are the product of valuing, and that valuing is something we do because it is relevant to us personally, not because it is a moral requirement. It is, of course, possible to hold deeply unhelpful values according to this definition, for someone could value self-harm, or driving exceptionally fast, with all the associated risks to self and others. However, in music therapy, the context is interpersonal encounter—being-in-relation in music—and the activity is giving shareable form to this therapeutic experience. Whilst harmful values are sometimes expressed in this work, for example there can be unsafely loud beating of percussion instruments, throwing of instruments, spitting and more, nevertheless the structures of music assert their own demands which can help in the search for re-experiencing and re-valuing the situation. Given the fact that shared music making is often a new experience for music therapy participants, from Sayer's perspective it could be argued that values would not yet be sedimented, or formed. However, I believe it is reasonable to argue that 'valuing' can occur in completely new situations and for that reason I feel it is a more useful term than 'value' in this study.

*What Systems of Value Recognition Operate in the Field of Music Therapy?*

This is a pivotal question for this study. Wood explores approaches to the evaluation of Community Music Therapy, developing a 'matrix' as a conceptual tool to help therapists consider the multiple discourses that occur in music therapy work. In the case study material Wood presents from a care home, he identifies seventeen possible discourses that coexist, or collide, in Community Music Therapy, encompassing foci as varied as 'personal biographical', 'sales', 'nursing', 'music specialism', 'management' and others (2016, pp. 104–121). This finding is significant for my own study, for it implies a corresponding number of systems of value recognition: for example, in Wood's work, music therapy was valuable to the director of learning and development because of the potential for successful 'knowledge sharing' (p. 115). Whereas, it was valuable to the housekeeping assistant because it was audible right throughout the building, giving others a chance to hear the participant 'being different from usual' (p. 109).

Whilst this is interesting and thought provoking, the values described are still individual, and/or role specific. The step from this to a 'system of value recognition' is a separate consideration. There was clearly a tacit, or explicit, valuing of shared music making by the people in the setting. Perhaps it was management-led, perhaps it grew from the people living and working in the home, perhaps from a combination of the two, or maybe from family feedback. For a music therapist, the absence of resistiveness to our practice can be tantamount to an explicit valuing of the work. Whatever the case may be, the system of value recognition which was clearly at play in the care home Wood describes was manifest in a great variety of behaviours—the allowing of the rearrangement of furniture; not complaining about noise; providing equipment; celebrating music therapy in PR; citing music therapy in sales material; expecting that music therapy could enrich the lives of residents and offer knowledge and skills to the staff. I suggest that all of these behaviours amount to a 'shared system of value recognition' in the home. Furthermore, if culture is the product of shared systems of value recognition, then it is fair to say that the culture of the care home was one which facilitated and celebrated shared music making and what it could bring to the lives of all involved.

### *What Can Be Understood of the Culture of Chloe's Rehabilitation Home?*

In Chloe's fictional rehabilitation home, the situation was very different. The prevalent valuing that happened in this setting was concerned with the body of medical and academic-therapeutic knowledge that underpins neurological rehabilitation. Furthermore, accountability was exceptionally highly valued and all staff were fully conscious of the part they had to play in this. It is essential to stress that the ethos was undoubtedly one of care: the working hours were very long, the toll on emotional resources wrought by continual proximity to tragedy was acute, yet staff members were highly caring and conscientious.

However, whilst individual staff members clearly recognised the humanity of the patients, attempts to engage with the spiritual and interpersonal dimensions of the patients' lives were tacitly regarded as 'off script'. To use Kitwood and Bredin's terms, the staff in this setting were operating from a 'frozen' mindset, possibly to avoid distress. As a result, the culture of the home was clinical and impersonal. It is unsurprising that the music therapist's attempt to foster the personhood of Chloe and her family was met with some alarm, mistrust and even fear. Furthermore, I suggest that whilst care was uppermost in the intentions of the team, their model of care was not closely aligned to an ethic of care, as I understand it (that is, giving from a place of humility with no expectation to receive in return). This is because the practices of the home were essentially transactional, not relational: the focus was somewhat contractual, whereby the staff team guaranteed to be highly accountable in delivering best practice therapies and in return expected the compliance and collaboration of the resident and their carers.

### *What Can Be Learnt from* Chloe's Story *about the Cultures of Music Therapy?*

I wish to re-emphasise that I am a music therapist who has worked in the UK for the last twenty-six years. In this chapter I am therefore considering 'what counts' and 'cultures of music therapy' with regard to what I have seen 'counting' in the 'cultures of music therapy' in the UK. The music therapy literature suggests that there are many shared motivations, principles and practices to be found in the music therapy work that happens around the world. I have found literature from Scandinavia, Australia and Israel that seems particularly aligned. It is clear that local social attitudes and histories will shape the discrete music therapy cultures in all regions, and that some may therefore appear very different. However, I am emboldened to share this case study of my experiences of UK cultures of music therapy and what counts, because I think it is likely to find resonances in other music therapy professions in Western or Westernised countries, and where it does not resonate I hope it inspires thoughtful reflection. I will not repeat 'in the UK' when I use these terms, but please bear this in mind.

So, what *can* be learnt from *Chloe's Story* about the cultures of music therapy? This is a difficult and uncomfortable question for a practitioner-researcher. As the music therapist in this story, I encountered an overwhelming personal integrity demand, which required me to validate the therapeutic experience of personhood which I believed had taken place. However, given the context, I translated this into functional, measurable evidence (I verbally reported the repeated turning of Chloe's head) in my feedback to the Senior Rehabilitation Therapist. Because of the fundamental necessity for all evidence to be validated by the whole team, and no others had seen this response, my evidence was rejected. This in turn resulted in a crisis of care for me, Chloe and her family: I followed instructions to deny the significance of the turned head, and the result was my own 'dis-integration', loss of hope for the family, loss of facilitating environment for the nourishing of personhood for Chloe and her loved ones, and frustration and exasperation for two staff members at the home, which even threatened the continuation of the music therapy provision.

The question remains whether this was an isolated incident of misaligned thought and expectation, or whether it reveals something more about the cultures of music therapy. I believe the latter is true.

### *The Cultures of Music Therapy I Have Experienced*

I want to emphasise that I do not believe there is a single culture of music therapy. Instead, I think there are likely to be micro cultures which grow from stakeholders' gradual, shared valuing of certain things in certain contexts, and from the development of systems for recognising and endorsing what is valued. For example, having worked in several pre-school settings and discussed this client group with music therapy colleagues with similar experience, and having read music therapy literature about the same, I suggest that there is culture of pre-school music therapy in which developmental progress is systematically valued through linear goal setting and outcome measurement, but in which child-led exploration and expectation of change are also valued. This system of valuing is recognised by practitioners through their ongoing work in this model and is also endorsed and perpetuated in music therapy training.

By contrast, my nine years as a music therapist in a hospice, and associated engagement with this strand of the music therapy profession, persuades me that what counts in this work is a profoundly person-centred, in the moment approach, which acknowledges a wide range of factors within the session, from creativity, to grief, play, spirituality and legacy making. Again, this is corroborated by writing on the subject which itself contributes to a recognising and systematising of this valuing (Hartley, 2001).

However, although I believe there can be approach-specific, setting-specific and client-group-specific cultures in music therapy, I do also think there are areas and instances of valuing within the profession as a whole that have become recognised and systematised into resultant, overarching music therapy cultures. With *Chloe's Story*, the other poems and vignettes, and my autoethnographic story as a backdrop, I have the following observations about these overarching cultures of music therapy.

### Chameleon Culture

My own experience as a practitioner leaves me in no doubt that we have a tendency to 'cave in' under pressure from other quarters. For example, our profession has an increasingly robust body of research, and clear theoretical foundations. However, in spite of this, I know from my own practice and from supervision with others that situations frequently arise in which we give way to competing attitudes. These attitudes may be ignorant, mis-informed, reasonable or just different, yet I believe that the therapist in us often seeks to honour the other person's standpoint, whilst the practitioner in us can feel disempowered when confronted with outsider-observer criticism or misunderstanding. As a consequence, I believe that we have developed a chameleon culture in music therapy, whereby we adapt our 'colours' to suit the prevailing thinking framework of the setting in which we work. Whilst this may be a pragmatic solution in a setting with a relatively 'fluid' mindset, it can be calamitous when the mindset is 'frozen', as *Chloe's Story* illustrates.

**Aspects of 'Frozen' Culture**

Following from the first observation, because of the dominance of 'frozen' thinking within our education and care institutions, as identified by Kitwood and Bredin, the prevailing thinking frameworks from these spheres which compete with our indigenous music therapy ideas tend to favour outcomes that are measurable by outside-observers: finding value as an insider involves a fluid mindset that is open to interpersonal and relational encounter. As a result, these outcome-driven expectations can powerfully inhibit the awareness of being-in-relation, which I argue is of such great potential value to music therapy participants. By meeting these outsider expectations, music therapy stakeholders are thus in danger of creating a 'frozen' culture of our own. The supervisee role I adopt in the story *Supervision* highlights this tension.

**Culture of Tension and Confusion**

Thirdly, and worse than this, we can find ourselves at the same time fostering therapeutic experience of personhood, yet failing to communicate this as valuable to our commissioners or in any way persuade them that it counts. In this way, we create and perpetuate a culture of tension and confusion. This undoubtedly matters, because participants such as Moon, Mehdi and the autistic boy in *Communication Difficulties* can have their music therapy discontinued if they fail to show evidence of developmental or functional improvement. Yet in the relational sphere, they may have powerfully communicated aspects of their personhood in audible musical form, and music therapy may be the only context which is conducive to this experience.

**Transactional Culture**

Fourthly, our historic tendency to adopt some of the priorities and 'frozen' thinking that have prevailed in medical models of care and in psychotherapy[24] has resulted in some profoundly transactional approaches. For example, we typically require consent forms from people attending therapy. They should be signed by the participant, or their carer if this is not possible. Technically, they can be revisited and consent withdrawn, however, this rarely happens. Instead, in effect the setting providing therapy uses the consent as a kind of insurance against complaint. Indeed, we actually are legally required to insure ourselves against our clients. I do not

[24] See Aigen (2014, pp. 18–22).

believe this is appropriate. The added dimension of asking music therapy participants who lack the ability to sign, to do so or be signed for, pales by comparison. Academia can also uphold some 'frozen' attitudes, in my experience, and in both these strands of my working life—as practitioner and researcher—I find a transactional culture deeply puzzling and uncomfortable.

### Culture of Ableism, Notwithstanding Growing Anti-Oppressive Awareness

Connected to the last point, I am concerned that music therapy actually has a culture of ableism in certain respects. I perceive the root of this as lying in the illness ideology that dominates Western healthcare, whereby 'the biopolitical state … makes its population sick by turning it into a mass of patients' (Groys, 2022, p. 34), and which has permeated music therapy in the UK (Rolvsjord, 2010, Chapters 1–2). In many contexts, music therapists adopt the role of experts (Flower, 2019, pp. 149–155, 234–239) because in many settings and models of music therapy, this is the presumed identity.[25] When this starting point is combined with some 'frozen', transactional thinking around care and illness and the need for outsider-observer evidence, it follows that the expert therapist will take control of the participant's journey: reasons for referral will be sought from other experts, the therapist will set goals, monitor them, measure progress and finally report on the participant in academic-style language that is often not meaningful to participants. These goals are typically focused on normative, ableist notions of what health and wellness are, and much emphasis is often placed on changing the participant's presentation (Groys, 2022, p. 3). This process also perpetuates a marked power imbalance between participant and music therapist, which is explored in the short story *Supervision* through the supervisee's discussion of Tyler. This is not limited to decision making regarding goals and reporting, but is present on a much deeper and systemic level whenever a therapist comes from a heritage, socio-economic, musical, age or gender background of privilege or non-marginalisation.

This is a gross over simplification of highly nuanced processes, undertaken on a case by case basis by deeply committed people, in most instances.

[25] In Community Music Therapy the role of music therapist is characterised by 'responsiveness' and 'responsibility' rather than by 'expert decisions informed by diagnostic information about the pathology of the individual' (Stige & Aarø, 2011, pp. 166–7).

Furthermore, there are clear examples where a music therapist, or a whole setting or service, have taken a stance against the illness ideology and expert persona: Procter describes how these things 'do not exist' at a setting he works in (2004, p. 219), and O'Grady and McFerran advocate 'Saying "No" to Referral Processes' (2006, p. 75). Nevertheless, although my recent conversations with newly qualified therapists and those in training[26] revealed a powerful growing awareness of multiple forms of oppression and the urgent need for the music therapy profession to engage with these issues, I observed the focus to be more on attitudes to music and to marginalised people working in the profession, rather than on the tried and tested expert-led practices we perpetuate as practitioners and which I argue foster ableist attitudes. Furthermore, Gilbertson (2019) firmly critiques such practices from a queer perspective, adding a 'nervousness' (p. 7) to my awareness:

> It seems to me that there is a dangerous innocence being acted-out concerning the use of behavioral/psychological/physiological/pathological attributes coded in terminology and textual (words and numbers) claims in music therapy. It is a severe power of responsibility to determine what another person is through one's own choice of terminology and terms of reference. Acts of oppressive codification are rife, and the field of music therapy has only fairly recently intensified in challenging potentially oppressive processes in research, practice, and education. (p. 17)

R: *(To Music Therapist)* That's pretty tough, you know, what you are saying there.

MT: Is that how it comes across?

R: Well, yes! Are you surprised? Music therapists are ableist, oppressive, frozen, confused...

MT: Uh ... no, please don't see it like that...

R: How, then?

MT: I'm trying to get at the systems of value recognition, because I do agree with Wilson that these are what define a culture. All I'm say-

[26] These conversations took place at the European Music Therapy Conference 2022 in Edinburgh, Scotland.

ing is that music therapists, *and others engaging in the field*,—so, commissioners, other professionals in the settings we work in, funders, other social scientists and natural scientists,—together we endorse certain things in certain situations in ways that amount to a system of value recognition.

R: Such as…?

MT: *(Looking frustrated)* … everything we've just been talking about!.... goal setting, assessment, measuring, reporting, insurance, being an expert, all that stuff. By agreeing to do things in the ways we do, all of us are basically saying 'this is what we value', or 'this is our culture'. We might not be aware we are agreeing, or we might actually *not* agree, but do it anyway—and that is the confusion and tension bit—but by doing it we are endorsing it, saying and showing that it counts in the world of music therapy.

R: *(Pause, thinking)* Then, in that case, the bit of the culture of music therapy that stands out most for me is just that: tension and confusion. Do you agree that you can have different systems of value recognition going on within one culture?

MT: Yes, of course. There will be valuing going on about all sorts of things, all at the same time.

*Long pause.*

R: I'm sorry, Music Therapist. I feel as if I've waded into a sore point.

MT: No, don't worry. It's in plain sight. I mean, when I was training in the '90s, there was a sort of cold war going on between psychodynamic approaches and music centred ones.

R: I know. That's a bit strong, calling it a cold war, isn't it?

MT: Probably. We've come a long way since then. What I'm worried about now is that the new generation of therapists coming through are so, so angry.

R: *All* of them?

MT: I don't know … no, of course not, … but some…

R: ...about what…

MT: About the in-built oppressive thinking and practice that the profession is built on—I think that's how they see it.

R: And how do you see it?

MT: I think they're right. Maybe. A lot of right. So much needs to change. People are hurting so badly,[27] whether they are practitioners, participants, people in supporting roles. There is a tidal wave of sadness and anger about the injustice that people of privilege have meted out on people with less power. It's not just in music therapy, it's in life as a whole,—you know that. And it's so overdue. It's right and it needs to happen. But it hurts and grates so much more in a profession that is claiming to do good.

R: So, why the 'maybe'?

MT: I don't mean that. All I mean is that some of us have been grafting for years, and others for decades, just to get music therapy on the map at all. It has been a fantastic working life in terms of time spent with participants. It is such a profound privilege. But I've found it quite soul destroying in other ways: people thinking you are fluffy and fringe; managers seriously suggesting that you come and work as a volunteer after they discontinue your post; co-workers sighing and rolling their eyes, even shouting at you, throwing things once; working in broom cupboards. And now the next generation is shouting at us for being patriarchal, biased, and perpetuating privilege and injustice … but we had to start somewhere—we tried to fit in just to get anything done at all … we can't cancel out all the good … Maybe I'm just tired … But they're right, … we've allowed a system to grow that can hurt people…

[27] See British Association of Music Therapy Diversity Report (Langford et al., 2020).

R: Yes. I don't know what to say.

M: I do. I say, you are trying to share what you love—music, the way *you* do it. It's got ten tons of baggage, but I think people recognise sincerity and authenticity. We can't stop. Imagine if everyone of privilege stopped sharing what they love and believe to be of value. Dire. It's the *sharing* that matters.

MT: You might be right. Do you mind if I go for a while?

C: Take a break. Caring is exhausting.

MT: I'm not caring. I'm not a carer. I can't even claim *that* moral high ground.

C: I'd say you are. You've just got a bit frozen. There will be time to think that through. Take a break.

*MT goes out.*

Dear Collaborator, this is Researcher again. I know I have already greeted you at the start of this message, but it feels a long time ago. I have found it particularly hard to avoid producing what Music Therapist termed a 'lecture' in this chapter, mainly because the ideas explored will be new to music therapists, I expect, and I very much want to do justice to Wilson, ACR and the notions of experience, culture and valuing that his thinking can offer to the field of music therapy. Plus, when the context is music therapy, it is vital that the overlap or inseparability of these concepts with the experience and fostering of personhood is recognised and considered.

And what has all this to do with nonverbal and arts-based knowing? Everything!

I am feeling, and imagine you might also be noticing, that this research has reached a sensitive point. Rather than tell you about the next message, which will in any case explain itself I hope, I will therefore close this message. Again, I would like to thank you for your time and patience. I have personally felt excited by the contributions of ACR to music therapy, but am mindful that the Roles have different histories and priorities and may find certain of the explorations more or less comfortable.

With best wishes,
Researcher

C: Researcher?

R: Oh hi, Carer—

C: Just a few things … You haven't talked about Musician's quote.

R: True. The quote … it's when Hamlet has seen his father's ghost and wants to persuade his friend Horatio that it really happened, but Horatio reckons it's imaginary. So, Hamlet says 'there are more things in heaven and earth, Horatio, than are dreamt of in your philosophy'.

C: Yes, I know, it's at the top!

R: But I didn't want to go into the ins and outs or bring in the supernatural: critical realism isn't supernatural…

C: So it just means 'listen up! We're going to search for what's not obvious'?

R: Pretty much.

C: Oh, OK. But literature search. Where's the literature search?

R: There isn't one. There are only a few studies I can find that use critical realism in music therapy research[28] and not a single one that uses ACR.

C: Oh, fair enough. But you've forgotten to talk about validity and reliability.

R: True. I'm pretty tired now. Oh never mind … I have attempted to be reliable and valid during this ACR section. But the only guidance I've found within critical realism for ensuring validity and reliability, is Sayer's 'practical adequacy',[29] oh, and for studies where evaluation

[28] See Chap. 1, Section "Direct Message 3".

[29] Sayer's notion of practical adequacy explores how theories and discourses 'relate to the constraints and opportunities of the context in which they are proposed' (2000, p. 25). A

is the focus, Pawson and Tilley[30] provide guidance, but my research isn't evaluative. Anyway, I see critical realism really as a process of unpacking *everything*: questions, answers, explorations ... there is always more underlabouring to do...

C: Do we need to do anything else, you know, to show we've thought about it?

R: I don't think so ... I've come to the conclusion that reliability, which asks whether the outcome of research could be repeated in a further study, isn't really a helpful concept in critical realism. The critical realist asks questions in order to explain things: it is unlikely that two thinkers would ask the same questions.

C: Maybe not...

R: On the other hand, validity *is* a useful notion, because it asks if a conclusion is accurate, or likely. But here our retroductive approach helps—it's designed for just that: to address validity. It's not enough to propose one generative mechanism for a phenomenon—it's expected that several explanations will be explored. The strength and safety, if you like, lie in the range of possible mechanisms that are studied. Then you can select the most 'valid' and helpful one as your conclusion, or a combination perhaps. Anyway, that's why we're using four methodological approaches. Does that help?

C: Yes, sure. Thanks, Researcher. Let's find the others.

## References

Abrams, B. (2010). Evidence-based music therapy practice: An integral understanding. *Journal of Music Therapy, 47*(4), 351–379.

practically adequate theory is one that is helpful or useful in developing knowledge, rather than one which claims to be true.

[30] *Realist Evaluation* (Pawson & Tilley, 1997).

Aigen, K. (2007). In defense of beauty: A role for the aesthetic in music therapy theory: Part I: The development of aesthetic theory in music therapy. *Nordic Journal of Music Therapy, 16*(2), 112–128.

Aigen, K. (2008). In defense of beauty: A role for the aesthetic in music therapy theory: Part II: Challenges to aesthetic theory in music therapy: Summary and response. *Nordic Journal of Music Therapy, 17*(1), 3–18.

Aigen, K. (2014). *The study of music therapy: Current issues and concepts*. Routledge.

Ansdell, G. (2014). *How music helps in music therapy and everyday life*. Ashgate Publishing, Ltd.

Ansdell, G. (2017). Practising Goethe's 'delicate empiricism' in music therapy research: Finding value and saving the phenomenon. In T. Stickley & S. Clift (Eds.), *Arts, health and wellbeing: A theoretical inquiry for practice*. Cambridge Scholars Publishing.

Archer, M. S. (2000). *Being human: The problem of agency*. Cambridge University Press.

Arstein-Kerslake, A., O'Donnell, E., Kayess, R., & Watson, J. (2021). Relational personhood: A conception of legal personhood with insights from disability rights and environmental law. *Griffith Law Review, 30*(3), 530–555. https://doi.org/10.1080/10383441.2021.2003744.

Bhaskar, R. (2016). *Enlightened common sense: The philosophy of critical realism*. Routledge.

Carless, D., & Douglas, K. (2011). Stories as personal coaching philosophy. *International Journal of Sports Science & Coaching, 6*(1), 1–12.

DeNora, T., & Ansdell, G. (2014). What can't music do? *Psychology of Well-being: Theory, Research and Practice, 4*(23), 1–10.

Dewey, J. ([1934] 2005). *Art as experience*. Perigee.

Dewing, J. (2008). Personhood and dementia: Revisiting Tom Kitwood's ideas. *International Journal of Older People Nursing, 3*(1), 3–13.

Dickens, C. ([1854] 2016). *Hard times* (Fourth international student edition, Norton critical editions). WW Norton & Company.

Flower, C. (2019). *Music therapy with children and parents: Toward an ecological attitude*. (PhD), Goldsmiths, University of London.

Frankfurt, H. G. (2004). *The reasons of love*. Princeton University Press.

Gilbertson, S. (2019). Imagining something else: A queer essay. *Voices: A World Forum for Music Therapy, 19*(3), 1–26.

gov.uk. (2023). *VATREG02100—Basic principles of registration: Legal meaning of person*. Retrieved January 13, 2023, from https://www.gov.uk/hmrc-internal-manuals/vat-registration-manual/vatreg02100

Groys, B. (2022). *Philosophy of care*. Verso Books.

Hartley, N. A. (2001). On a personal note: A music therapist's reflections on working with those who are living with a terminal illness. *Journal of Palliative Care, 17*(3), 135.

Ikäheimo, H. (2010). Making the best of what we are: Recognition as an ontological and ethical Concept. In H.-C. Schmidt am Busch & C. F. Zurn (Eds.), *The philosophy of recognition: Historical and contemporary perspectives* (pp. 350–353). Lexington Books.

Jiang, C., Liu, F., & Wong, P. C. (2017). Sensitivity to musical emotion is influenced by tonal structure in congenital amusia. *Scientific Reports, 7*, 7624. https://doi.org/10.1038/s41598-017-08005-x

Kirschenbaum, H., & Land Henderson, V. (Eds.). (1989). *The Carl Rogers reader*. Houghton Mifflin Harcourt.

Kitwood, T., & Bredin, K. (1992). Towards a theory of dementia care: Personhood and well-being. *Ageing & Society, 12*(3), 269–287.

Krumhansl, C. L., & Shepard, R. N. (1979). Quantification of the hierarchy of tonal functions within a diatonic context. *Journal of Experimental Psychology: Human Perception and Performance, 5*(4), 579. https://doi.org/10.1037/0096-1523.5.4.579. Source: PubMed.

Lahdelma, I. (2021). Separating the cultural from the universal in harmony perception. Retrieved from https://musicscience.net/2021/09/12/separating-the-cultural-from-the-universal-in-harmony-perception/

Laing, R. D. (1990). *The politics of experience and the bird of paradise*. Penguin.

Langford, A., Rizkallah, N., & Maddocks, C. (2020). *British Association of Music Therapy diversity report*. Retrieved from London: https://www.bamt.org/resources/diversity-report

Lee, C. (2003). *The architecture of aesthetic music therapy*. Barcelona Publishers.

McCormack, B., Roberts, T., Meyer, J., Morgan, D., & Boscart, V. (2012). Appreciating the 'person' in long-term care. *International Journal of Older People Nursing, 7*(4), 284–294.

Nordoff, P., & Robbins, C. (1973). *Therapy in music for handicapped children*. Victor Gollancz.

O'Grady, L., & McFerran, K. (2006). Birthing: Feminist community music therapy, the progeny of community music therapy practice and feminist therapy theory. In S. Hadley (Ed.), *Feminist perspectives in music therapy* (pp. 63–80). Barcelona Publishers.

Pawson, R., & Tilley, N. (1997). *Realistic evaluation*. SAGE Publications Ltd.

Procter, S. (2001). Empowering and enabling—Music therapy in non-medical mental health provision. *Contemporary Voices in Music Therapy*. https://doi.org/10.15845/voices.v1i2.58

Procter, S. (2004). Playing politics: Community music therapy and the therapeutic redistribution of musical capital for mental health. In M. Pavlicevic & G. Ansdell (Eds.), *Community music therapy* (p. 214). Jessica Kingsley Publishers.

Rolvsjord, R. (2010). *Resource-oriented music therapy in mental health care*. Barcelona Publishers.

Salimpoor, V. N., Zald, D. H., Zatorre, R. J., Dagher, A., & McIntosh, A. R. (2015). Predictions and the brain: How musical sounds become rewarding. *Trends in Cognitive Sciences, 19*(2), 86–91.

Sayer, A. (2000). *Realism and social science*. SAGE Publications Ltd.

Shakespeare, W. (1986). *The complete works*. Oxford University Press.

Smith, C. (2011). *What is a person?: Rethinking humanity, social life, and the moral good from the person up*. University of Chicago Press.

Stige, B., & Aarø, L. E. (2011). *Invitation to community music therapy*. Routledge.

Tsiris, G. (2008). Aesthetic experience and transformation in music therapy: A critical essay. *Voices: A World Forum for Music Therapy, 8*(3), 10.15845/voices.v8i3.416.

Vuvan, D. T., & Schmuckler, M. A. (2011). Tonal hierarchy representations in auditory imagery. *Memory & Cognition, 39*, 477–490.

Wilson, N. (2020). *The space that separates: A realist theory of art*. Routledge.

Wood, S. (2013). Evaluation of community music therapy: Why is it a problem? In L. O. Bonde, E. Ruud, M. S. Skånland, & G. Trondalen (Eds.), *Musical life stories. Narratives on health musicking*. Centre for Music and Health Publication Series (Vol. 6). NMH-publikasjoner. Retrieved from http://hdl.handle.net/11250/196825

Wood, S. (2016). *A matrix for community music therapy practice*. Barcelona Publishers.

CHAPTER 6

# Loosening the Threads Along the Way 4

## Direct Message with Interruptions

### *Complexifying Evidence, Experience and What Counts with Arts-Based Research*

Now does my project gather to a head.[1]

Dear Collaborator,

In this book, I am concerned with nonverbal and arts-based knowing and whether this can be construed as evidence in music therapy, and if so, evidence of what. In order to explore this, it has been necessary to investigate what kinds of experience occur in music therapy, because knowing of any nature is inextricable from experience, whether of reading, thinking, singing or anything else.[2] I realise it is not a straightforward question. Indeed, it contains three main foci, relating to the words 'what', 'kinds of' and 'experience'.

[1] Shakespeare, *The Tempest,* Act 5 scene 1 (1986, p. 1336).

[2] See my proposed theory of four phases of experience in Chap. 4 in which 'knowing' is the third phase.

**Supplementary Information** The online version contains supplementary material available at https://doi.org/10.1007/978-3-031-86220-5_6.





J. Atkinson, *Insights From Music Therapy Practice and Research*,
https://doi.org/10.1007/978-3-031-86220-5_6

1. Addressing the question from a 'what' perspective, I have needed to describe and illustrate different music therapy experiences for different stakeholders, including myself. I have attempted to do this throughout the book and I analysed many of these descriptions in the autoethnographic section (Chap. 3).
2. Addressing the question from a 'kinds of' perspective, I have needed to (1) analyse what is experience and what is not, and (2) categorise different types of experience with appropriate ontological and epistemological explanations. I have used phenomenology and Aesthetic Critical Realism to underlabour in this way.
3. Addressing the question from an 'experience' perspective, I have needed to acknowledge that experiences themselves need to be experienced. This in turn has led me to recognise that this book itself must provide ways for experiences not just to be described and analysed, but also experienced by those engaging with it.

I had not noticed the complexity of the question when I first identified my topic. Indeed, I have only discovered the necessity of these three approaches through actually doing retroductive[3] analysis.

*The Final Cycle of Retroductive Analysis: Arts-Based Methodology*
This current cycle of retroduction is concerned with focus no. 3, above. I will discuss how I used arts-based research methodology and introduce the remaining arts-based work that I have undertaken for this enquiry. In this way I will revisit my own *experiences* of arts-based experience, and at the same time offer you the opportunity to experience further arts-based work within the context of methodological discussion.

There is a broader purpose to this endeavour, however. Certainly I am interested in arts-based experience, but more importantly I am motivated by the *implications* of arts-based experience for music therapy practice, the cultures of music therapy and for notions of evidence in music therapy. In this chapter, when I offer you arts-based experiences I am doing so in order to ask the question:

- are you aware of the phenomenon of your own experience of this arts-based work?

[3] See Chap. 1, Section "Direct Message 3".

Furthermore, I am asking

- is there anything about your experience of this book, and in particular of this section of arts-based discussion and experiencing, that you are valuing?

By valuing, I refer to Wilson's notion of approach-avoidance motivation (2020, pp. 99–101).[4] In addition, I am asking

- does this experience of arts-based work afford you any sort of experience of being-in-relation, with self, other or natural necessity (the structures of the world)? Or, if not, can you imagine that arts-based experience *could* afford this even if it is not doing so right now, separated as you are from actual interpersonal relationship?

If you feel that you *are* experiencing any of these things, then I suggest that you are either in part, or wholly, experiencing what Wilson calls an aesthetic experience, and what I regard as a part of therapeutic experience. The remaining part which is necessary for an experience to be therapeutic is the interpersonal *responding* that occurs between people engaged in music therapy, which I construe as an affirmation of personhood. Perhaps you have actually responded in some way to aspects of this book and feel that the experience has been therapeutic and affirming of your personhood. It is frustrating that I am unlikely to know. (If this thought worries you, ethically, please keep reading.)

That is not the primary concern, however. What is important to me is this chance to theorise and demonstrate what therapeutic experience *could* be. If there is any agreement that therapeutic experience is an aim of therapy, then it is a short step to the claim that therapeutic experience is evidence of both personhood and therapy itself. It is no secret that I long for a culture of music therapy in which therapeutic experience of personhood can *count* as evidence.

*Revisiting Ethical Considerations in ABR*

I have discussed my ethical approach to this investigation at various times during this book. I am aware that I have just made direct reference to your own responses and experiences, Collaborator. I wish to reiterate, that I am fully conscious that you are neither a research participant nor a participant

[4] See Chap. 5.

in therapy, and that there has been no informed agreement between us regarding your participation. However, it is perhaps a finding of this enquiry, that where the topic of study includes an experience of arts-based work, and the mode of sharing the study includes an experience of arts-based work, there is a somewhat thin dividing line between your involvement as an outsider-engager, and an insider-experiencer. Of course, I have no expectation of any feedback and hope therefore that my using the term 'Collaborator' has not felt oppressive and inappropriate.

MT: When is this going to end?

R: Oh, is it *that* bad?

MT: No, no, I don't mean that. How are we going to know when it's finished?

R: Finished? It'll be when we have completed the four cycles of retroductive analysis—you know, looked at experience with all four methodological approaches…

C: …and checked our motivations to see if we have done what mattered to each of us…and checked our promise to be sure we have done it in the *way* we intended.

R: Sure—and just as important, we need to revisit our topic to make sure we've stayed on task, and not wandered off and investigated something else. The quotation does what it says on the tin: this journey is in its final phase. I asked Musician to find one about drawing to a close. I can't pretend I've conjured up tempests and caused the environment to sing, like Prospero does, but I have been on a voyage of my own.

MT: Yes. *We* have. But what's with all these ghosts and magic? I thought you were trying not to appear fluffy … d' you think it's going to help!?

R: (*Looking shocked*) Do you really think it's an issue? I could take out the quotations… I just thought, you know, 'suspend your disbelief' and all that. Someone whose comfort zones are linear model work, and 'outsider'-outcome measurement, may not credit arts-based experience with the potential for meaningful therapy. So they would need to 'suspend their disbelief' in a modest way when engaging with this book, like if you were going to the theatre or reading fiction … (*Thinking*) I'm worried now.

*Pause.*

C: (*Looking at MT*) Is something on your mind?

MT: I guess…

C: Are you worried about the people who come to music therapy, and whether this will help them at all?

MT: I suppose so. It all feels a bit abstract. I'm right that there won't be any kind of 'therapeutic experience evidence sheet' that other therapists can actually use, will there?

R: No, there can't be, really. It's not that sort of enquiry.

C: This is all about the principle of the thing, isn't it, Researcher? D' you remember when you went to that ableism seminar and one of the hosts basically owned up that nonverbal research participants weren't on their radar and never had been?

R: Yes.

C: Well, every little helps. You always said this was only going to be a tiny drop in the ocean.

MT: I know.

R: Let's carry on … is that OK? Otherwise we'll all get worried…

*Embracing Arts-Based Methodology*

I had always intended to use arts-based methodology because music therapy is itself an arts-based phenomenon, and because I am keen to avoid the automatic assumption that research investigations and any resulting knowledge are dependent upon verbal language. Shortly after COVID-19 lockdown began, and once the shock of being legally bound to stay at home was sinking in, I began painting. It was nothing to do with my enquiry, but felt an important part of making sense of the present time. In the summer of 2020, the first wave of coronavirus was coming to an end in the UK. Restrictions were mind-bogglingly complicated, involving four different tiers around the country, calculations concerning groups of six—from two households, or was it six households, meeting outside, but allowed to use toilets, wearing masks, two metres away from one another and always washing, washing, washing hands. As a family, we were able to go away and 'bubble' with another family in Yorkshire. During this time I began to write poems as data for my enquiry. They were about fictionalised music therapy experiences and interactions, and I wrote them in an unplanned and improvisatory manner. Looking back, I embarked on this phase of arts-based data collection-creation in much the same way that I was trained to embark upon a music therapy session: you enter the space with the other person or people, fully equipped with relevant information, theory, musical skills, imagination, overarching purpose, and above all with deep awareness of the importance of listening. But for therapists who work in an emergent way, you do not in fact know what you are going to play, or indeed why—these things happen and you make sense of them in the moment, or after the session. This was how the poetry phase began, and I cannot honestly say that I was seeking to write in response to any particular question. The poems, vignettes and short stories that resulted have been shared in Chap. 2, Section "Poems, Stories and Vignettes".

It is important at this point, to share my understanding of arts-based research methodology and the ways I situate myself within this tradition, as an autoethnographer.

*Arts-Based Methodology and Methods*

### My Choice of Terminology

The word 'practice' can occur in a confusing array of connections with 'art(s)' and 'research': art-based practice research; art practice research; art(s) research, art(s)-based research.[5] In addition, many authors reflect upon the fact that all research is a 'practice' and that the arts, social sciences and natural sciences all involve craft and share many common features (Leavy, 2009; Smith & Dean, 2009; Barone & Eisner, 2012; Nelson, 2013).

[5] It is important to clarify that I am not using Practitioner Research as a methodology. Practitioner Research tends to focus on organisational 'practice problems' and can involve participants in the co-creation of new knowledge for specific areas of practice (Fox et al., 2007, p. 94).

I am choosing to refer to my approach as 'arts-based research' (1) because it is unambiguous about the involvement of arts-based work in the investigation and (2) because I wish to include the created product, albeit as a feature of the arts-based process, and 'practice' seems to prioritise the pre-product process. I like Michael Compton's comment that 'all works of art can be thought of just as what the artist leaves when he has finished working' (1979, p. 56). It echoes Wilson's belief that the '"artwork" is, in effect the "means" (a tool—and very often, an extremely skilful one, at that)' to achieve aesthetic experience—i.e., the experience of a phenomenon, of being-in-relation and awareness of this, and of valuing (2020, p. 102).

In my opinion, the purpose of the arts-based product, whether developed through research enquiry or not, is to engage with others in multiple sensory and cognitive ways, peculiar to that arts-based expression. Barone and Eisner (2012) comment:

> The meanings located in a story, the qualities generated by a symphony, and the cadences that are made meaningful in a poem are all sources of enlightenment in arts-based research. This suggests that the concept of literacy needs expansion from a process concerned essentially with the making of meaning in language to a process in which meaning is made through the interpretation of forms in whatever media they happen to appear. The ability to deal meaningfully with visual art, for example, is not the same as the ability to deal with music. Each form of representation has its own demands and exacts its own requirements. This suggests that if research methodology is to be expanded and diversified that the students will need to be prepared in more than one "language". (p. 62)

For me, it is this possibility of research findings to speak through arts-based products that is particularly exciting. By saying this, I reiterate that I am not subscribing to the dominant Western concept of 'the arts', which seems to define what is and what is not an art work, on monetary grounds. Instead, I regard all humans as potentially creative artists, and regard art making as something that happens between people, in processes of collaboration and sensory perception. The relationship of audience to arts-based product is one such process of collaboration, but a hugely powerful one that can bring experiences that are lost to traditional written research.

**A/r/tography**

There is a growing literature concerned with arts in research (Knowles & Cole, 2008; Smith & Dean, 2009; Nelson, 2013; Leavy, 2017). The methodological approach that I am taking in this book is close to that of a/r/tography. A/r/tography is an approach which explores the ground where art practice, research enquiry and art education and pedagogy meet (Carter et al., 2011; Irwin, 2013). It was originally developed from the work of visual art practitioners who are also educators and researchers and it draws on image making, arts practice and arts-based enquiry. Rita Irwin developed the approach in her work at the University of British Columbia, Canada, and with her co-researchers cites the 'rhizomatic' theory of Deleuze and Guattari (1987 cited in Irwin et al., 2006 p 4) as an inspiration. The rhizome, like a map, has no definite borders—everything is linked to everything else. Irwin et al. explain,

> rhizomatic relationality effects how we understand theory and practice, product and process. Theory is no longer an abstract concept but rather an embodied living inquiry, an interstitial relational space for creating, teaching, learning, and researching in a constant state of becoming (see also Britzman, 2003). For a/r/tgraphers this means theorizing through inquiry, a process that involves an evolution of questions. This active stance to knowledge creation informs a/r/tographers' practices making their inquiries emergent, generative, reflexive and responsive (de Cosson et al., in press; 2003; Sinner 2004). Moreover, products and processes are conceived as relational. (Irwin et al., 2006, p. 5)

In a later article (2017), in which they reflect on the growing global interest in a/r/tography, Irwing et al. state

> most importantly, it is a form of inquiry that is different from research that posits questions in order to discover what already exists. A/r/tography continually asks questions in an effort to engage with ongoing practices in art and education in order to create knowledge rather than discover it. (p. 2)

The reasons for my sense of affinity with a/r/tography lie in these reflections. Both quotations could be describing my experience of music therapy as both a practitioner and participant. The 't' in a/r/tography refers to 'teacher', which itself is a catch-all term for educator, pedagogue, learning-sharer. It could, however, stand for 'therapist', in that a therapist seeks to facilitate learning, in the broadest sense of 'knowing and experience of self and other and music', which happens in and through music making and relationship. Even when the music therapy process is strictly functional, focusing on the acquisition of fine motor skills through the practice of rhythmic finger movements, for example, the learning taps into the personal bodily experience of rhythm, both physical and sensory, which is facilitated through a relationship with the therapist as s/he musically supports the exercise. In the participant, a new knowing of musical, physical and sensory self emerges, which is audible and observable to the therapist; in the therapist, a new knowing of the actual and potential scope of both parties' musical and personal learning is possible, which is communicated to the participant in the unfolding therapy. Significantly, music therapist Stuart Wood draws on Deleuze and Guattari's conceptualisation of music *itself* as rhizomatic, indeed as an 'ideal of rhizomatic behaviour' owing to its inherent multiplicity of lines, connecting points, new shoots, entry points and ruptures ([1987] 2004, pp. 13–14 cited in Wood, 2016, pp. 94–95).

Often, people who participate in music therapy have had little experience of music making, creativity or the ways of being which can arise through musical relationship. For this reason, the self-knowledge and musical knowledge that is gained in music therapy *is* new knowledge and the therapist has to be continually reflexive and responsive in order to afford the widest experience and avoid limiting the scope of the learning. Similarly, the therapist is engaged in on-the-spot, real-time theory making as they listen, respond and creatively imagine what the participant might need, musically and personally, as the therapy unfolds—all of which characteristics are also true for a/r/tography.

*Why Is A/r/tography Appropriate for My Enquiry?*

The fact that a/r/tography closely reflects my experience of music therapy practice does not necessarily mean that it is an appropriate philosophical approach for my enquiry. However, I believe there are reasons why it is.

In light of the explanation above, I believe that music therapy actually is a form of a/r/tographic research. The findings are the unfolding and intimately related processes and products of the musical therapeutic journey. These are available to me through my experiences and through my observations of others' experiences. My study is autoethnographic: the different roles that I experience in my music therapy work (Musician, Carer, Researcher and Music Therapist) co-exist and each have their own integrity demands. This division of Roles is not merely a conceit for the purposes of this book—I really do observe myself functioning from different roles at different times. For this reason, I believe it will be useful to keep in mind the knowledge-creating and theory-building purposes of a/r/tography in my exploration.

*Four Types of Research Involving Practice*

Up to this point in the book, I have used the phrase 'arts-based research' to describe one of the methodologies I am using. However, the phrase covers many different approaches, and it is important to identify which approach I am taking.

Skains (2018, pp. 85–6), herself a creative writer, identifies four ways in which 'practice' is involved in research. By 'practice', Skains is referring to creative artistic work. In each of the four ways, Skains emphasises that the research question needs to guide the study.

The first way is '*practice as research*'. This form of research typically results in an artefact—a film, book, video game, etc. There is no accompanying theoretical and reflective analysis because the creating of the product *is* the research process: inherent in the drawing, dancing, designing, etc., are procedures which, for that medium and art form, constitute the research steps of data collection, analysis, meaning-making and communication.

The second way is '*practice and research*'. Researchers in this instance are also arts practitioners. They undertake two separate activities—creative work and critical research into artefacts by other practitioners. For example, a dancer creates her own choreography. Meanwhile, she researches the choreographies of other dancers and brings her own creative knowledge into the research process.

The third and fourth ways have a particular focus on analysing and understanding the creative process itself.

The third way is '*practice-led research*'. Here, the purpose of the research is to illuminate some aspect of the creative process. Creative practice is used in the exploration, but is not necessarily included in the presentation of findings.

The fourth way is '*practice-based research*'. In this instance, the research seeks to demonstrate its findings in the artefact itself. 'Critical exegesis' is a fundamental part of the research and the analysis and meaning-making of both the process and product are presented in 'critical discussion'. It is essential that the critical discussion is included in the findings, otherwise this becomes 'practice as research' (see 'first way' above). It seems to be implied that the critical discussion is verbal.

Whilst different authors and researchers use a variety of terms to express these ideas, I find Skains' definitions helpful and believe that my enquiry encompasses both practice-led research, because my exploration began in music practice, which has led me into verbal exploration of my experiences, and practice-based research in that I explore themes and demonstrate findings in creative forms. Indeed, drawing, creative writing, painting, glass fusing, mobile making and video making are the methods of data collection, analysis and meaning-making. Critical verbal reflection accompanies all these approaches, contributing the second strand to my 'practice-based research'. It is interesting, in light of Skains' explanations, that Barone and Eisner (see below) regard 'reflection' after the experience of the art as an essential stage in arts-based research (2012, p. 60).

*My Study: The Choice of Art Form*

I am aware that my methodology is perhaps unorthodox: from my exploration of the literature, I believe it is probably more usual, when conducting practice-led and practice-based research, either that an arts practitioner explores some aspect of their own creative process by using the *same* art form that they usually practice, or that an arts practitioner has a research interest which is not art focused (for example the experience of refugees) and employs their own art form to explore this.

*Four Reasons for Multiple Art Forms in My Study*

In my enquiry, however, I am deliberately exploring an arts-based practice (music therapy), through other art forms that are not my named professional practice. The reasons for this are various. Firstly, as discussed many times, I want to reflect the fact that many of the people I work with do not use language and I wish to allow some of their experience to be shared in nonverbal ways. Music could be one way, but I have been drawn to other nonverbal art forms.

Secondly, I have often thought of my work as 'creativity therapy in music' and am accustomed to using drawing, story-telling, movement and poetry in my work as musical stimuli. Moreover, songs themselves use two creative art forms.

Thirdly, I am interested in different forms of knowledge: as music therapists we make claims that music therapy can bring self-knowledge. If this is true and if this is valid, then it must be possible for it to be nonverbal because we recognise this knowledge in our nonverbal clients. I am interested in the extent to which I can lead an audience to knowledge, or knowing,[6] in ways that are not verbal.

[6] I am wondering whether 'knowledge' is somehow regarded as public, 'out there', shared and corroborated (in the academic field, 'peer reviewed'), whereas 'knowing' is personal, intimate, yet recognisable in self and others.

Fourthly, Leavy draws attention to the discovery by Sinner et al. (2006 cited in Leavy, 2009, p. 4) that the many a/r/tographical dissertations in the University of British Columbia were found to focus on 'highly conceptual topics', such as 'love, death, power, memory, fear, loss, desire, hope and suffering'. I believe that my interest in experience and evidence is similarly 'conceptual' as a topic and that the largely (but not exclusively) visual art-based thinking within the a/r/tographic academy will help my project.

C: You're happy when you talk about arts-based research, aren't you?

R: D' you think so?

C: Yes, definitely. There's a sort of spring in your step.

R: Is it so different to the other sections?

C: Oh, they're fine. I'm not saying anything's bad. It's just it has all been quite serious for quite a long time. And you seem more playful now.

R: I really did have a good time doing the glass fusing!

C: I remember! Sorry, I just wanted to comment. I'll stop talking now…

R: No, thanks. It's fine … where was I?…

*Questions of Permission*

An issue which has concerned me is the extent to which I am 'allowed' to use art forms other than music in my enquiry. I am a trained musician—I have a post-graduate diploma in performance and have undertaken professional concert work. I am also a trained music therapist with 26 years' experience. I feel this gives me permission to use music in my data collection, analysis, meaning-making and presentation of findings.

To what extent do I have permission to use creative writing, visual image making, video? There are two ways that I look at this. Firstly, if I am seeking professional validation, then I have a degree in modern languages: I have explored, in depth, the whimsy of the written word, what it can represent, how its context is or is not relevant and to what extent it can be rendered in another language. As part of this degree, I explored poetry, plays and other prose writing in depth in English, German and Italian. I have always written a little at times of confusion—poems, ramblings and more recently in this investigation, dialogues. In addition, I am extremely visual in the way I understand things: if I do not have a mental diagram of a process, I cannot understand it; concepts, feelings and ideas invariably develop an image and a soundtrack in my mind. I had art tuition since I was five years old: at first my father painstakingly taught me the principles of composition, perspective, mark making, shading and media every holiday, and as an adult I have sought art classes. I have no background whatever in glass fusing or video-making.

Barone and Eisner devote a chapter of their comprehensive book *Arts-based Research* to the question of who might feel entitled to undertake this work (2012, Chapter 4). They conclude that formal training is not the main criterion for considering whether someone is eligible to engage in arts-based research. Instead, they propose that anyone is appropriate, whose work fulfils the primary purpose of arts-based research, namely to

> [invite] members of the audience into experiencing aspects of a world that may have been otherwise outside their range of sight and to thereby cause them to question usual, commonplace, orthodox perspectives on social phenomena. We believe that someone who can produce such work—by first carefully observing facets of the world and then recasting them into a meaningful cultural form—is at the time of that creation operating as an artist. The more powerful the work in achieving this goal, the higher the degree of artistry involved in its making. (p 55)[7]

[7] I agree with Barone and Eisner's dismissal of professional training as prerequisite for engaging in arts-based research. In addition to these authors' reasons, my critical realist research philosophy (Bhaskar, 2016) and, in particular, the theory of Aesthetic Critical Realism (Wilson, 2020)—see Chap. 5—leads me to challenge the mainstream concept of 'artist'. Certainly, there are 'professional' arts practitioners who make a living from their creative work, but I could not engage in music therapy if I limited my understanding of 'musician' to professionals in the field. For, a cornerstone of music therapy is the belief in the musician in each human being, regardless of impairment or difficulty. Furthermore, my experience of improvising with people in music therapy suggests to me that an untrained music-maker can certainly attain and share musical experience. For these reasons, I am keen to validate the creative expression of all people and am equally keen to avoid the notion that an arts-based researcher must be professionally trained in the arts used.

*Making a Mobile*

I am struggling to determine the purpose of this section of retroductive analysis. By now, I have certain ideas as to the significance of arts-based methodology within my exploration and the experience it affords. I am aware that I could lead you through the arts-based processes that I undertook to make a mobile and video it, in such a way that I guide your experiencing and thinking in order to persuade you of my own. But I am not sure whether this would be ethical or fruitful: for me, the significance of using arts-based work in this book lies in what *you* make of it, and what *we* make of it together. Music therapy is a relational encounter experienced in music making. I feel this chapter should reflect that.

I therefore plan to take you through my activities and reflections at the time. In Chap. 4, I drew upon the analytical reflections that I wrote whilst making the painted images. I also wrote reflections for the whole process of making the mobile and in greater detail than previously, and it is these that I will share now, in the order in which they were written. For each of the art forms, I tended to undertake and extended period of arts-based making, and reflect analytically in written documents on my laptop after the event.

The first document was written on 6 April 2021 after several weeks of researching into mobile-making, materials, and different techniques for making pendants. I wanted to capture this preparatory experience on the first day of five that I had set aside in the holiday for glass fusing. The indented text below contains the major part of these reflections. I have removed a passage relating to reliability and validity as I will address this later. The headings and subheadings are original.

It is important to note that the focus of this book which I have mentioned throughout,—i.e. experience and evidence in music therapy and its relationship to arts-based and nonverbal knowing—had not crystallised at the point I wrote these reflections. As you will read, I was still conceiving a focus on integrity and integrity demands (Chap. 1, Section "Direct Message 5") as the main topic. I have discussed the fact that creating a sequential narrative for my enquiry has been an act of 'reconstructed logic' (Chap. 1, Section "Direct Message 6"), that is, a post-hoc endeavour.

### ***Rationale for Creating a Mobile***

*Accessibility and Inclusivity*

> ***Initially, I had strong views that I would like to create visual-only arts-based data. This was because so many of the people I work with in music therapy do not use language and I wanted to generate work that was fully accessible to***

*them, in acknowledgement of the inspiration they are for me in this research process. However, as detailed elsewhere, the figurative line drawing that I undertook for this purpose only ever illustrated thoughts and ideas that I had already formulated: I found I was gaining no new insights from this art work and thus it did not contribute to data and data analysis and was more relevant to infographic sharing of findings.*

*I also spent a week of research time attempting to learn animation so that I could bring these line drawings to life as a short film. I found I was particularly slow to learn the technology and only produced a three second video at the end of a week….I do not think I could create art that I believed to be 'good', or even 'good enough' if I were to persevere with animation as an art form. I therefore decided to abandon the idea.*

*However, my wish to create a visual, moving image—albeit not narrative—remained. At this point I started considering what other visual art forms might offer movement (flags, kaleidoscopes) and I quickly realised that a mobile would. Besides, I have always loved mobiles and am drawn to watching the changing patterns they offer.*

## *The Relevance of Mobile Structures to Music Therapy and Music Therapy Research*

### *My Arts-Based Methods Revealing Relationship as a Dominant Theme in My Experience And Research*

*My interest in creating a mobile for this research is based on considerations far deeper than my liking mobiles, however. Indeed, the impetus for the decision came directly out of the acrylic paintings which I made, and these paintings were direct responses to the written poems and vignettes that I created. When I was writing, as I discuss elsewhere, I became aware that what I was exploring in almost every case was relationship. Often, this was the relationship between therapist and participant or other individual related to the work, as I experienced it. It is important to remember that I have been a music therapy participant, a carer of someone experiencing music therapy, a fund raiser for music therapy, a care taker for music therapy spaces, a supervisor, a supervisee, a lecturer and a student, and a co-therapist who supports the main therapist. Consequently, in my fictionalised 'participant/other' characters, I am not merely imagining the experience, but am bringing first-hand experience to it, and to the relationship(s) generated.*

*… in some of the writing, I realised I was exploring the relationship of a participant to music, or the relationship of a support worker to music therapy, or my relationship as a therapist to certain features of working life, such as fund raising. I found this hugely liberating: for years, I have wondered what to draw and when to develop the drawings into something else. I have always imagined*

*that I needed to draw something visible. However, having discovered that I am motivated to draw the experience of relationship between people or things, I constantly see opportunities for this beyond my research!*

## *Mobile-Making as a Way To Further Explore Relationship*

### *Uncertainty and the unexpected in relationship*

*Given, then, that relationship lies at the heart of my interest, mobiles as an art form seem ideally suited. Always in a relationship there is uncertainty—we know what we bring ourselves to a relationship, but can never be sure what another will bring. Even when we conceptualise our relationship as being with a thing, eg fundraising, such things are actually the actions and ideas of people, and uncertainty can appear at any moment in these perceived features. It is essentially this uncertainty which makes a relationship interesting and draws us to human company over that of robots: even the smartest robot would lack the full range of unpredictability—to move to America, say, or get a tattoo. Our interactions may sometimes feel routine—go to work with others on the bus, say hello to colleagues, attend meetings—but they are in fact subtle variations on themes, which include countless unexpected incidents and relationships.*

### *Uncertainty and the unexpected in mobiles.*

*A mobile sculpture is an artwork that relies on movement for its effect. This movement cannot be predictable because the movement of air which causes a mobile to move will vary from moment to moment, day to day. A mobile therefore relies upon uncertainty and unexpectedness, the same two features that lie at the heart of human relationships. For this reason, making a mobile seems appropriate for an arts-based research project that is interested in relationship. As the pendants on the mobile turn, they move with respect to one another and new relationships can be discerned. Furthermore, the viewers can themselves move round the mobile and perceive different relationships in this manner as well.*

### *Uncertainty and the unexpected in music improvisation.*

*More important, still, is the connection between music therapy improvisation and the uncertainty and unexpectedness inherent in human relationships and mobile sculptures. This connection is far from coincidental. Indeed, a music therapist is trained to 'meet and match' the participant in musical improvisation, by imitating the participant's sounds and situating them in a musical tonality and genre where appropriate. So far, the therapist has received an unpredictable communication, and by reflecting it audibly, has effectively rooted the relationship in listening. At a moment judged by the therapist, the next stage is for the therapist to offer something new, – a new sound, motif, genre or tonality. This is the therapist's chance to bring unexpectedness into the relationship. And the participant responds in their own way, predictable or otherwise.*

*What this illustrates, is that music therapy improvisation is bound to contain uncertainty and unexpectedness, because it is a musical out-working of the relationship between therapist and participant(s). For this reason, making a mobile feels like an inspiring way of further exploring the relationships I have identified in my research - described above.*

### *Transparency, Shadow, Reflection and The Ripple Effect*

*When considering the materials I would like to use for the mobile, I was immediately drawn to transparent materials. There are various reasons for this. When seen in directional light, a mobile will cast a shadow. Where different hanging arms rotate at different positions and suspend diverse pendants, the movement of shadows can be complex as the shadows can fall upon floor, ceiling, and walls, depending upon the position of the light source(s) and upon the location of the mobile inside or outside. The speed of movement appears magnified because the distance a shadow travels around its surrounding space will be considerably greater than the distance that the sculpture itself moves. I am excited by this prospect but am still more excited by the opportunity of creating reflections through transparent pendants, rather than shadows from opaque ones.*

*There are reasons for my preference for transparent materials, which again relate to my experience of music making in music therapy. Music therapy does not happen in a bubble. Participants all bring their identities, histories, past relationship to music, current concerns and issues into the therapy room, as does the therapist. If I created opaque pendants, it would be like saying 'the music therapy all happens here, in the therapy space represented by the mobile sculpture, and at best you will see a colourless shadow beyond this space'. However, by allowing the pendants to be viewed through each other, and by making it possible for coloured reflections to fall upon and move around the surfaces of the space, it is possible to visually represent the realities that (i) things from outside come into music therapy and colour it (ii) music therapy creates a 'ripple effect'* (Pavlicevic & Ansdell, 2004, p. 15; Pavlicevic et al., 2015)—*ie it impacts the people and places surrounding it because it is embodied, audible, and takes place in time, all of which is true for the mobile's reflections.*

*I am aware that it is necessary to be a sighted person in order to experience the visual mobile sculpture that I wish to make. However, I also intend to create a musical soundtrack of a video of the mobile in motion,*[8] *which will be accessible to visually impaired people who can hear.*

[8] I do provide a version of the mobile video that includes a soundtrack. However, as I explain in Footnote 14 of this chapter, I do not include the soundtrack as part of the research data.

*The Choice of Transparent Material*

*I have described elsewhere the process of my writing and image making: I live with the ideas for a long time and when there is finally time to commit them to paper, they usually appear as I want them in the first draft and have little or no editing. I have been through a similar process in choosing the material for the transparent mobile pendants that I wish to make. The following substances were all considered and rejected:*

*Perspex—somewhat late in the day, I began to think about the environmental impact of my research and in particular the acrylic paints I was using. I realised that I feel my use of acrylic paints is not consistent with an ethic of care. The tubes and paints themselves are plastic and I am unhappy that I have contributed to global problems through my environmentally unfriendly choice. Perspex also falls into this category and was therefore discounted.*

*Sugar glass—this was an exciting, sustainable option. The process of making sugar glass appears fairly easy. However, I discovered that it dissolves around four days after making, and I wish to create a permanent sculpture.*

*Stained glass—I quickly discounted this option as cutting and mounting the glass in lead needs such skill that I do not have. Whilst the glass could be off-cuts and therefore environmentally friendly, lead is a sought after element and I felt my project could not justify its use.*

*Recycled plastic—this option seemed environmentally acceptable. I could cut shapes from used food packaging, for example, and colour them with appropriate ink. However, I was aware that the end result would be flimsy and the pendants could be prone to flapping in a breeze.*

*Pre-shaped glass—I spent considerable time imagining how I could make the pendants from pre-existing glass beads with wire holding them in place. I was attracted to this idea, which could throw interesting reflections from the different planes of the surfaces. However, it is important that the pendants should as far as possible be made to the designs of the acrylic paintings, thus creating continuity from the writing, to the painting, to the mobile. I did not think this would be possible with beads, so rejected this idea.*

*Found glass—there is a style of jewellery that uses the smooth glass pieces found on the beach. It is often held in place with wire that winds round the glass piece into a loop for the necklace chain, so it needs no drilling or sticking. For the practical reason that I do not live near to a beach, and that it often takes a long time to find these pieces, I did not pursue this idea.*

*Painted glass—it is possible to buy glass medallions, whether round or square, which can be painted with glass paints. I was drawn to this idea because it was environmentally sustainable and would allow for fairly accurate depictions of the acrylic designs. However, what I realised was that this material and approach would place me firmly in control of the process: there would be little uncertainty or unexpectedness in the creation of the pendants, even if the movement and casting of reflections would inevitably be unpredictable. This seemed out of tune with the spirit of the venture.*

*Fused glass—I finally chose this option. Fusing glass involves placing small glass pieces on top of each other to a given thickness. This is then fired at very high temperatures and the process is possible in a domestic microwave kiln. There is an element of chance in the result—the microwave kiln fires the glass unevenly, causing somewhat different degrees of fusing. At times, fused glass appears totally melded together, sometimes this process is partial, and other times, the glass pieces remain in a pile, albeit permanently fused. Each of these results would give rise to different surface contours and degrees of transparency, which in turn would result in different types of reflection through and off the glass, as well as different appearances of the pendants. All my knowledge so far comes from internet searches of examples and YouTube videos of the making process. I made my choice of this material based on these, as they seemed to allow for the unpredictability I wish to explore. In this way, a new relationship is emerging—that of researcher to the chemistry of glass fusing!*

### *Ordering the Materials*

*It was necessary to buy the materials in advance of a week that I had set aside for the next phase of my arts-based research. I therefore bought all the below for £102.*

- *Medium size microwave kiln*
- *8 clear round precut shapes*
- *10 clear square precut shapes*
- *One jar of mixed colour glass offcuts*
- *One starter set of 8 frit (glass sand for colouring) samples—different 'summer' colours*
- *One pair of protective gloves*
- *One sachet mixed colour glass confetti*

*All the above glass pieces and frit are compatible; they all melt and expand at the same rate. I borrowed a basic microwave as my investigations have suggested that the simpler the better and we do not have a microwave at home.*

## ***Thoughts on My Credibility as a Fused Glass Artist and Mobile Maker!***

### *Qualifying as an Artist*

*I am returning here to* Barone and Eisner's (2012) *discussion of who qualifies as an artist.*

[Here, I briefly explored those quotations from these authors' writing that I discuss above and I reach the same conclusion contained in Footnote 7 that, although inexperienced, I have 'permission' to pursue arts-based methods.]

*A Deliberate Choice of Inexpertise*

*I hope I fall into the category of artist that Barone and Eisner describe. However, it is more than a convenient excuse for not being experienced in the art form I am choosing. For, when I made the decision to pursue mobile making with fused glass pendants, I realised I would be able to share the experience of almost all those I meet in music therapy sessions: that is, they have no expertise in music making but are willing to participate, all the same.*[9] *It is people's familiarity with the building blocks of music (pulse, rhythm, motif, melody, harmony etc) which equips them to be the musicians they can be in music therapy music-making. In the same way, though untrained, I am familiar with colour, composition, balance, light and am trusting that this acquaintance will enable me to make a mobile with fused glass that says what it needs to say.*

*The very choice of items in my online shopping basket demonstrates both my inexpertise, and my familiarity with the building blocks of visual image and sculptural form. Perhaps frit will not stick to my glass rounds, perhaps the confetti will fuse into a brown lump, perhaps my microwave will not reach heats that result in high levels of transparency. But something about the pendants and the way I hang them will make reference to my experience of colour and form, notwithstanding the unpredictability I am embracing in the process.*

## *A Final Question: Do I Need To Make a Mobile? What Will The Mobile Add to My Research Process?*

*The answer is, I am not sure. In keeping with the a/r/tographic belief that research in this approach creates, rather than discovers knowledge, I strongly feel that the arts-based data collection cannot finish yet, with simply the writing and the 2D images. Slightly worryingly, I have become unsure what my research question is.*[10] *It has been conceived as an enquiry focusing on integrity, ie undividedness, in music therapy. However, in pursuing arts-based research, I find I am obedient to the arts process first and foremost, and am keeping the original research question in mind, rather than the other way round.*[11]

[9] In a further set of reflections that I made after the glass fusing, I repeat this belief that by undertaking an unfamiliar arts-based activity, I am putting myself in the same position as many participants who make music in music therapy sessions. Later, I refer to this as '*a sort of accidental act of solidarity with the people I work with*'.

[10] This comment pre-dates my move to focusing on experience and my associated interest in evidence and the cultures of music therapy.

[11] Regardless of the research question or focus of study, this statement remains true, that '*I find I am obedient to the arts process first and foremost*'.

*Emergence*

> *What I do know, is that my experience of many aspects of music therapy has to do with emergence. I rarely see music therapy in the linear terms in which it nowadays likes to describe itself. Even apparently linear processes such as business development and fundraising seem to have such emergent potential which can be lost with linear thinking.*

*Risk*

> *Two things are needed if emergence is truly to be respected as a valid process in gaining insight, understanding and knowledge: risk and trust. They are in essence two sides of the same coin. On many levels, arts-based research involves taking risk. Will it be taken seriously? Will it yield any findings? Will the artworks have validity? Do I qualify as an artist? In truth, it is impossible to know any of these things before the work is done, so trust is needed even to embark on the journey.*

*Trust*

> *I believe it is trust that links my choice of approach (arts-based research and autoethnography) to my field (music therapy) to my original research focus (integrity demands). All three are, in a sense, like pendants on a mobile, moving in and out of central focus. At present, having taken the risk of arts-based methods, I am trusting the process... I am inclined to trust these processes and their inner integrity because I work in exactly this way: for years I have embarked on risky, exposing musical journeys because I trust that new musical relationship will grow as a result. And this emergent relationship in turn creates a fertile space for the growth of personal and shared insight, but only if we remain obedient to the integrity of the musical process. Indeed, I trust this because I know I have gained such insight through such a process.*[12] *If we abandon the integrity of music making, I believe we cannot be confident of our purpose ... and for this reason, I can say I feel sure the arts-based data collection is not finished and I need to pursue making the mobile.*

I am struck by the complexity of themes that arose from simply thinking about making a mobile, before a single arts-based activity had taken place. I also wrote brief reflections on glass fusing after the week of this adventure. However, as I look back, I am surprised that these do not refer to the experience of fusing the glass at all. Instead, they rehearse the thought processes that I have already shared in the pre-activity analytical reflections. I will therefore not duplicate them here.

[12] I (and all Nordoff Robbins trainees at the time) received my own music therapy during my training.

*Validity*

Collaborator, it seems important to consider validity, because whether or not a trained artist is doing arts-based research, I accept that it must have some validity for it to be useful.

I like Sinner et al.'s suggestion that research approaches involving arts practice require a move 'away from "rigor" and toward "vigor"' (2006, p. 1252 cited in Leavy, 2009, p. 16). She further proposes that 'the aim of these approaches is resonance, understanding, multiple meanings, dimensionality and collaboration' (p. 16). I am drawn to the notion of vigour ('strength, energy or enthusiasm' (Cambridge Advanced Learner's Dictionary and Thesaurus online, 2023)) as a methodological goal because it is an attribute which is also central to a therapist's work: a music therapist requires strength, energy and enthusiasm and must often employ them subtly and trustingly, in the face of considerable resistance.

Barone and Eisner (2012) insist that arts-based research requires 'criteria' for evaluating validity and not 'standards', which lead to statements of quantity (pp. 146–7). They argue that criteria are 'much more slippery' and require 'judgement regarding significance or value' (p. 147). They suggest that the following qualities in arts-based research can be considered as criteria for assessing the validity of the research:

> incisiveness; concision; coherence; generativity; social significance; evocation and illumination. (p. 148)

And they argue that 'thematic' cohesion is necessary (p. 59).

Leavy (2009) proposes a somewhat different set of features which must be present for arts-based research to have validity:

- Theory—re-evaluated concepts of 'truth', 'knowledge' (citing Jones, 2006, p. 1), 'good art' and 'good research' (citing Sinner et al., 2006, p. 1229) are necessary (p. 17).
- Methodology—attention must be paid to the 'artistic craft' (citing Faulkner, 2005) and such criteria as are used in that art/craft for evaluating work (p. 17).
- Interdisciplinary approaches—in order to 'maximise the aesthetic qualities and authenticity of the work' (p. 18).
- Audience response—ascertaining and engaging with audience response can contribute to validity of the research (p. 18).

- Attention to emotions—researchers can use emotions (in self and others) as 'validity checkpoints' (p. 19).
- Use of theory in data analysis—this can allow things to be seen that might otherwise remain unseen (p. 19).
- Literature reviews—these can add 'micro and macro contexts' and 'multiple voices' to a research study which might otherwise have a focus on the artist-researcher (p. 19).
- Cycles of analysis—attention to ongoing cycles of analysis during the research process can root the project as a *research* enquiry (p. 20).

*Validity and Reliability in This Book*

Whilst I find Barone and Eisner's criteria a little abstract, I hope my arts-based enquiry will have some social significance in its advocacy for nonverbal ways of communicating and knowing, and I hope that it is evocative, incisive and coherent. The features that Leavy proposes are easier to use when I try to assess the validity of my own exploration. The one that is in some ways missing in my work is 'audience response'. I fully accept the idea that response from an audience can provide important feedback to the arts-based researcher and I acknowledge that in some ways I have lacked this response. At the time of investigation, I was at pains to share every aspect of my project with some kind people who agreed at different points to engage with it. But more importantly, the reason for my direct approach to messaging you, Collaborator, is to invite and encourage you to respond to the arts-based content, not only to the verbally expressed ideas.

The feature that is perhaps most elusive and hardest to employ systematically and with confidence is 'attention to emotions'. As a Nordoff Robbins trained music therapist, I have learnt the discipline of not attributing emotional states to the presentation and behaviour of others. For example, if someone roars noisily in a session and throws a drum beater across the room, we take care not to refer to this, or think about this, as the participant displaying anger. The reason is that one person can never know the emotional state of another, nor the intended emotional communication within a given behaviour. The roaring and throwing may, in fact, signify exuberance, excitement, pain, insecurity, boredom or a host of other things. Of course, some participants are able to use language and can assert that they feel angry, verbally. In this case, it is reasonable to accept this self-description. But for many participants, this is either not possible, or if they do use language, their emotional vocabulary may be limited by the picture cards they use, for example.

I am drawn to the idea that emotional responses can provide powerful and important feedback. However, I am also wary of the danger of expecting an emotional response, on whatever level. For example, as a young therapist I once walked into a hospital ward with my violin, expecting to be greeted with interest and hoping to offer something positive and different to the usual auditory backdrop of machines and radio. As soon as I entered, however, the older patient opposite the door called out in alarm, 'Get that thing (violin) out of here! You remind me of my dead husband'. This was before any arts-based experience had been shared: merely the sight of a component of music-making triggered overwhelming associated emotions.

On the other hand, I recently shared one of the fictionalised stories from Chap. 2, Section "Poems, Storiees and Vignettes" at a conference. I felt unconfident and insecure as to whether it would be taken seriously in the context of an academic setting, but an audience member told me afterwards that it had moved them to tears. This felt affirming, validating and encouraging, not only because I felt that the fictionalised character's voice had been heard, but also because I believed that the use of story as a medium for sharing had actually made space for this emotional reaction, in a way that a more formal case study might not have.

I include this background and these examples to explain why I am both wary of 'attending to the emotions', but also believe that emotional responses can bring significant insight and experience in their own right. As a practitioner, I have had so many experiences of feeling moved in music therapy sessions that I am perhaps in danger of believing that meaningful therapeutic experience *requires* this emotion. I will therefore remain mindful of this complexity when I consider emotional responses to arts-based research.

*The Emerging Mobile: Pendants*

The week that I had allocated to glass fusing provided a steep learning curve. I will share the challenges and successes in detail because they all contributed to my emerging experience and understanding of art-making as a research methodology.

To fuse glass in a microwave, you have to experiment with settings and times. It is therefore easier to use a simple, mechanical microwave, than an advanced, digital one. Fortunately, mine was the former. The first challenge is to heat the glass until the small hole in the top of the kiln (1 cm diameter) glows red hot. At this point, you can open the microwave, remove the kiln, open the kiln wearing appropriate gloves and observe whether the glass is fusing evenly, unevenly or at all. Frequently, a corner of the glass might glow red at this point.

The next stage is to repeat the process until the hole is glowing a very light, bright orange. This indicates a far higher temperature. Once again, it is wise to observe whether the glass is fusing, or behaving unexpectedly. I encountered unexpected results as a direct result of my inexperience: I did not know that iridescent glass surfaces repel each other. In my second attempt at fusing I wanted to fuse two iridescent glass squares to one another. I was astonished to find that the top layer had slid off the lower one during fusing and moved its way up the side of the kiln. A hurried phone call to the kind and helpful supplier explained my mistake and gave me strategies for rescuing the kiln and avoiding the problem in the future.

A fascinating feature of glass fusing is the chemical fact that glass wants to re-form into a ball shape when it is heated. As a result, if you leave the glass too long in the hot firing, the original glass base shape you are fusing will actually shrink in size and grow in thickness, as part of its journey towards a ball formation. This was surprising for me, but also led to a couple of interesting results. Furthermore, if you use confetti glass to create a pattern pre-fusing, this confetti will be totally absorbed into the thickness of the glass when it is over-fired in this way. I presume that this is how marbles are made. Frit (a sand-like colouring agent) seemed totally unpredictable to me—at times it would dissolve and bond, at other times, it remained as a rough and raised surface on the glass.

Although the process of fusing is astonishingly quick—three or four blasts of two to three minutes on a high setting seemed to suffice—the process of cooling is very slow. When you remove the kiln from the microwave after the last blast, it is important not to lift the lid to speed the cooling. This is because the contrast in temperatures between the kiln and the room will cause the glass to crack as it cools. It is therefore necessary to leave the kiln for three hours after each fusing.

I was making this voyage of discovery at the same time as attempting to represent the original acrylic paintings, which were themselves responses to the poems, stories and vignettes, in glass form. I enjoyed the process of imagining the fused effect of different combinations of glass base (which could be opaque, iridescent, transparent, patterned or textured), confetti glass and frit. However, the laying out of confetti, cut glass and frit on a glass base was frustrating because the slightest jog or movement could send the pattern awry.

Figure 6.1 illustrates the finished glass pendants.

**Fig. 6.1** Fused glass mobile pendants based on acrylic painted images. (a) Therapist's relationship to self (b) Carer/care-receiver relationship after massive trauma; (c) The participant as I (as therapist) experience them; (d) Therapist's relationship to commissioning; (e) Carer/care-receiver relationship; (f) Therapist's

*The Emerging Mobile: Beams and Fastenings*

In all honesty, during this period of my research, I was totally preoccupied with making something that was satisfying as an arts-based phenomenon. I became absorbed with sourcing the right kind of fastening, beams, adhesive and thread, as I recorded at the time in further reflections:

> *I had a concept in mind for how I wanted to suspend the mobile pendants. I was seeking a traditional system of hanging pendants from beams, which in turn would hang from other bars. A family member who had previously made a mobile recommended 2 mm stainless steel poles for the beams: they are strong and relatively easy to cut by an amateur with a hacksaw. I sourced these from a manufacturer in Sheffield and sourced clear nylon thread for hanging. I was given some clear 2 mm bore-diameter flexible plastic tubing which can be used to fasten thread to poles.*
>
> *I spent a long time deciding how to fasten the thread to the pendants. Initially, I did not want to use pendant bails (fastenings) that included a flat plate that you stick to the back of the pendant. The reason for this was that I did not want the shadow of the pendants to contain the form of the metal plate. I therefore took advice from a stained glass supplier and tried to stick metal loops to the upper edge of the pendants with a strong epoxy glue. I used spare fused glass pieces and was glad to have done so as this was totally unsuccessful—the glue ran down the pendants and I could not find a way of keeping the metal loop in place in the wet glue. I therefore went back to the bails with metal plates, found some unobtrusive ones, and used these.*
>
> *All these materials were fairly easy to source, but it took a lot of time to research them and find the best solutions, and delivery was not always fast. I therefore had to plan this part of the project carefully, particularly as I only had small periods of time to work on the mobile, that I had to pre-book in the family calendar!*

In addition, there were further material considerations relating to a couple of the original acrylic images:

**Fig. 6.1** (continued) relationship to fundraising; (g) Multidisciplinary team member/therapist relationship; (h) Mia and her relationship to music; (i) Theresa and her relationship to music therapy; (j) Mr. B and his relationship to music, music therapy and the music therapist; (k) Supervisee/supervisor relationship; (l) Communication difficulties!?

> *Two of the pendant designs contained protruding linear shapes. I had in mind creating beaded wire representations of these shapes that could show the colours intended and maintain rigid form. I therefore sourced wire that I hoped would remain rigid under the weight of the beads and found beads whose hole would allow for the wire to pass through (0.7 mm). In addition, I needed a system for fixing these beaded wires to the relevant pendants and therefore decided to buy some clear glass, square section beads to do this. Being square section, there would be maximum surface area for gluing to the pendant itself, thus securing the strongest bond.*

The final activity in making the mobile was creating a hanging design that worked in the ways I wanted it to. I recorded some brief reflections on this, as well:

*Designing the mobile hanging structure*

> *I initially drew a design of how many beams I wanted to use and which pendants I wanted to hang on which beams. There was careful thought in the groupings of pendants: I wanted certain pendants to be connected by the same beam, for example, and in one case, I wanted a pendant to hang alone on a beam.*[13] *However, having constructed this design, I had to re-think: it looked clumsy and all the pendants seemed to be hanging at the same level so that the overall effect was visually uninteresting. In addition, several of the pendants collided as they turned and I was not able to adjust the threads to overcome this.*

I am surprised, in retrospect, that I did not write a fuller account of this process. The pendants were quite difficult to suspend because of their weight. It was necessary to take over the living room carpet and build a support of music stands, chairs and anything at hand that could bear the weight of different beams whilst I created the structure. The moment of testing whether the beam would hang in balance was always stressful, because of the risk of glass pendants crashing into each other and breaking or chipping, but fortunately, in spite of numerous crashes no damage was done.

The placing of different pendants is deliberate: I wanted to have two separate main beams because the designs afforded by single beam mobiles do not allow nearly as much complexity of relationships between pendants. Each main beam has two further beams suspended from it, as well as two separate, individual pendants. The individual pendants were chosen

[13] As outlined below, in the final design, four pendants hang alone on the second tier beams.

because the images they portrayed all had connotations of isolation for me: *Mia and her relationship to music* seemed to capture the solitude of Mia in her music making. *Mr B and his relationship to music, music therapy and the music therapist* seemed to convey the discomfort felt by someone who is volunteering in order to overcome loneliness. The image *Multidisciplinary team member/ therapist relationship* conveys my own experience of isolation in an institution in which my priorities, and what I care about, are questioned and marginalised. *Theresa and her relationship to music therapy* depict the deeply compassionate care of a cleaner who does everything she can to mitigate the deep separation from normal life experienced by families with children whose medical needs require frequent hospitalisation. She is suspended in a solitary position because she makes these connections on her own.

The three pairs and one trio of pendants that hang from the two main, second tier beams are also intentionally placed. *Supervisee/supervisor relationship* needs to occupy one of these smaller third tier beams because they are rendered visually as a pair of interconnected circles and I chose to create this with two discrete glass bases, rather than 'drawing' the image with frit on a single base. *Therapist's relationship to commissioning* and *Fundraising* occupy another of the smaller beams and are paired because they both relate to the financial and business side of music therapy, which I personally find challenging.

The trio of *The participant as I (as therapist) experience them*, together with *Therapist's relationship to self*, and the ironically named *Communication difficulties!?* to my mind forms the healthiest selection of relationships: they are dissimilar, each has its own identity, but they belong together and are in balance. Each is transparent, which feels significant, though I am not sure why. The final pair shows *Carer/care-receiver relationship after massive trauma* with *Carer/care-receiver relationship*. I find it painful to look at the former pendant, even now. It is based on the characters of Chloe and Callum and the rough edges, shard-like point and zig-zag 'rupture' pattern convey the pain, shattering of normality and despair. The other pendant, on the other hand, shows the type of relationship that is seen in carer/care-receiver relationships where the carer has had sufficient time, or capacity, or both, to accept the unexpected reality and find hope. This is portrayed in the story of *Mehdi*, or in the poem *Carers*, for example. By juxtaposing these two manifestations of carer/care-receiver relationship, and by using the intense reds and oranges, I have sought to highlight the profoundly demanding experience of caring-with-an-ethic-of-care that makes up the daily lives of these carers.

The following page illustrates the suspended mobile (Fig. 6.2).

You may wish to play the video of the mobile in motion at this point, without soundtrack.[14]

MT: I feel you could go on talking about the mobile for hours.

R: Sorry.

MT: No, I don't mean you shouldn't. I mean, you never seem to run out of things to say about it, or ways of thinking about it. You don't struggle with it, like you have done with other aspects of this enquiry.

R: You're probably right.

MT: I suppose I am just interested to know why? What is it about the mobile that matters to you?

R: Well ... (*Thinking*) ... I suppose it tells me things.

MT: How? What sort of things?

R: When I look at the mobile, I'm not in charge. *It* is in charge. It goes where it wants. It's very humbling. I'll try to explain ... but I want to explain to Collaborator, really. Can you listen? We can talk again afterwards?

MT: Sure, but don't you think Collaborator might need a break? They could listen to us for a while?

[14] I have excluded the improvised soundtrack from my arts-based data. As was the case with my drawing of insects, I found that improvising did not reveal anything new to me and that I was simply 'illustrating' in sound certain ideas that I already had about the mobile. I had therefore not intended to include a version of the video with a soundtrack in this book. However, the objections from Musician were overwhelming. She refused to be part of a music therapy project with no music in it. And she reminded me I had made a promise to include a soundtrack so that visually impaired people could get a sense of the mobile from listening. You will therefore also find a second version of the video, with soundtrack, to watch and listen to if you wish.

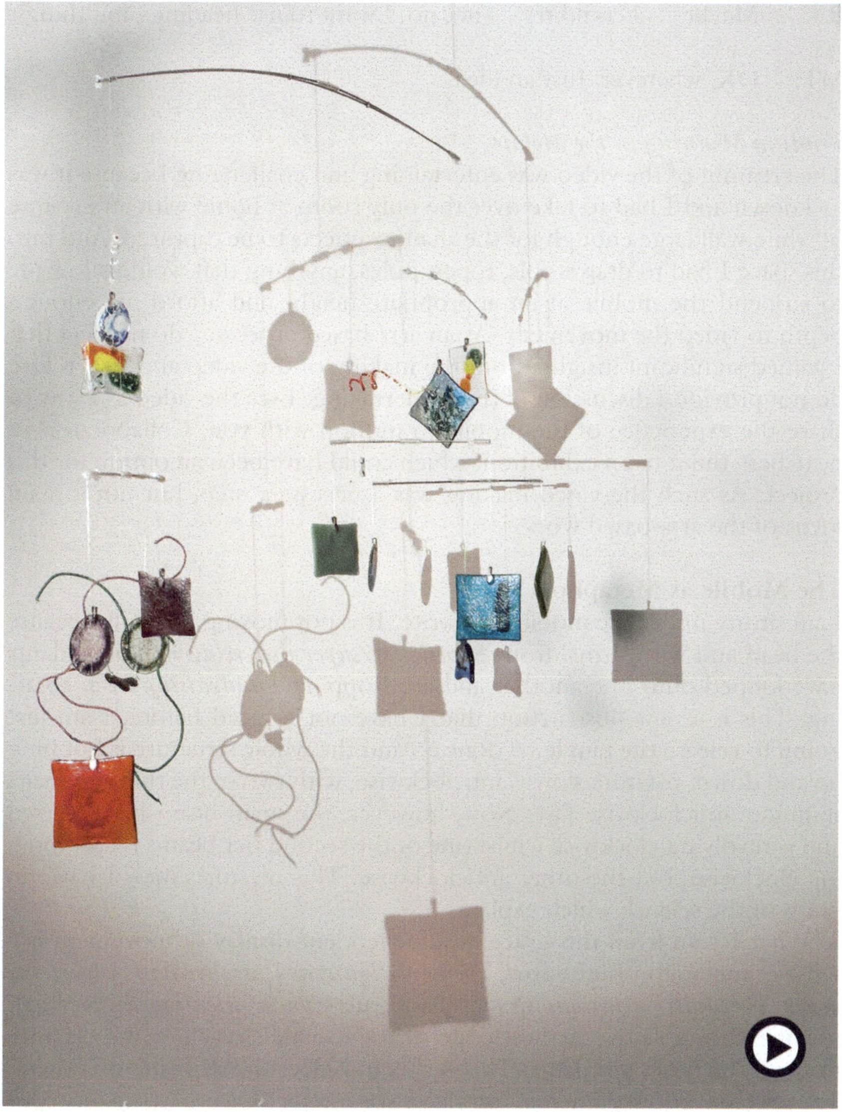

**Fig. 6.2** Suspended mobile

R: Maybe … I could try … no, no, I want to use headings and things.

MT: OK, whatever. Just an idea.

*Finding Meaning in the Mobile*
The creating of the video was entertaining and challenging because it was lockdown and I had to take over the only room at home with an expanse of white wall large enough for the shadow effects to be captured. And into this space I had to drag stools, ropes, poles, anything that would allow me to suspend the mobile at an appropriate height and afford me enough depth to video the movement. As an arts-based process, I do not feel that I gained significant insights from the making of the video and I therefore do not provide a discussion of this undertaking. I see the video as a way to share the experience of the mobile in motion with you, Collaborator—a next-best-thing to an exhibition, which could have been an option for this project. As such the video making was a necessary step, but not a main focus of the arts-based work.

**The Mobile as Metaphor**
I am sitting under the mobile as I write. It is not moving properly because the bead and wire 'arms' from *Supervisor/supervisee relationship* pendants have looped onto one another and are stopping *Fundraising* from rotating. This is a new obstruction that I have not noticed before. I am just going to release the tangle … done … and the whole structure is bobbing up and down, rotating slowly anticlockwise, with two of the third tier pairs spinning anticlockwise fast. Now, however, the main beam has reversed and is revolving clockwise whilst one of the second tier beams is also moving clockwise, but the other anticlockwise. This mystifies me—I have no grasp of the science which explains it.

What I gain from this graceful, independent display of movement is a sense of metaphor. Right now, *The participant as I (as therapist) experience them, Therapist's relationship to self* and the *Communication difficulties!?* trio is rotating at the farthest edge of the mobile's reach, some distance from all the other pendants. This seems to reflect the daily life of a therapist providing music therapy services: we interact with participants, discover their health and wholeness, work for development and change where appropriate, move together in the ebb and flow of music, all largely unconnected to the complexity of interactions, relationships and activities which create the conditions for our work.

Now, though, I have been distracted by a near-miss: *Carer/care-receiver relationship after massive trauma* is positioned such that this pendant is subject to collisions with *Fundraising*. I found this tendency to collide genuinely distressing at first—from the perspective of mobile maker, I was worried the pendants would damage each other, and I was dissatisfied with my poor mobile-making technique which had resulted in this inbuilt flaw. From the perspective of arts-based researcher, I was unhappy that the arts-based work was so obviously imperfect and I was uncomfortable about what that would mean for my credibility as an arts-based researcher and the validity of the work. From the perspective of a music therapist, I was truly upset by this collision because of the particular pendants involved. It triggered memories of frustration and distress in numerous services, at times when funding for a participant's music therapy has run out, yet I and the participant have felt the work to be unfinished. Furthermore, it triggered a painful consciousness that the long-term accommodation and care of people like Chloe are actually dependent not upon the broadest understanding of their need, but upon constraints of funding.

I spent a lot of time thinking about this collision. In the end, rather than dismantling the mobile and re-hanging the pendants, I decided to leave the collision as an unintended by-product of the work. The reason for this is that the tensions that this collision triggers for me are real, not just for me as a researcher, art maker and music therapist, but crucially for the people like Chloe and her loved ones who have experienced devastating loss. I did not want to tidy away these experiences for these people—it did not seem fair.

### Insights from Metaphor

The mobile is suspended from a pole above our sofa and has become entangled with violin bows, hair and clothes at different times. It is received in different ways as a feature of our home. There is generous agreement that people enjoy looking at it. Often, visitors seem to like touching the pendants and feeling the cool glass. Family members find it annoying that they keep bumping into it. But nobody has yet asked for it to go (it has been there for over four years).

For me, it is something like a tangible inconvenient truth: it has become something that I often spend too long absent-mindedly watching. And when I do I always notice things. Right now, *Mr B's*[15] bead and wire arm

[15] To facilitate reading, I am contracting the pendant names to just the characters, or features of music therapy, involved in the depicted relationships (some relationships are with me, some with each other).

has looped onto the nearest thread, from which *Commissioning* and *Fundraising* are suspended. This provokes questions: what is the contribution made by volunteers to the field of music therapy? I suspect it is vast, encompassing hospital volunteers who keep therapy spaces tidy, to expert financial volunteers who steer small service providers, to in-session volunteers who facilitate music making. Do we acknowledge this contribution? Do we celebrate and applaud this work? It represents a significant act of care, from a care ethic perspective which expects nothing in return. But should it be paid? Is *Mr B* grasping *Commissioning* and *Fundraising* for a reason, to make a statement?

And every time I look up, *Supervisor* and *Supervisee* are in a new and different relationship to the other pendants. Yet they are permanently far away from *Multidisciplinary Team Member/Therapist*, because all these pendants are suspended from the same second-tier beam. However, unlike *Supervisor* and *Supervisee*, the *Multidisciplinary Team Member/Therapist* pendant does not hang from a third tier beam (it is one of the isolated, single pendants) and the stakeholders depicted in this relationship are denied the opportunity of rotating independently towards *Supervisor* and *Supervisee*. Why did I position these pendants in this way? *Supervisor* and *Supervisee* are a strange and complex, connected, three-dimensional object. Yet their movement in relation to each other is quite limited because they are joined by the beam at the top, as well as by the brown bar (that is meant to represent a see-saw) at the bottom. Does this say something about the experience of giving and receiving supervision? Is supervision constrained in some way for those involved? Perhaps the supervisee does not feel at liberty to explore aspects of their work because of a combination of legal scrutiny and organisational foci, such as safeguarding, accountability and best practice? Perhaps the supervisor feels bound by these foci and the transactional type of interaction that they demand? Perhaps the supervisor-supervisee relationship is experienced by other stakeholders as impenetrable and exclusive? Perhaps it needs to be? Maybe not?

*Relating the Meaning of the Mobile to The Focus of This Book*

### The Mobile Defines Unperceived Kinds of Experience

I notice a pattern to my ponderings of the mobile:

1. by looking at the mobile, I spot visual phenomena, such as all those just described;

2. these visual phenomena prompt me to articulate what I have seen, such as the somewhat daunting, complex, and exclusive appearance of the *Supervisor/supervisee relationship*, or the total isolation of *Mia's relationship to music*;
3. these observations in turn provoke me to question why I have represented these stakeholders, and my relationship to them, in these ways, and what this tells me about the status quo in the cultures of music therapy.

I would not have become aware of many of these phenomena if I had not made the mobile. As a result, the mobile independently generates insights that are separate to my prior understanding, by enacting and illuminating additional experiences in music therapy.

**The Mobile Provides Evidence of Cultures of Music Therapy**

What I want to suggest is that making the mobile and slowly watching it move over a period of time has provided me with insights into different aspects of music therapy, which were there all along and therefore constitute aspects of the cultures of music therapy, but which I could not have apprehended or imagined without the mobile. Why, for instance, did I place isolated and vulnerable *Mia* in an isolated and vulnerable position? Yes, I was trying to illustrate a feature of what I imagine to be her reality, but providing individual music therapy behind a closed door and allowing her to opt out and not return (i.e. the fictionalised context of her therapy)—what does this say about the concept of care in my music therapy practice? Is this caring? Or might it have been more appropriate to encourage Mia to share her personhood by taking me to a social setting which played meaningful music for her? Would this experience have connected her more powerfully to the wholesome qualities of musical engagement than an expert-led session at the piano, however caringly it was conceived? And would it have addressed her extreme isolation more effectively?

I am confronted at this point with an uncomfortable realisation: as music therapists, we use the word 'evidence' to refer to a deliberate and demonstrable outcome of therapy. Even if my preferred notion of evidence as therapeutic experience of personhood were to become accepted, this would still be something that is expected and hoped for by those involved. What the mobile has revealed in visible form, however, is that other things can emerge as 'evidence' in music therapy—unexpected and perhaps unwanted things. Once again, this begs the question, 'what is the evidence *of*?', and in this instance, the emergent evidence is of the unconscious or unchallenged status quo in the cultures of music therapy: the mobile is providing evidence of certain things we take for granted in the field. It is reasonable to argue that any research, per se, is likely to uncover evidence of how things are, or the status quo, but there is something about the status quo playing out in space and time, colour and shadow, above your head and all over your walls, floor and ceiling, that is particularly impactful, I find.

### The Mobile Complexifies What Counts in Music Therapy

The mobile has led me to contemplate how, when and why it is that things *count*. It has illustrated two ways in which music therapy stakeholders let things count: (1) in some circumstances we are aware of and therefore actively seek, foster and endorse certain things so that they are known to count—this is the case in music therapy sessions when practitioners set goals and measure outcomes; (2) often, we are not actively endorsing something, but neither are we challenging it, and therefore it counts as part of what is normal. For example, my relationship with fundraising is complicated because it is often necessary to ask participants for consent for filming, or for case study material, when this is for the purposes of a grant application or corporate sponsorship approach and not of direct benefit to the participant. Such compromises have become just part of what we do in music therapy, they are normal, but do we really want to let this kind of experience 'count' in music therapy?

#### *Returning to Wilson's Concept of Culture*

Wilson's definition of culture as that which grows from our 'systems of value recognition' (2020, p. 137) is relevant again, here. When applied to the field of music therapy, I believe the mobile illustrates some of these systems, and clarifies how tacit and acknowledged cultures co-exist. For example, the very fact that there are pendants that depict my relationship with fundraising, with commissioning, with a cleaner, with a multidisciplinary team member, all point to cultures which are to a greater or lesser degree consciously accepted.

For example, fundraising and commissioning are connected to the culture of professionalism in the field: the work is seen as professional, highly skilled and important and therefore needs to be regarded and remunerated as such.

The involvement of multidisciplinary team members and cleaners demonstrates a culture of dispersed therapy: it is akin to the cultures of secondary and tertiary care in the NHS in which the patient travels to the major hospital for planned and emergency services. I suspect there is less conscious realisation of this culture in music therapy. It was not inevitable that music therapists' work should 'bolt on' to secondary and tertiary medical care services, schools and other institutions. In many ways, it seems more logical to develop numerous, local music therapy hubs resembling GP surgeries, where regular visits, self-referral and preventative care are the norm. However, I believe that generations of therapists have highly valued the interest of tertiary medical care practitioners and other professionals and have adapted to those models rather than pursuing a more holistic, arts-based model. The consequence is a somewhat unconscious culture of dispersed therapy. This example illustrates how the act of valuing one element of music therapy (e.g. approval from other professionals), when systematised can have significant consequences with regard to another element (e.g. availability of music therapy and ease of access for participants).

The contribution that the mobile has made to my research has been to greatly complexify the topic. Just looking at the mobile and the experiences it embodies provokes the query '*What are my observations evidence of?*' When thinking about the kinds of experiences that occur in music therapy, and which of these count as evidence within current cultures in the field, the mobile leads to a new question that has been implicit throughout this book: *who decides* what can be named evidence *of what*? That is, who decides *what counts*?

In response to this question, I have tried to illustrate the ways in which shared valuing becomes systematised, thus creating cultures of practice, of understanding or of organisation. In this way, all stakeholders who do not actively challenge a part of the valuing and the status quo that it supports are wittingly, or unwittingly, contributors to the notions of what counts. This is as true concerning concepts of evidence as it is concerning concepts of record keeping or session format. However, I expect that when asked what evidence is in music therapy, many would very likely respond that it is proof that the therapy has worked, i.e. that a goal has been reached.

If evidence as a concept were broadened to encompass evidence of assumptions, expectations and biases, as well as evidence of acceptance of received wisdom in music therapy, whether tacit or otherwise, I suspect we would have the chance to re-examine the entire field, not merely the part we currently call evidence. I believe this would be the case for all stakeholders, not just therapists: supervisors could reimagine supervision, carers could reimagine their roles, fundraisers could reimagine their purpose and so on. Indeed, returning to a critical realist form of thinking, I believe this is what the cultures of music therapy would ***need to be like***[16] for those music therapy experiences that do not currently count as evidence to do so.

*What Have Other Researchers Discovered About Combining Arts-Based Research and Music Therapy?*

**Theorising ABR in Music Therapy Research**

I am struck by these complex insights and by the gradual and unexpected ways in which the mobile has revealed them. I believe this is an a/r/tographic example of arts-based research creating, rather than revealing, knowledge. I realise that I am not alone in combining arts-based methodology and music therapy research, although this is not as frequent an occurrence as I would expect, given the arts-based nature of music therapy.

Already in 2005, in the second edition of a volume dedicated to music therapy research (ed Wheeler), there is a chapter focusing on arts-based research (Austin & Forinash, 2005 Chapter 36, p. 458) within 'Part IV. Types of Qualitative Research'. The authors comment on the potential for ABR to 'capture subtleties and enrich the rendering of experiences' (p. 470). There is a second mention of the importance of ABR to the examination of experience:

> Artistic forms are closer to the irrational world of the unconscious and the source of creativity and therefore come closer to capturing experience than the more rational world of words. (p. 470)

Although I find this a somewhat bold statement and my instincts are to unpack several concepts within it, including rational/irrational, conscious/unconscious, artistic forms, experience, I believe it is basically trying to find words for phenomena such as my learning from the mobile and its complexifying of my research questions.

In this 2005 edition, Austin and Forinash state that 'arts-based research has not been widely used in music therapy' (p. 460) and they draw mainly on two examples. However, in the third edition of this volume (Wheeler & Murphy, 2016), arts-based research is once again discussed in 'Unit 7:

[16] See Chap. 1, Section "Direct Message 3" and Chap. 5.

Interpretivist designs. Natural Setting Approaches, Chapter 44' (Viega & Forinash, 2016). Here, Viega and Forinash cite numerous examples of ABR research in arts therapies and nine music therapy examples in particular. Through these examples, they illustrate a diversity of art practices that music therapists use in research—mixed arts including creative writing, art, and audio (Rykov, 2008), poetry and performance (Kondo, 2003), music improvisation, writing, poetry (Vaillancourt, 2011), for example.

In addition, like Ledger and McCaffrey (2015, p. 443) and Kenny (2015, p. 475), Viega and Forinash deliberately define the potential for arts-based research as a methodology, not merely a set of 'adjunctive' methods:

> For researchers who frame ABR as a methodology, transformative and pluralistic worldviews are employed. A pragmatic approach is utilized within the artistic reconstructions of a social phenomenon so that the art can shape and shift social consciousness. (2016, Epistemological Foundations section)

This is helpful for my study and explains the role of arts-based work in my research. However the authors go further, and propose that ABR can be used in circumstances where 'art' is a 'radical event in research':

> For researchers who see the role of ABR to radically and subversively change to [sic] social constructs, art is not valued as an object from which knowledge is to be constructed. Rather, art is seen as an event that demonstrates epistemological states that are constantly changing. Here, discourse of art in research stems from ontological and axiological concerns, challenging the role of epistemology in research. (Variations or Types section)

I am puzzled that Viega and Forinash attribute the value of ABR to *either* constructing knowledge, *or* challenging the role of epistemology. I would argue that using art in research can be useful for both of these ends. Furthermore, I suggest that art is not primarily valuable as an 'object' or an 'event' but as a *process*.

Conceiving 'art as a radical event in research' implies that ABR can have a political dimension, and I agree. Viega and Forinash seem to imply that a significant arts event is required for this to be the case, for example a performance or an exhibition. Although my arts-based enquiry is not performed outside of this book, I believe that more modest styles of presentation such as mine can also have a political purpose. For me, this purpose is to challenge transactional thinking in research, bring nonverbal research participants onto the 'radar', attempt to offer ally-ship through an anti-oppressive approach and challenge the status quo in the understanding of experience and evidence in music therapy.

*ABR Approaches Used by Other Music Therapy Researchers*

I am conscious of your patience and commitment, Collaborator, in engaging with these four explorations of my topic, each from a different methodological perspective (Chaps. 3, 4, 5 and 6). They are nearly at an end. But before moving to some form of conclusion, it feels important to acknowledge the work of other music therapy researchers whose investigations have involved arts-based research.

Diane Austin's study of Alcoholics Anonymous (AA) is a seminal work in this area and is fascinating in both content and methodology. At the time she undertook this study, *Grace Street* (1991–1998), Austin was a music therapist, former actor and friend of people living with alcoholism. She observed AA meetings and wrote a musical for three characters, involving monologues and songs. In her article (2016) describing the revival of the play in 2015, she presents a narrative of the process of creating the work, and shares the full script and songs. Austin states that there were initially several performances of the musical, but the results of the research were not published because there was no technology for sharing a video of the work (Austin et al., 2016). The 2015 revival was a response to this dilemma.

I am struck by a different sort of complexity in Austin's work. She shares very few methodological reflections and presents the retrospective narrative somewhat in the manner of autoethnography. There is ambiguity regarding the nature of the performance: there is a question and answer session afterwards, but it is not stated whether the audience is participating in the research. However, Austin comments that Kenneth Bruscia (a well-known music therapy researcher) encouraged Austin to add a song to the original score because she was 'still collecting and analysing the data' and would continue to do so every time someone asked her a question (Austin et al., 2016 p. 48). Furthermore, the actors who present the revival performance are referred to as 'artists'. They were auditioned from a cohort of music therapy students and their reflections display therapeutic awareness and self-awareness (pp. 49–51). It is not stated whether they were also research participants, or if these were only the original actors involved. It is clear that the characters in the play are fictional, but they are drawn from participant observation at AA meetings.

Austin invites the reader of her article to 'enter into the play as an audience member' through the video, script and score, and 'to reflect and find meaning through the listening experience' (Austin, 2016, p. 14), and one of the actors refers to the performance as the '"results" of our process' (Austin et al., 2016, p. 49). I see several parallels with my own research: I recognise the same impulse to give voice to people whose voices are often silenced or obscured and to present their experiences; there is a sharing of these voices in story form; there is an expectation of an experience on the part of those encountering the sharing. In addition, I perceive an added layer of complexity because there are actors playing the fictionalised characters, who bring ideas and responses and make demands of their own. Austin reflects tantalisingly little on these aspects. Her focus seems fully directed at the topic of AA meetings and those involved and she does not relate whether she discovered things she was not expecting through this process.

Over the last few years, there has been a noticeable interest in ABR amongst music therapy researchers: two special editions have been published, which have addressed this topic from multiple angles—in the Journal of Music Therapy (2015 Vol 52(4)) and in Music Therapy Perspectives (2016 Vol 34(1)). Written with a music therapy readership in mind, the former presents an editorial and five articles from five different practitioner-researchers from five different countries. Woven into thought-provoking descriptions of arts-based research journeys, involving the casting of musicians' hands (Gilbertson, 2015), or imaginary dialogues with inspirational colleagues (Kenny, 2015), there is discussion that enquires which art form is appropriate, when it should be used, how to understand ABR and what the audience's role is, as well as the relationship between ABR and epistemology (Ledger & McCaffrey, 2015), and the ways in which ABR enhances researcher reflexivity (McCaffrey & Edwards, 2015).

The 2016 special edition contains an equally inspiring collection, including written description (Kay, 2016), reflection, analysis of product and process (Beer, 2016; Kay, 2016; Viega, 2016a), exploration of supervision of ABR (Forinash, 2016) and theory (Viega, 2016b). Elsewhere, Haire and MacDonald's decision to use ABR to explore humour in music therapy involves a process of visual sense-making that feels similar to my own (2021), whereas the clearly defined 'systematic approach' to 'arts-based reflexivity' in music therapy research that Schenstead proposes feels less familiar: Schenstead appears to create 'artistic responses' to 'burning questions … [and bring] continued introspection … [into her] reasoning' (2012 Steps … section), whereas my experience was more akin to having a gut feeling that I wanted to create arts-based work, followed by a gradual dawning of its meaning, through sensory perception and insight.[17]

Whatever the process, the sense is of a methodology that is gaining momentum within the profession.

*Threats to ABR That Could Impact Music Therapy Research*

McCaffrey and Edwards published a case study with an extensive review of arts-based methodological concepts and applications in which they describe ABR as a research field that currently enjoys freedom from convention:

> We resist the consignment of ABR to a numbered list of types of media or purposes, and contend that since it exists in the margins of contemporary research (Jones & Leavy, 2014) it might be anticipated that it enjoy an extensive time of flourishing in music therapy before an inevitable *social closure*[ii] occurs by which expertism and exclusion frame it more rigidly through the hegemonic and colonizing actions of traditional scholarship. (2015, pp. 5–6)

The footnote contained within this citation is significant:

> ii Social closure is a concept devised by the philosopher and sociologist Max Weber (1978) to refer to the way groups act to assure the best commercial interests of a particular behaviour or activity. It is regularly used as a theory to understand the behaviour of professional groups in credentialing, training, and professionalizing; creating a system in which some can be included and others are excluded (Edwards, 2015). (McCaffrey & Edwards, 2015, p. 24)

What I perceive here is Edward's and McCaffrey's description of what I regard as a music therapy *culture*—that of education and research. It is not clear whether they regard the 'hegemonic and colonizing actions of traditional scholarship' to be the results of deliberate, conscious actions, or tacit agreements to a status quo among stakeholders. Either way, I believe

[17] I was struck by similarities in my own experience and in Carless and Douglas' discovery of 'waves of embodied engagement' (2017, p. 4), in their 'art-based' research into women's physical activity and sense of belonging—*Across the Tamar*, of which the first two waves are (1) embodied engagement of researcher/s with the research setting and participants (in my case fictional engagement) (2) embodied engagement of researcher/s in sense-making processes.

such 'actions' constitute a shared valuing, which when systematised becomes a culture.

The prediction that this culture of arts-based research will become *evidenced* through the 'credentialing, training and professionalizing' of arts-based research such that 'some can be included and others are excluded' is clearly as worrying to Edwards and McCaffrey as it is to me. For this reason, I suggest that it would be of enormous benefit to the music therapy field to deliberately search for *evidence* of *what counts* in extremely diverse areas, including power relationships, hierarchies of communication systems, aims for therapy, concepts of the therapeutic frame, record keeping and reporting and much more, but also in specific approaches to research and knowledge gathering, such as ABR. At the same time, however, it will be essential that *what counts* is not confused with *what is codified and manualised.*

But, that is another project. For now, I have reached the end of this last cycle of retroductive analysis. I think it is my favourite. It would be interesting to know which was yours, Collaborator. I will message again before this book ends.

With many thanks, again—
Researcher

C: Do you think it's time?

R: For a conclusion?

C: Yes,—a sort of drawing together of ideas.

R: I feel nervous...

C: Oh, Researcher, you don't need to. It'll be fine. Good luck!

R: Thanks, Carer.

## References


Austin, D. (2016). Revisiting Grace Street: A retrospective account of an arts-based research study of Alcoholics Anonymous. *Music Therapy Perspectives, 34*(1), 14–25.

Austin, D., & Forinash, M. (2005). Arts-based research. In B. L. Wheeler (Ed.), *Music therapy research* (2nd ed., pp. 458–471). Barcelona Publishers.

Austin, D., Mahoney, J., Courter, A., Ryan, K., Starace, J., & DeFeo, N. (2016). Artists' reflections on preparing and performing the arts-based research study Grace Street. *Music Therapy Perspectives, 34*(1), 48–51.

Barone, T., & Eisner, E. W. (2012). *Arts based research*. SAGE Publications, Inc.

Beer, L. E. (2016). From embedded to embodied: Including music in arts-based music therapy research. *Music Therapy Perspectives, 34*(1), 33–40.

Bhaskar, R. (2016). *Enlightened common sense: The philosophy of critical realism*. Routledge.

Carless, D., & Douglas, K. (2017). Art-based research as waves of embodied engagement: Reflections on 'Across the Tamar'. *Journal of Applied Arts & Health, 8*(2), 241–253.

Carter, M., Beare, D., Belliveau, G., & Irwin, R. L. (2011). A/r/tography as pedagogy: A promise without guarantee. *Canadian Review of Art Education: Research and Issues, 38*, 17–32.

Compton, M. (1979). *Looking at pictures in the Tate Gallery*. Tate Gallery Publications Department.

CUP. (2023). *Cambridge advanced learner's dictionary and thesaurus* Retrieved May 3, 2021, from https://dictionary.cambridge.org/dictionary/english/vigour

Forinash, M. (2016). On supervising arts-based research. *Music Therapy Perspectives, 34*(1), 41–45.

Fox, M., Martin, P., & Green, G. (2007). *Doing practitioner research*. SAGE Publications Ltd.

Gilbertson, S. (2015). In visible hands: The matter and making of music therapy. *Journal of Music Therapy, 52*(4), 487–514.

Haire, N., & MacDonald, R. (2021). Thinking through improvisation: How arts-based reflexivity can offer new knowing about music therapists' experiences of humour in music therapy. *Voices: A World Forum for Music Therapy, 21*(2). https://doi.org/10.15845/voices.v21i2.3104

Irwin, R. L. (2013). Becoming a/r/tography. *Studies in Art Education, 54*(3), 198–215.

Irwin, R. L., Beer, R., Springgay, S., Grauer, K., Xiong, G., & Bickel, B. (2006). The rhizomatic relations of a/r/tography. *Studies in Art Education, 48*(1), 70–88.

Irwin, R. L., Pardiñas, M. J. A., Barney, D. T., Chen, J. C. H., Dias, B., Golparian, S., & MacDonald, A. (2017). A/r/tography around the world. In G. Barton & M. Baguley (Eds.), *The Palgrave handbook of global arts education* (pp. 475–496). Springer Nature.

Jones, K., & Leavy, P. (2014). A conversation between Kip Jones and Patricia Leavy: Arts-based research, performative social science and working on the margins. *Qualitative Report, 19*(38), 1–7.

Kay, L. (2016). Research as bricolage: Navigating in/between the creative arts disciplines. *Music Therapy Perspectives, 34*(1), 26–32.

Kenny, C. (2015). Performing theory: Playing in the music therapy discourse. *Journal of Music Therapy, 52*(4), 457–486.

Knowles, J. G., & Cole, A. L. (Eds.). (2008). *Handbook of the arts in qualitative research: Perspectives, methodologies, examples, and issues.* SAGE Publications, Inc.

Kondo, S. (2003). *Special moments: Attending to a dying person during the music therapy session in the intensive care unit.* (Masters), Simon Fraser University.

Leavy, P. (2009). *Method meets art: Arts-based research practice* (1st ed.). Guilford Publications.

Leavy, P. (Ed.). (2017). *Handbook of arts-based research.* Guilford Publications.

Ledger, A., & McCaffrey, T. (2015). Performative, arts-based, or arts-informed? Reflections on the development of arts-based research in music therapy. *Journal of Music Therapy, 52*(4), 441–456.

McCaffrey, T., & Edwards, J. (2015). Meeting art with art: Arts-based methods enhance researcher reflexivity in research with mental health service users. *Journal of Music Therapy, 52*(4), 515–532.

Nelson, R. (Ed.). (2013). *Practice as research in the arts: Principles, protocols, pedagogies, resistances.* Palgrave Macmillan.

Pavlicevic, M., & Ansdell, G. (Eds.). (2004). *Community music therapy.* Jessica Kingsley Publishers.

Pavlicevic, M., Tsiris, G., Wood, S., Powell, H., Graham, J., Sanderson, R., et al. (2015). The 'ripple effect': Towards researching improvisational music therapy in dementia care homes. *Dementia, 14*(5), 659–679.

Rykov, M. H. (2008). Experiencing music therapy cancer support. *Journal of Health Psychology, 13*(2), 190–200.

Schenstead, A. R. (2012). The timelessness of arts-based research: Looking back upon a heuristic self-study and the arts-based reflexivity data analysis method. *Voices: A World Forum for Music Therapy,* 12(1). Retrieved from https://voices.no/index.php/voices/article/view/2035/1779

Shakespeare, W. (1986). *The complete works.* Oxford University Press.

Sinner, A., Leggo, C., Irwin, R. L., Gouzouasis, P., & Grauer, K. (2006). Arts-based educational research dissertations: Reviewing the practices of new scholars. *Canadian Journal of Education, 29*(4), 1223–1270.

Skains, R. L. (2018). Creative practice as research: Discourse on methodology. *Media Practice and Education, 19*(1), 82–97.

Smith, H., & Dean, R. T. (Eds.). (2009). *Practice-led research, research-led practice in the creative arts*. Edinburgh University Press.

Vaillancourt, G. (2011). Creating an apprenticeship music therapy model through arts-based research. *Voices: A World Forum for Music Therapy, 11*(1). https://doi.org/10.15845/voices.v11i1.341

Viega, M. (2016a). Aesthetic sense and sensibility: Arts-based research and music therapy. *Music Therapy Perspectives, 34*(1), 1–3.

Viega, M. (2016b). Science as art: Axiology as a central component in methodology and evaluation of arts-based research (ABR). *Music Therapy Perspectives, 34*(1), 4–13.

Viega, M., & Forinash, M. (2016). Arts-based research. In B. L. Wheeler & K. M. Murphy (Eds.), *Music therapy research* (3rd ed.). Barcelona Publisher.

Wheeler, B. L. (Ed.). (2005). *Music therapy research* (2nd ed.). Barcelona Publishers.

Wheeler, B. L., & Murphy, K. M. (Eds.). (2016). *Music therapy research* (3rd ed.). Barcelona Publishers.

Wilson, N. (2020). *The space that separates: A realist theory of art*. Routledge.

Wood, S. (2016). *A matrix for community music therapy practice*. Barcelona Publishers.

CHAPTER 7

# Arriving Somewhere

## Conclusion

No epilogue, I pray you.[1]

M: How are we going to do this? I mean, there are so many themes—caring, care ethics, integrity, experience, evidence; there are four Roles; four methodological approaches plus a research philosophy—that's a lot of combinations!

MT: Yes, and we've taken up quite a lot of Collaborator's time already.

M: That's an understatement!

MT: I think we should let Researcher get on with it. We can stay around … help where needed.

C: Good plan…

[1] Shakespeare, *A Midsummer Night's Dream*, Act 5 scene 1 (1986, p. 374).



J. Atkinson, *Insights From Music Therapy Practice and Research*,
https://doi.org/10.1007/978-3-031-86220-5_7

Dear Collaborator,

I am aware that this book has been somewhat philosophical and that it has taken effort to keep my thinking focused on the topic of *other* arts-based and nonverbal *knowing*, as well as experience and evidence in music therapy. This was particularly true when I was engaging in arts-based image- and mobile-making: I have already explained that the demands of the art form tended to shout louder than the demands of the research topic.

At this point, it is necessary to reach some kind of summary of what I have learnt. I have included findings in each of the sections of retroductive analysis (Chaps. 3, 4, 5 and 6). All I intend to do here, therefore, is to draw these findings together in conclusion.

### *What Kinds of Experience Occur in Music Therapy?*

The table below summarises the different kinds of experience that emerged through the book and identifies the research methodology from which they have arisen (Table 7.1).

**Table 7.1** What kinds of experience occur in music therapy?

| *Kind of experience* | *Which methodology revealed this finding* | *Explanation and examples* |
|---|---|---|
| Experiences of phenomena unfolding in time, recognised and shared verbally. | Autoethnography | The experiences we recognise and choose to share determine our personal and interpersonal narratives. They may arise from any of the four phases below.<br>Examples from study:<br>The events of my own research story; the events that form the 'plot' in the poems, stories and vignettes. |
| First phase of experience: event | Phenomenology | Experiences in the 'event' phase are the pre-conscious encounters with phenomena.<br>Examples from study:<br>Mia encounters the phenomena of pitch, phrase sound, timbre etc.; I encounter my emotional response to Chloe's participation. |
| Second phase of experience: awareness | Phenomenology | Experiences of awareness can be sensory, physical, spiritual but this phase occurs before the cognitive phase of knowing.<br>Examples from study:<br>Moon becoming aware of therapists' music making; Anna's instinct to pray; my feeling of dividedness when the service for families was ended; my watching the mobile, unconsciously noticing patterns. |

(*continued*)

**Table 7.1** (continued)

| *Kind of experience* | *Which methodology revealed this finding* | *Explanation and examples* |
|---|---|---|
| Third phase of experience: knowing | Phenomenology | Experiences of knowing can, but do not need to be verbal. They can also be sensory, physical, musical, interpersonal.<br>Examples from study:<br>Young autistic boy realises/knows he needs to reach out to his peer; Mehdi knows the inevitable shape of the music and ends the improvisation; I recognise/know that my image-making *is* nonverbal eidetic reduction; I watch the mobile and discover evidence of tacit cultures of music therapy. |
| Fourth phase of experience: sharing | Phenomenology | Experiences of sharing can, but do not need to be verbal. They can also be sensory, physical, musical, interpersonal.<br>Examples from study:<br>I write a book for others to engage with; Chloe turns her head to share her awareness and participation; young autistic boy kisses his peer's head; Moon shares his personhood through music making. |
| One experience related to another as a 'generational offspring' | Autoethnography<br>Phenomenology<br>Arts-based research | Every phase of experience is a part of the four stages (from event to sharing). But each can also be considered a new event (phase 1), experienced in its own right, and the starting point for the further phases.<br>Examples from study:<br>My writing of stories etc. involved all four phases. But, the act of writing (event) also inspired me paint (a 'hunch' not a conscious decision at first). Painting became a fresh event. The awareness and knowing it afforded about arts-based process became a new event-experience that gave rise (not consciously at first) to my awareness, knowing and sharing about evidence and personhood.<br>The unfolding of shared, improvised music making in sessions also involves these generations of experience. |
| Experience of awareness of being in relation | Aesthetic Critical Realism | We can experience being-in-relation with self, other, and natural necessity (the underlying structures of the world)<br>Examples from study[a]:<br>Chloe's parents experience being-in-relation with Chloe, and with musical structure, within musical improvisation; Theresa experiences being-in-relation with the cycle of life and death, self and other when she listens to music therapy in the hospice. |

(*continued*)

**Table 7.1** (continued)

| *Kind of experience* | *Which methodology revealed this finding* | *Explanation and examples* |
|---|---|---|
| Experience of valuing | Aesthetic Critical Realism | If we experience an approach-avoidance motivation during our awareness of experiencing being-in-relation, this constitutes valuing.<br>Examples from study[a]:<br>Moon experiences valuing by 'conducting' the music making whilst it happened; Supervisee recognises the powerful connecting that occurs in improvisation and values it in shared discussion, afterwards. |
| Experience of personhood | Aesthetic Critical Realism | Personhood is experienced as relational: our personhood does not depend on others, but an experience of being-in-relation with others is essential for personhood to flourish.<br>Examples from study[a]:<br>Mia's isolated, distressed self begins to be heard in the music improvisation; Tyler's robust, creative personhood is shared in music making. |
| Therapeutic experience | Aesthetic Critical Realism | Therapeutic experience (synonymous with Wilson's 'aesthetic experience') is proposed as the combination of (i) an initial phenomenon (ii) awareness of being-in-relation, and (iii) valuing.<br>Examples from study:<br>Chloe's family experience shared music making (phenomenon), are aware of new interconnectedness (being-in-relation), and value this experience (audible through their participation and verbalised afterwards); Chloe experiences the same but demonstrates valuing through turning her head.<br>NB Dr JJ does not have therapeutic experience of Chloe's session because he has no opportunity for being-in-relation. |
| Experience of nonverbal knowing | Arts-based research | Mehdi, Mia, Tyler, Anna, the autistic boy, the participant described in 'Communication difficulties', Chloe, Chloe's family, myself as therapist all demonstrate nonverbal knowing of self, relationship, other, musical structure, natural necessity through our musical relationships in shared music making. |

[a] I focus on examples from music therapy sessions as these contribute to the exploration of evidence.

### *In What Ways and Under What Circumstances do These Experiences Count as Evidence?*

The enquiry I have undertaken has not sought to consider music therapy experiences alongside notions of evidence in every case, as pre-determined by relevant stakeholders. This would be a different but interesting project. In other words, if I look for examples of the ways in which the particular kinds of experience listed above are currently regarded as evidence in music therapy, then it is only in *Chloe's Story* that this issue is confronted. This story contains the only example of music therapy in this book in which there is an explicitly specified notion of what evidence in music therapy might be: multidisciplinary-team-agreed proof of outsider-measurable function, in relation to a specific therapeutic goal. It could be argued that *Communication Difficulties* and *Moon* poems contain implicit notions of what evidence might be in music therapy: outsider-measurable proof of some kind of development in these characters that challenges their 'labels'.

This discovery highlights two important findings:

- I believe a crucial component is frequently omitted from searches for, and discussions of, evidence, namely the question 'evidence *of what*'
- It has become clear that there are two positions from which evidence is measured, that of outsider, and that of insider.

With respect to the first bullet point, I have observed that generally, when evidence-based music therapy practice is discussed or planned, what is prized is evidence of *measurement*. Such measurement is regarded as reliable and useful because it is observable. Significantly, I would argue that measurement, per se, is neutral—it involves no valuing. This is unproblematic in work or research which is measuring water levels on flood plains, or consumption of tea, for example. However, another word is frequently used interchangeably with evidence—outcome.[2] Furthermore, in a puzzling way, measurement is often even regarded as an outcome, whether it is measurement of finger movement, or frequency of initiation in musical question and answer activities.

[2] Indeed, the two concepts are often run together as 'outcome measures'.

This is problematic for me, because unlike value-neutral measurement, I would argue that outcomes are *desirable*—that is, they are based on valuing. Therefore, to my mind,

1. before an outcome is even measured, its conceptualisation reveals considerable *evidence* relating to the systems of value recognition within the culture of the music therapy being provided
2. by pre-setting a desirable outcome, it is only possible to define what is already imaginable and measurable—so, emergent, nonverbal experience of personhood (awareness of being in relation with self, others and the world, including the phenomenon of music) is excluded because it cannot be pre-imagined
3. questions must be raised regarding *who* sets the outcome, and whether it is appropriate or ethical for the language-based values of 'powerful' therapists to determine the therapeutic journey of the 'weaker' participant, particularly when they do not use language

If these issues were taken into consideration, answers to the question 'evidence *of what'* might be surprising.

With respect to the second bullet point, the second important finding concerning the question 'in what ways and under what circumstances do these experiences count as evidence?', revolves around the positioning of those who measure evidence. Moon's experience and apparent valuing of the music therapy as an insider is analysed in depth in the Aesthetic Critical Realist analysis (Chap. 5). It is significant that Moon's four phase journey of (1) experiencing a phenomenon (shared music-making) (2) becoming aware of being-in-relation (3) knowing this experience to be valuable, and (4) sharing personhood through arts-based participation, was exactly replicated in my own arts-based research journey: I encountered an arts-based phenomenon (creating stories, images, a mobile), I became aware of being-in-relation with self and the structures of art methods and materials, valued this experience, shared this experience albeit with you, Collaborator, whose responses I cannot gauge.

The intense fulfilment and valuing that I experienced as an insider in this process (which I am not trying to frame as a therapeutic process, as it was solitary), and that I believe I witnessed in Moon's fictional insider process, would not be measurable to someone outside the experience. Perhaps you can sense it, Collaborator, but perhaps that would be because

I have shared it with you in a way as close to that of an insider as has been possible.

The position of outsider has already been discussed, above. As a result, I therefore conclude that the circumstances under which different kinds of evidence count in music therapy are predominantly situations in which an outside-observer can measure perceivable distance travelled in pursuit of a therapist-set outcome. The insider-observable therapeutic experiences of personhood, with which this study has been particularly concerned, largely do not enjoy circumstances in which they count as evidence. I propose that music therapists should provide greater clarity when reporting evidence, by identifying which form of evidence their measurements refer to:

- outsider-measured linear evidence of a therapist-set outcome
- insider-measured emergent evidence of therapeutic experience of personhood

### *What Can be Learnt About the Cultures of Music Therapy from the Kinds of Experience That Count as Evidence?*

I have already discussed these findings in Chap. 5 and am keen to reiterate that everyone I know in the field of music therapy is striving to give their best to others who need music therapy support. I therefore propose that the first finding, regarding the cultures of music therapy, is the following:

- Culture of well-intended effort, skill, service, and commitment to people and to learning.

However, if the kind of experience that counts as evidence tends to be outsider-measured linear evidence of a therapist-set outcome, then I believe this demonstrates that there are also cultures of music therapy with the following characteristics:

- Chamaeleon culture, in which music therapy stakeholders 'cave in' to other professional theoretical frameworks.
- Aspects of frozen culture, whereby music therapy stakeholders perpetuate frozen thinking from borrowed theoretical frameworks, (e.g. pursuing linear goals and outcomes) that are detrimental to emergent therapeutic experience of personhood.

- Culture of tension and confusion in which music therapy stakeholders recognise and value emergent therapeutic experience of personhood, but marginalise this experience in discussion and reporting, in favour of outsider-measured linear evidence of a therapist-set outcome.
- Culture of ableism, notwithstanding growing anti-oppressive awareness, which can be found in pervasive Western illness ideologies and healthcare-professional-expert-persona identities among therapists. Normative attitudes to health, wellness, illness, recovery and ability can be seen in professional goal setting. Power imbalances favouring the 'well' professional can be found in outcome measurement, reporting and consent.

In addition, this study has identified a further culture of music therapy, although the finding comes less directly as a result of defining those experiences that count as evidence. I mind about this culture, and therefore wish to name it so that we can address it in the profession through an ethic of care:

- Transactional culture, whereby different parties to a music therapy arrangement transact from individualistic positions. This can be seen in the requirement for signed consent, financial arrangements, and insuring against client legal action, for example.

I am fully aware that all stakeholders providing music therapy need to earn in order to live. I do not have answers as to how to move these aspects of the field closer to an ethic of care. However, there are instances of music therapists only requesting verbal consent (which is all that is required by UK general practice doctors).

### *What Would the Field of Music Therapy Need to be Like, for Those Music Therapy Experiences That do Not Currently Count as Evidence to do So?*

My enquiry suggests that the music therapy field would need to develop the following characteristics, in order that music therapy experiences that do not currently count as evidence could do so:

- As an arts-based therapy, it would be helpful for therapists to expect the music making to lead to the creation of knowledge, in the a/r/tographic sense, not merely the discovery of what already exists. This would require therapists to pay attention to all emergent experience in music therapy as a valid focus of the work, and in particular to insider-measured emergent evidence of therapeutic experience of personhood.
- As a therapy concerned with the phenomenon of interpersonal music making, it would be helpful for therapists to engage with the concept of four phases of experience, that this enquiry has identified, together with the concept of generations of experience, whereby any phase can itself become the 'event' for a new set of four phases. This is important because I have encountered considerable lack of clarity regarding reporting of, and research into, aspects of the musical encounter: often 'experience' is used to describe the fourth phase (sharing), and the earlier three phases are glossed over or inappropriately merged into the shared experience. This is particularly problematic in instances in which participants are nonverbal and the sharing constitutes a therapist description of their own experience.
- As a therapy that relies on musical relationship, even in instances where linear goals for functional gain are in place, it would be helpful if Wilson's theory of Aesthetic Critical Realism could become familiar. I have reformulated Wilson's theory as one of therapeutic experience of personhood, but the components of this and Wilson's theory of aesthetic experience, are the same: (1) experience of a phenomenon (2) awareness of the experience of being-in-relation with self, other, natural necessity (3) valuing of the experience. I suggest these three components correspond to the phases 1, 2 and 3 of my concept of four phases of experience. The sharing phase which I conceptualise, is theorised by Wilson as an ongoing process of metacognition (i.e. a process of experiencing our experiences) which is shared through the unfolding of being-in-relation, and through 'giving shareable form to our aesthetic (therapeutic) experience': for Wilson, this is the definition of *what art is* (2020, p. 110). If this theoretical framework were to be embedded into music therapists' thinking, it would help to clarify when and where the *therapy* is happening: I suggest it begins in the awareness and valuing phases (2 and 3), as these allow participants to affirm what matters to them as people-in-relation. Therapy continues in the sharing phase (4) whereby person-

hood, based on a participant's valuing, is shared musically, verbally, or in other ways. Indeed, these experiences provide evidence of the participant's personhood.

- If music therapy were to reclaim the flourishing of personhood as a primary focus, music therapists could gain much from explorations of autoethnography. The notion of autoethnography as a political act, whereby the autoethnographer asserts their own story as a unique contribution to an infinitely diverse map of personal stories, could embolden music therapists to affirm and endorse insider-measured emergent evidence of therapeutic experience of personhood. By regarding a participant's music making as their personal, musical autoethnography the uniqueness of the participant, rather than conformity to wellness ideals, could become a priority.
- For this priority to be added to the priorities in music therapy practice (I do not wish to 'trump' other priorities, or to propose a binary of 'good' emergent experience versus 'bad' linear outcomes), music therapists would need more time in their schedules to share thinking, offer insider arts-based experiences to those in positions of power and avoid 'caving in' to competing ideologies. This would be necessary until such time as all stakeholders are comfortable with emergent experience of personhood as a valid priority and form of evidence in music therapy. I suggest that music therapy researchers would also have a significant role to play.
- A vital concept that music therapists would need to embrace and share with other stakeholders is the above-mentioned difference between outsider and insider measurers of evidence in music therapy.

A theoretical framework that I believe could significantly help to validate this approach is the capabilities approach (Sen, 1993). It seeks to identify what it is that people 'have reason to value' and can be applied to relational creative engagement (Wilson et al., 2020). By deliberately addressing those things that participants in music therapy themselves value, however they indicate this valuing, whether verbally, through behaviour, music making or other means, music therapy stakeholders could be empowered to seek alternatives to linear goal setting.[3]

[3] It is important to emphasise that participants' wishes are frequently included in music therapy goal setting. However, in my experience in the health and education systems, the overarching 'heavy hand' of prevailing illness ideologies, financial constraints and notions of

Collaborator, it is time to end. I sincerely appreciate your continued time and engagement. I know I have made considerable demands.

Thank you.
With best wishes,
Researcher

MT: Researcher, thank you for this. I'm so relieved that you have managed to condense all these pages into something useable.

R: Do you think it is?

MT: Well, I think it is if you read the rest as well!

R: What about our motivations?

M: I'm happy—this does it for me—it *does* seem to show that nothing contributes to the fullness of life the way music does!

C: And I think it will probably help in the long run. If people in the field do manage to advocate for something more experience-led, then people who need this might have more access to music therapy.

R: Music Therapist?

MT: Yes, we have definitely found out about what kinds of experience happen in music therapy, what they're like, and what they are evidence of.

R: And I feel further down the path of understanding cultures of music therapy and how they affect what is and isn't counted as evidence.

accountability can make it very hard for a music therapist to advocate foci which rely on insider measurement. It is also relevant that Nordoff Robbins trained music therapists and those identifying with the music centred approach typically place high value on musical experience as a focus of therapy. However, in my own training and subsequent discussions with Nordoff Robbins colleagues, I have encountered a lack of clarity regarding the ontology of experience and how it relates to therapy and evidence of therapeutic outcome.

MT: I feel we kept our promise of our own ethic of care, too. I mean, it's more than a promise isn't it? It's an integrity demand for each of us. I really hope that the bits that critique music therapy don't come across as negative. I really very much want to avoid that … So … job done?…

M: No…

R: What?

M: I want to talk about oranges…

C: Oranges?

M: Yes. It's what it seems to come down to. You see, there are many people who need to know about the peel—if it's healthy, if it is allowing the orange to grow properly, whether the zest smells right, how big an orange it is covering, therefore what size of packing box is needed, how many boxes, transport logistics etc.

MT: Go on…

M: And that's fine.

R: Good! (*Exchanging puzzled glances with Music Therapist*)

M: But other people are hungry, some of them are very hungry. And they need nourishment and company … they need to eat the segments with other people and relieve their hunger. It's the food within that counts for them.

C: Oh, … I see. You mean for some outsiders, music therapy experience is confined to the peel—they can see and smell and check it. But for insiders it's all about the delicious taste and the shared meal?

M: Exactly…

R: And…

M: That's all.

R: Oh! Well, thanks Musician. I'm not quite … maybe … d' you know, I'm really tired. It'll be food for thought.

MT: Ha ha!

R: Sorry?

MT: It's OK. Let's go. What are you going to do now, Researcher?

R: Sleep.

MT: Musician?

M: I think I'll play my violin.

MT: Carer?

C: Finish my book whilst there's a lull.

R: And you, Music Therapist?

MT: Not sure … I think I'll write a poem…

R: Really?

***Mobile***
*By Music Therapist*

Colours glide,
Phrases to the eye,
Casting shadows in rhythm,
Resonant with purpose, undisturbed.

We are still a 'we',
Conscious of you
And of time.

So many words, and yet
What we remember is
The sound of hope,
Of us all.

Deep knowing,
Flighty, not for capture,
Shared, dependent, free,
Sensed between, yet scarcely seen
Beyond…

## References

Sen, A. (1993). Capability and well-being. In M. Nussbaum & A. Sen (Eds.), *The quality of life* (pp. 30–53). Oxford University Press.

Shakespeare, W. (1986). *The complete works.* Oxford University Press.

Wilson, N. (2020). *The space that separates: A realist theory of art.* Routledge.

Wilson, N., Gross, J., Dent, T., Conor, B., & Comunian, R. (2020). *Re-thinking inclusive and sustainable growth for the creative economy: a literature review.* Retrieved from https://disce.eu/wp-content/uploads/2020/01/DISCE-Report-D5.2.pdf

# Index[1]



[1] Note: Page numbers followed by 'n' refer to notes.



J. Atkinson, *Insights From Music Therapy Practice and Research*,
https://doi.org/10.1007/978-3-031-86220-5_7

The manufacturer's authorised representative in the EU is Springer Nature Customer Service Centre GmbH, Europaplatz 3, 69115 Heidelberg, Germany. If you have any concerns regarding our products, please contact ProductSafety@springernature.com

Printed and bound by CPI Group (UK) Ltd, Croydon, CR0 4YY
30/09/2026
02225567-0003